# JENS
# LEHMANN

## The madness is on the pitch

# JENS
# LEHMANN

## The madness is on the pitch

*With Christof Siemes*

*Translated from the German by Ceylan Hussein*

First published as a hardback by deCoubertin Books Ltd in 2017.

First Edition.

deCoubertin Books, Studio I, Baltic Creative Campus, Liverpool, L1 OAH
www.decoubertin.co.uk

ISBN: 9781909245624

Cover design and typeset by Leslie Priestley.

Printed and bound by Jellyfish.

# Contents

# The Most Important Match Of My Life

THE NOTE. I HAD STUDIED IT CLOSELY BEFORE THE MATCH AND tried to memorise some of the names and information about the penalty takers. Long run-up, left corner, that sort of thing. It was like learning vocab, really – at least, that was how I tried to approach it. Sounds simple: a handful of names, a few phrases thrown in, done. But it was like in the old days at school: do the words and phrases still come to you if you are standing alone at the blackboard? My board was huge, 7.32m x 2.44m – the goal. And the lesson had already lasted 120 minutes. It was stifling hot on this early summer's evening; I had already lost three kilos in weight since kick-off two hours ago.

On top of that, there were not thirty or forty fellow pupils sitting in this classroom of mine, glad that it was my turn rather than theirs. No, in my classroom, there was a febrile crowd of 81,675 maniacs. Even before full time, they had been whistling and booing so loudly that I had to cover my ears. Neither before nor after had I ever heard such noise. And now, as Ivan Zamorano took the ball, everything became louder. It was 1–1 after extra time as the Chilean international stepped up to the first penalty. 'Hang on,' you might say, 'Chile? But the game with the note was against Argentina! We've known all that for ages, the Sommermärchen, a story told a thousand times: the 2006 World Cup quarter-finals in Berlin, 1–1 after extra time, with goals by Roberto Ayala and Miroslav Klose.'

Yes, quite. But there is another piece of paper in my life. And it was even more important to me than the one from Schlosshotel Grunewald, the one auctioned off for a million euros after the World Cup and donated to a German Museum of History in Bonn. Apparently, such notes belong to my success just as prayer books belong in church. The paper that helped me with the most important match of my life was written by Huub Stevens on 21 May 1997, in Milan, or was it written at Hotel Costello di Casiglio in Erba, at Lake Como? Occasionally, the details within these big moments get lost, so intense is your focus on the game.

Legends surround what is said and done before a game or in the dressing room during half-time. I must admit: the minutes in the dressing room were of no great significance to me. I did not have any particular rituals – even the order in which I put on my socks was irrelevant to me. The only exception was that I would carry on using the same gloves until I lost a game while wearing them. There was a period in England when I wore one pair 49 fixtures in a row – I had taken good care of them, so that they would not fall apart. Apart from that, I concerned myself with my boots and considered which studs to choose – the long ones? Or maybe the short ones, as the pitch was dry? Then, my thoughts centred only on the warm-up and the match. Everything else was darkness, periphery.

I remember holding the Milan note before the game. But was it written in the Guiseppe Meazza dressing room and not, after all, at the Hotel Costello di Casiglio in Erba? The German national team had resided there during the 1990 World Cup, and that was to be a good omen for us, the Schalke side, too. This one single game alone stood between us and the greatest achievement in the club's history – the UEFA Cup. Back then, that was anything but 'the losers' cup', as Franz Beckenbauer called it dismissively later on. Before the introduction of the Champions League, this was where – bar the national champions – Europe's best sides were playing. Arsenal, Valencia, Glasgow Celtic, Beşiktaş, AS Roma, Lazio and Bayern Munich – they had all stepped up with us in autumn 1996 in the first of six rounds. We were the underdogs: for the first time in almost twenty years, a Schalke side had qualified for a European competition, and our Bundesliga form was average (we came twelfth at the end of that season). Apart from Olaf Thon and Marc Wilmots, barely any of us had any international experience; no one knew names like Yves Eigenrauch, Michael Büskens or me, Jens Lehmann. At the start of the campaign, we as players had seen to the sacking of our manager, Jörg Berger – the side had lost trust in him. No orderly circumstances any more, then, and there was little to indicate that within a few months, this team of nameless men should become legendary in Schalke history.

Our new manager came from Roda JC, our first UEFA Cup opponents, of all places. Two weeks after we had eliminated his Dutch side, Huub Stevens started with us. Rudi Assauer, our Director of Football (DoF), appointed him and it proved a lucky find. Stevens' programme matched his haircut – the man combed his hair with a ruler and a compass. To us, he had given the decisive 'little bit more': more discipline, more technique, more organisation. This was topped with our irrepressible will, probably born out of spite and a feeling of inferiority. For many of us, it was the last chance to prove that we had been unfairly overlooked by managers of other big clubs. We wanted to prove that, with comradeship and better organisation, we average players were able to compete at the highest level. With Stevens, we put together a run that had never been seen in the UEFA Cup: in all our home games, we didn't concede a single goal. 'The sheet must stay clean,' Stevens' contribution to the war chest of immortal footballing lines, was created during that season: 3–0 against Roda, 1–0 against Trabzonspor, 2–0 against Bruges, 2–0 against Valencia, 2–0 against Tenerife – none of the star-filled teams had ever managed that. Finally, there were only two sides left: us and Inter Milan. It was the last time that the cup winner would be determined over two legs. We stepped up at the Parkstadion first, where we had to keep a clean sheet again if we were to stand a chance at all. And we did. Putting it nicely, it was an uneventful game. He who combs his hair with a ruler and a compass upheld his reputation and only brought on a second forward 23 minutes before full time: Martin Max. During this season, Huub Stevens simply did everything correctly – just three minutes after that change, Marc Wilmots found space 25 yards out and drilled the ball into the corner to make it 1–0. 'S04 – one hand on the cup,' the screen read after the final whistle.

The second leg, that would become the most important game of my life, began for me hours before kick-off – in a house of worship. There is a little chapel at the hotel in Erba; that's where I went on the morning of 21 May 1997. Faith is something too personal to talk about much, but one thing is certain: you do not pray to God if you do not think he's listening. Maybe, sitting there, I was waiting for guidance from above; instead, Charly Neumann walked in, one of our team officials. He had been a Schalke figurehead since those days in the 1950s when Charly, a trained baker, would bring Ernst Kuzorra – the club's legendary pre-war striker – fresh rolls. And because you're meant to be quiet in a house of worship, Charly, who was never at a loss for words and rarely at one for tears, sat next to me silently. Only on the way back to the hotel did it burst out of him: 'Jeez, would you have thought we'd play here one day?' 'No, Charly, not at all,' I replied, 'But now, we have to win!' 'Don't worry, the good Lord will have an eye on us,' he reassured me.

It was routine for me to sleep before an evening game, and normally I would drift off as if by the push of a button. Later in my career, if I was playing in an evening international game, I would start thinking about it at 7 pm at the earliest, sometimes even later (and at times, I would not even be excited by the time kick-off arrived). But on this day, things were still completely different. True, I was 27 already, which by today's standards is relatively old, but in those days, immediately after the Bosman ruling, transfers happened at a slower speed; you would stay with one side for longer, and careers rarely went off like rockets. I was not to receive my first cap until about a year later, and even after ten years at Schalke I could in no way be sure of my position as number one. So, I lay in bed in my small Erba room and stared at the wood-panelled ceiling until I knew every knot-hole by name. What if I did not play well today? Would the gaffer bin me? And then what?

An hour and a half before kick-off, we were finally at the stadium. I had phoned my family and my girlfriend, who were all in Milan and told me that the square at Milan Cathedral was packed with Schalke fans singing nonstop, all afternoon. In the end, even the Italians were applauding. We knew of our fans' loyalty, and yet we were overwhelmed when we first stepped onto the pitch. Even today, I get goosebumps thinking of this moment: a home game, 900 miles away, 20,000 Germans. Of course, during the bus journey through the city, we had also seen Italian supporters showing us their hands with extended fingers: 'We'll get five!' But over the years, things like this had only stirred my blood more. You wait, you little Italians, I'll show you!

We played towards our fans in that first half. Maybe the blue-and-white sirens' song had turned Italian heads; maybe we were simply better – in any case, the sheet stayed clean on the road too. Eighty-five minutes altogether, up until that throw-in just before full time on my right-hand side. Somehow, the ball cheated its way through our defence and Zamorano reacted quickest, touching a shot into the top corner. That's no proper shot, I thought, more a sideways push. But it flew in: extra time. In such a situation, your body is so full of adrenalin that you do not feel anything – no pain, no exhaustion; but at the same time, no brilliant ideas enter your mind. We could have done with some, though, as we were now a man up. Inter's Salvatore Fresi had been sent off. We were reluctant to take risks, and so it happened as it probably does on every ground in the world: we were making the running, but it was Inter who had the chances. There were eleven minutes left to play as a sliced shot flew into my penalty box – I went out, the ball jumped, and Maurizio Ganz lobbed it over me. Shit, I thought, watching. There are some scenes that have been burned into my memory like the final duel in High Noon, and this is one of them. I was not sure if it was going in – if it did all would be lost. Mike Büskens chased the ball, and everyone – players, officials, spectators – just stood and watched until it dropped onto the bar and Büskens was able to hoof it away. We put up the shutters and waited for the final whistle.

Penalty shoot-out, then. Goalkeeper's hour, they call it – allegedly because the keeper has nothing to lose. But that is rubbish; the pressure on him is immense. In secret, every team expects their own keeper to save at least one. And you're supposed to have nothing to lose? Not to mention the fact that this was my first shoot-out as a professional; my last had been with Schwarz-Weiß Essen, my youth team.

Instinctively, I did what I would do again and again in later years: I sat down at the halfway line, took a sip of water, and focused. There are colleagues who, at this stage, make jokes or provoke the opponent. You need intuition and a strong nerve in this situation; every distraction is poison. Unlike a pistol duel, this is not about speed – on the contrary, it is about who can delay the decision before the shot longest. There is a split second between the moment a taker has opted for one corner and the moment a ball is hit. There is no return for either him or the keeper. That is the instant in which I have to react. Only then do I have a chance of saving the shot. Of course, other factors play a role too. You experience a player over 90 or 120 minutes, see his course of movement, register how and where he shoots, particularly in pressure situations. And the pressure during the final shoot-out is comparable with nothing in our sport.

Ingo Anderbrügge took the first penalty for us and tucked it away: 1–0. The note. Hubert Neu, Stevens' assistant, showed it to me again. 'Zamorano, long run-up, left corner,' it said. The referee blew his whistle and, indeed, the Chilean was first to grab the ball. It was a long run-up, swift, steady. That meant he was not going to make a sudden change to his decision. He would stick to his guns – or would he? Zamorano lunged, his leg moving towards the ball; I dived to my left. I saved and walked away. No high-fives with the opposing keeper now. This was a game of life and death – there was no way I could wish the opponent luck. But I watched him – and our takers. Olaf Thon scored too and I had noticed already that Gianluca Pagliuca was a typical Italian keeper, always moving early. I had my own little psychological theory: at a squeeze, the Italians were not as strong-nerved. I was, unfortunately, to experience an exception sometime later in my career. But for now, it was the turn of a Frenchman in Italian service, Youri Djorkaeff, who scored, as did Martin Max after him. Inter's Aron Winter took the ball next. It is on now, I thought, reaching into my bag of mind games. I approached Winter, standing in front of him so he could see just how big I was. 'I keep standing in the middle,' I said. Was that fair? It did not matter; no one would ask me about it afterwards. Winter remained silent, watching only the ball; the pressure was on him now. I stood unmoving, standing and standing, going right at the last moment. He, however, had sussed me out and shot to my left. But Winter had opened his body too much and the ball missed the far post. Then, Marc Wilmots scored and when I saw him wheeling away in celebration, I knew that we had won.

Wins like this always prompt television reporters to ask how you are feeling. What are you supposed to say? In our case, everyone started running around, screaming senselessly at each other – all the emotion needed to come out, especially because no one could have anticipated this victory. Even Rudi Assauer, who rather enjoyed playing the tough, macho DoF, stood crying on the pitch. Really, our team was only average, and yet the cup belonged to us now. Later, we players were joined on the pitch by our wives and girlfriends. An hour after the final whistle, we took a lap of honour for the Schalke fans, who were still present and still singing. The Italians were long gone and home by this point. I will never forget the images of the fans crying with happiness, just as I won't forget Maurizio Ganz's shot hitting the crossbar.

The mood in the changing room after such a win is hard to describe. The rooms at the San Siro were rather ugly, no good place for celebrations. But this win was so significant to us, to the club, that the surroundings did not matter at all. All the pressure, the ambition, the desperation had fallen off us; again and again we lay in each other's arms; some were crying. Eventually, someone started singing one of the club anthems: 'Blue and White, how I love you' or 'Stand up if you're Schalke'. The latter had been invented by a drunken fan during the quarter-final against Valencia: he had simply stood up and sung that one command, to the tune of the Village People' '*Go West*'. Around him, ten people rose to their feet; in the end, the whole Parkstadion was standing. Since then, fans from all across the country had been singing it for their club.

At some point, amid the hubbub of feelings, a question emerged: okay, what does this match mean to me now? It was my first big victory, and that sticks to you. From now on, everyone else knew I was a winner, and that was worth a lot. What came next – the titles with Dortmund and Arsenal, the World Cup, and the European Championship – stemmed from that experience in Milan and a piece of paper, of which I do not even know where it has disappeared to. But one thing is certain: it too would have deserved a spot in the Bonn museum.

# Stretching For The Ceiling – How I Turned Professional

ON THE EVENING OF 8 JULY 1982, MY DECISION WAS FINAL: I WAS going be a professional footballer. At that moment, Alain Giresse had scored, and the German national team was hopelessly behind in the semi-final of the World Cup in Spain. At 3–1 to France during extra time, what was left to happen? I was sitting on the sofa in my parents' living room in Essen-Heisingen, and although it was late and I was only twelve years old, I was allowed to – I had to – watch this game to the bitter end.

My God, I thought, we could not be knocked out here now. Surely, they had to do better. But Rummenigge did not score; Schumacher did not save; the match seemed lost. And suddenly, this thought formed in my mind: somehow, some day, I had to do this better. I wanted to become a goalkeeper. I wanted to play for the national team.

At that point, I had been playing football for almost ten years already. I had started at age four, on the street. Two years later, I received my first goalkeeper's kit. To this day, I have in my nose this smell of fresh grass and mud, which henceforth belonged to our matches in the garden like the scent of spaghetti Bolognese belonged to the Lehmanns' Saturday afternoons. My first teammates had been my father, my brother Jörg (two years my senior), and my cousin Jochen, four years older than me. Today, I have to say that none of them played extraordinarily, but of course, I had not noticed that at the time. I just wanted to play, always – no matter where, no matter how well, no matter with whom. A few years later, at ten, I had joined my first club, DJK Heisingen under-11s. We lived only fifty yards from their ground; my brother and cousin played there too, so no need for a great family meeting for me to be part of it. Another form of sport had been in line, really: I could have been rowing on the Baldeneysee or playing tennis, but they were too expensive: joining fee, bats, all the clothes; the list went on.

We did live in a rather posh part of town – Heisingen, the peninsula in Essen's south surrounded by the Ruhr, lies right next to Werden and Bredeney. Back then, the majority of Germany's millionaires lived there, people who held important positions within the corporate headquarters of Krupp, Thyssen, RWE, or Ruhrkohle. We, though, were a completely normal middle-class family: my father was working in sales at Henkel; my mother gave up her job when my brother Jörg was born. We grew up in an idyllic world, but like many younger brothers, I had my clothes handed down from my brother or cousin. I did not have lots of kits of my favourite club hanging in my wardrobe; at the time, the term 'fan merchandise' did not even exist. I did once own a Borussia Mönchengladbach shirt, and a Wolfgang Kleff top along with it – green with black stripes. But running around in such clothes all day or even wearing it to school as is common practice today was unthinkable. In any case, I would not have been able to decide on a club to support: I was simultaneously a fan of Mönchengladbach and 1. FC Köln, which, really, is a no-go. Today, we have to be thankful for those vast brown coalfields forming natural barriers between the two cities, or the fans would constantly be smashing each other's heads. Viewed from Essen, however, these two were equally admirable and, during the mid-70s, played the most beautiful, most successful football. In my home town, I could never quite decide between Rot-Weiss and Schwarz-Weiß. The former were a little better, but had never been in the Bundesliga; the latter was where I played later in my youth – my stepping stone into 'big' football. In the end, I became a Schalker Junge; more of that later.

As a young person, some of my convictions were as flighty as a flag on the terraces; initially, I could not even decide what I finally wanted to be – forward or goalkeeper. Most of the time when we were having a kick-about on an afternoon, with the great matches and their stars playing parallel in those children's heads of ours, I was Klaus Allofs, Pierre Littbarski, or Karl-Heinz Rummenigge. I was a forward in the first club match I can remember: we played with our under-14s against SV Kupferdreh, on the hill across the Ruhr. They were good and were beating us 6-0. The result annoyed me so much that I grabbed the ball in front of our own goal, marched across the pitch, dribbled around all opponents, and made it 6-1. I could not prevent the defeat with this, of course, but I did save my self-esteem. 'Really, in the end, I am better than that lot,' I told myself afterwards. And it has stayed that way to this day: humiliations are like power plants – ugly things, really, but you do draw energy from them. Straight after the match, I received my first offer – from Schwarz-Weiß Essen, to play as a forward.

Initially, however, I did not get beyond a trial session. The glorious Schwarz-Weißen trained on a narrow cinder pitch circumscribed by a hip-high wall, out of which a forbidding steel fence rose. Immediately during the first session, someone tackled me into this bit of misplaced prison architecture; I left a mark on it with my shoulder. I was completely perplexed at the way I, an innocent triallist, was being treated, so that my decision was certain at once. 'No, I'm not coming again,' I told the head of youth, Georg von Wick, who was feared among the entire Essen FA as the personification of pressure, achievement and coldness. At the time, I could not have guessed that under his aegis I would win my first title – for after just one more year in Heisingen, I ended up at Schwarz-Weiß Essen all the same, in goal for the under-15s.

By now, I was attending Schwarzwald Gymnasium, and my future coach, Martin Annen, was my class-mate in school, albeit a few years above me. He badgered me, asking whether I would play again. I did, as long as I would be far away enough from the damned wall. And there was only one safe position: in goal. So, I stood in there and did what I had been doing well since primary school: caught balls. During dodgeball, I would keep standing at the halfway line when the opponent was in possession, trying to hit me. If I caught a ball, they were suddenly easy prey. With this talent, it went so well in goal that I became my under-15s' captain and we won the Essen city cup at the end of the year.

Catching confidently, throwing quickly – it was a principle to which I would remain true through all my professional career. Rapidly, however, it became clear to me that catching balls alone did not make a good goalkeeper. I just had to look at Toni Schumacher in that semi-final: he appeared locked up in his kit, which, strangely, was in France's colours: a red shirt and blue sleeves with the three white stripes across. A brightly coloured powerhouse. When he knocked out poor Patrick Battiston in the sixtieth minute of the World Cup semi-final, I did not feel as much compassion for the heavily injured forward as I felt admiration for the courage with which Toni had come out of his goal. No one does that, I thought, if they do not have absolute trust in their body's resilience. Then, it was Schumacher's time to shine: Karl-Heinz Rummenigge closed the gap, and Klaus Fischer scored the equaliser by bicycle kick, leading to a penalty shoot-out in one of the best games in World Cup history. And Toni Schumacher, my hero and role model, saved Maxime Bossis' penalty – 'we' were in the final, because we had a strong goalkeeper, in every respect.

I was as drained as probably all German football fans that evening; in any case, I could not go to bed immediately and made the second path-changing decision that day: I needed to become stronger. From a squatting position, I did three jumps to the ceiling of my bedroom and four times twenty press-ups on top. During the next four years, I would do that every other day. The sound of the jumps nearly drove my parents to insanity but, as with everything, they got used to it. Later, I was even given dumbbells for my birthday, to train my upper arms more.

Initially, I told no one of my decision to turn pro. My parents did know that I could play football fairly well, but no one in my family had a serious sporting past and could not even remotely imagine me one day making money by flinging myself into the mud. In those days, a professional footballer was no more highly regarded than a prize fighter. The Bundesliga, after the great betting scandal surrounding Schalke and Bielefeld in the 1970/71 season, had the reputation of a smoke-filled bookmakers, and brawls between fans were part of the routine. Some stadiums were regarded as war zones. And that was where I wanted to work one day? 'You should do an apprenticeship,' my father kept saying, 'At the bank or as a trader. Then, you can study if you fancy it. You don't have to, though. Your decision.'

Until that day in July when West Germany won the World Cup semi-final at the expense of France, I had never really spared any proper thought for what I actually wanted to be. I had thought of being a bus driver, but only for the sake of convenience: whenever I missed my bus on the way to school in winter, I would freeze my tail off. When a second one finally arrived and opened its doors, I would go green with envy at the driver's workplace. I thought I wanted to be there one day too – but eventually, my bedroom jumps began hitting the ceiling.

Parallel to my hand-made strength training, I prepared a schedule for myself: at fourteen, within one year, I would be playing at Schwarz-Weiß Essen. At 18, I would be their reserves' number two; at 21, I would be first choice; and at 23, 24, I would make it into the Bundesliga. The masterplan was the national team. I can't quite put my finger on what actually drove me all those years. It was probably the longing for recognition and the ambition to be on that TV show yourself one day, the football highlights we would watch every Saturday evening at 6 pm Money played a small role too. At that time I might have had no clear idea how much was made in which profession, but one thing had always been certain: most of my friends and the children around me had more money than I did. In my parts, as a boy from a normal background, you quickly realised that you had to work hard in order to even keep up remotely with the kids from better homes. Many teenagers my age would never have to earn their own money. True, we were fortunate to live in our own house but, unlike the cool kids at school, I was not walking around in polo shirts by Lacoste or Benetton. The height of highs was a yellow Marco Polo fleece my dad had bought me. And while the others got scooters on their sixteenth birthdays, for me, it was just enough for a *mofa* [moped], a Hercules Prima 5S. That was doing thirty – especially after I had souped it up a bit – but it did stay just a *mofa*, as much as I tinkered with it. The others, no matter where we were going together, were always there ten minutes earlier. I didn't have a rear seat either, which meant no girls on the back. Especially when it came to courting the prettiest girls, those from 'normal' backgrounds were often left standing. The sixteen-year-olds in my class were picked up by eighteen-year-olds in a Golf GTI, while a *mofa* wally like me was not paid any attention.

I promised myself never to become as aloof and out of touch, but at the same time, it was probably exactly those experiences that shaped me. 'I'll show you,' was the chorus of the anger-song inside me. A quarter of a century later, my aggression and grimness on the pitch showed me that, apparently, I still had not shed this mentality. 'I'll show you' – to this day, that sentence explains almost everything. My critics will now hold against me the impression that I seem not to have risen above my teenage stage. On the pitch, this might even be the case, but in those decisive years in which a personality is formed, I learned something else: respect and tolerance. In the evenings, at the pub, I realised that not all wealthy youths were idiots. And in football, where I myself was one from a 'better home', I came to meet and value many who were of humble upbringing. In the game, you are reliant on everyone, no matter where they are from. My success is their success and vice versa. Football is a proper school for life and has an incredibly integrative effect. This is not just one of the guidelines of the DFB (Deutscher Fußball-Bund – the German FA) – for me, it was the truth on the pitch, day after day.

Eventually, I could no longer keep my doggedly pursued career-wish a secret at home. I pulled myself together, as if wanting to come out of goal in a hairy situation. My parents, without further ado, declared me unworldly. Years previously, they had not accepted one of my decisions. At the time, that was fortunate for me: I was dying to attend a *realschule* [in the German education system realschule is the mid-ranking secondary school, between Hauptschule (lowest) and Gymnasium (highest)], simply because all my friends were going there. Of course, I didn't know how different it would be. My parents, however, were more long-sighted – and unyielding: 'You'll be attending a gymnasium,' they decided, no matter how much I protested and whined. Eventually, I did acknowledge the importance of a good education, and now I know that professional footballers too can only profit from it. During my time at Arsenal, I saw young players who had contracts at fifteen, sixteen, and were only given two or three lessons a day by a teacher hired by the club. Accepting and absorbing new things, focusing over a longer period – young players are no longer taught any of this nowadays. But as a top player, you have to possess exactly that: a sense for new things – dietary habits, fitness exercises, and the ability to concentrate. Only if you are still alert, even in the 120th minute, can you write good exams – and win big games. Most successful footballers with whom I played over the course of my career – Thierry Henry, Dennis Bergkamp, Cesc Fàbregas, Oliver Bierhoff, or Christoph Metzelder, to just name a few – are intelligent people. They were able to think for their team-mates; it was what made them great. There is hardly a player left in modern high-speed football who is as daft as a brush.

'Health, school, sport – in this order, Jens, is how you live your life.' That was my father's eternally reoccurring litany. Often, when he struck it up, I could have strangled him. Today, I tell my children nothing different. Really, for my parents, my footballing obsession had a pleasant side effect: I was incredibly disciplined. When I had been given the *mofa*, I did not, of course, just drive the short distances to school and to training at Uhlenkrug, where Schwarz-Weiß Essen still play today. With greater mobility, a larger circle of friends became accessible to me. We would drive to Bredeney, where the girls where prettier than those in Heisingen (or perhaps, they were simply more unknown). There, we always went to Johnny's, a pub that was actually called 'Putzbachtal', but that at the time was the coolest of all places – with a landlord called Johnny. Mind you, I was never part of the properly cool lot. I always passed on the joints doing the rounds, did not even smoke and only drank cola. Sometimes, of course, I perceived my abstinence as a bit of a sacrifice, but the obligation towards my coaches and teammates was simply greater. I had a goal: professional footballer. And they did not smoke and drink – at least, that was what I thought back in the day; over the course of my career, I learned better. Every time, I said my goodbyes just before 10.30 pm at night. My parents ran a tight ship; 10.30 pm was my curfew. 'The sleep before midnight is the most important,' my father would say; besides, I had to complete my training schedule.

At first, whenever I said goodbye as promptly as if I had swallowed an alarm clock, my friends would look at me stupidly. 'What the hell are you doing? Why is it always that bloody football with you?' they would ask. I could never say more than, 'It's fun.' In time, they got used to the fact that hashish, cigarettes, and alcohol were wasted on me. I was accepted as peculiar – that might not have been cool, but better than to be laughed at or snubbed. Only the girls did not really want to have anything to do with an odd one like me. Admittedly, at fourteen, I had my first girlfriend – Katrin. But apart from a bit of snogging, there was not much going on; I just was not ready yet. Less than a year later, it was over; apparently, mere snogging had not been enough for her. In any case, she was not interested in me any more, not even during our end-of-school trip to Lake Garda in Italy. Instead, on the way there, another girl had already said: 'I'll get to work on that Jens this week.' She went with someone else after all, though – I was shitting my pants and did not know how to act. In the evenings, I sat on the beach with the cool stoners from my year; at least during this one week, I belonged. True, it eventually came to nothing, of course, as I was realising that it was another world – nice lads, spoiled and bored, smoking hash and drinking. Once, I could not resist after all, during an outing to a restaurant high above Limone sul Garda. It was the first drunken stupor of my life. Not many were added to it, or nothing would have come of the football.

No chance with the girls, only tolerated by the cool ones – of course, those were disappointments almost every teenager had to suffer. But for me, they turned into additional motivation. I realised that you could not achieve much in life without determination. Hence, that would run through my life like a common thread. After every low blow I received during my time in football, I always had the confidence that everything would get back on track. The majority of this 'basic trust' I owe to my parents. They were strict, of course, but also very loving and reliable. I'm sure that these orderly circumstances allowed me to become a successful athlete. It was not that my parents were standing on the sidelines during every game, roaring, 'Run! Pass! Tackle!' The yelling is counter-productive anyway; many of my former teammates lost interest when their parents piled on the pressure. I do not even recall whether my parents came along at all – though my mum claims that, often enough, she had kicked her heels on some sort of recreation ground; I cannot remember any of it. I profited in a different way. Over the course of my career, I saw teammates who had suddenly cracked completely in absolute pressure situations; who had entirely unexpectedly failed to perform during finals, a relegation battle, a penalty shoot-out. Often, those were people who came from more unstable circumstances – the parents divorced, the father disappeared, things like that. They lacked something I call basic trust. When they were on a knife edge, they would think, 'This is going to go belly-up again.'

In my head, it's always the exact opposite: Ah, it will be all right. For whenever I toppled over, my parents picked me up again. Whenever my brother or I needed our parents, they were there for us. When we came home from school, food was on the table, usually something with potatoes. In retrospect, I feel as if I ate nothing but potatoes for years on end – maybe that is how I got a keeper's build in the first place, since my parents are of rather average height: my father is 1.76m, my mother 1.70m. Sunday was church attendance, followed by a roast – those were two further benchmarks of this 'safe all-round package'. Of course, I did not always attend church voluntarily, but for a while I was even an acolyte. And because I do nearly everything I begin incredibly intensely, I occasionally even went three or four times a week – carrying candles, bringing the chalice to the altar, ringing the bells during consecration. I do not know whether I really learned faith in a greater justice in church, one that may prevail on the pitch too. But one thing I did learn there, something that would still benefit me as a pro: discipline and willpower.

At fourteen, I drove to Alsace for three days with the scout group. It rained as if the world was ending, and I lugged around a seabag, which instead of proper carrying straps only had some drawstrings. After three hours, I had bloody welts on my shoulder; I could barely walk for all the mud. But we moved along somehow; on the last stretch, my brother gave me a piggyback, and his friend carried my sea bag for me.

My brother and I were the children described by Florian Illies in his book *Generation Golf*. On Saturday mornings, the family car was washed: initially, a K70, later perhaps an Opel or a Passat – classic German cars. In the meantime, one of us had to sweep the drive and the pavement drain. Afterwards, it was time for spaghetti Bolognese, because I had read in a football magazine that the pros ate pasta before the games – and indeed, I would do so to the very end of my career. The afternoon was usually filled with a match. Back home, expecting her warriors, my mother would already be standing in front of the basement door with the laundry basket. In bad weather, she sprayed the ash from our clothes with the garden hose or stuck everything directly into the washing machine. The bath tub was already filled; then, watching Sportschau or Wetten, dass..?, the sun would set slowly on our idyll.

'Health, school, sport' – over the next years, father's litany was my law. I was the only one of my side at Schwarz-Weiß Essen who was allowed just one game a week even when two were scheduled – my father remained steadfast there, much to the anger of my coaches. On the cinder pitch near us, I was allowed to play as often as I wanted, but only if I was done with my homework and my marks added up. Luckily, I had always been a B-to-C kind of student without having to do too much on the side. My favourite subjects were maths and PE, but ultimately, not much of my school days has stuck in my memory. There was only thing for me: football. I was obsessed with it. I did not even want to go on holiday, because I would not be able to play there. Between thirteen and eighteen, I only ever went away once, to Italy, which was a football tournament with the under-19s.

Until the age of sixteen, however, I was average at best. I might have been playing in the Niederrheinliga as keeper of Schwarz-Weiß Essen's under-15s, but so had many – and many better ones, too. During my step up into the next age group, I stumbled: instead of competing with the B1 in North Rhine-Westphalia's highest league, I trudged about below with the B2. Not until shortly before the end of the season did a colleague's misfortune prove to be my luck: while making a save, Klaus Bagh jumped against a post in such a hapless manner that the poor chap broke his lower jaw. So, inevitably, I was promoted – but I was above average neither in terms of my performances nor my stature: I belonged to the group of rather smaller goalies. Since I was continuing my special domestic training, though, and firmly believed in becoming a pro, it went uphill step by step.

Goalkeeper training, at the time, did not deserve that name; in truth, it was an ordeal. Like most clubs in the Ruhr Valley, Schwarz-Weiß Essen only had a hard cinder pitch. Be it -3° or 30°, I always wore the same clothes: two padded keeper's trousers and two keeper's tops, on top of each other. In the summer, you would lose four pounds in sweat from simply standing around; in the winter, the clothes would soak up all the way to the top and end up weighing almost a stone. A lead vest was never needed; the rain above Essen took care of that for free. When I was eighteen, an orthopaedist predicted that thanks to all the hard landings on the Ruhr Valley's cinder pitches, I would get solid hip problems by the time I was thirty. Thank God he was not that good a diagnostician; I have not yet had to give up the upright walk.

But that may also be down to the fact that from May, we Cinder Children got access to paradise: the Schillerwiese. A wonderful, public green in Essen, freshly mown, the Wembley of my adolescence. Together with my first coach, Martin Annen, and the brand-new, blazing-fast 'Tango' ball, I went on a pilgrimage there. Martin would take aim, and at last, I was enjoying my job. From that moment on,

I knew: if only I got the chance to play on grass regularly, I would instantly be 30, 40 per cent better.

My former class-mate Martin Annen – who first suggested I become a goalkeeper rather than a forward - gave me something else to take along, something from which I still profit immensely to this day. After school, he began to study philosophy. At first, I didn't understand how this was supposed to correlate: that football obsessive a fine thinker? Shouting at the boys on the pitch to go full throttle, but studying Kant at home? Still, it worked. Bit by bit, the shelves in his room filled with the main works of the great German and foreign philosophers. Whenever I visited him, I would see Martin reading. I had a look at one or two of the volumes, but quickly left it at that – too difficult. And yet, he developed me with his example: because I was reading other books, I became not only enriched but convinced that reading enhanced my ability to concentrate. The regular evening glance at my father reading in his armchair reinforced this. On his lap were historical books, the *Spiegel*, whatever, but he would always read completely for himself. Readers are hard to distract, and for a goalkeeper the ability to concentrate is the most important parameter in order to access constant performances over long periods of time. I could only become the keeper I am today by being a reader.

The first time I realised that my decision to go pro was not a megalomaniacal crackpot idea was during the moment I finally stood in goal for Schwarz-Weiß Essen's under-15s first team. That was no longer an organic team grown over the years, but instead a strategically assembled hodgepodge of the best players from all of Essen, systematically headhunted by the club. Otherwise, there would have been hardly a way of standing against teams like MSV Duisburg, Fortuna Düsseldorf, or Borussia Mönchengladbach. During a knock-out game against Bayer 05 Uerdingen, we were even able to qualify for the German under-15s championship, albeit we were considered total underdogs. At the time, Uerdingen were putting a lot of their Bayer money into their youth teams – and yet, we won the first leg 1–0. Before the second leg, there was only one thing being said about us: 'Watch out, they're taking you seriously now; you're getting five past you!' But we drew 0–0 – and for the first time I had the feeling that 'that football thing' might actually work.

18

In the second round, though, I learned what downsides my sport could have if there was too much ambition in play. During the return leg of the quarter-finals against Hannover 96, one of the opposing forwards kicked off half my ear. Not a quarter of an hour had been played when I was already on the way to hospital. But we went through, and after turning round a 1–4 home defeat in the quarter-finals with a 5–0 win in Berlin, it was Paderborn-Neuhaus in the semi-finals. Years later, I reminisced about the game in Berlin with Martin Annen. After my injury, what with my bandaged ear, I had really only joined the trip to the return leg to support the team. But during final training in the afternoon, I told our coach, Friedhelm Slomke, and the head of youth, Georg von Wick, that I was bent on playing. However, the *Neue Rheinische Zeitung* journalist who had travelled along was certainly not allowed to report that I had started, because my parents read that paper. So, after our 5–0 triumph, the coverage merely said: 'The goalkeeper (no name!) provided stability for the defence; there is a strong will in him.'

The shoot-out in Paderborn-Neuhaus was my last until the UEFA Cup decider in Milan. I saved two penalties, which meant the finals for us. There, however, we lost to 5–0 to VfB Stuttgart – perhaps there is a higher sense behind the fact that, of all places, at the tail-end of my career, I ended up at the club to whom I owe my first great defeat.

For a small club like Schwarz-Weiß Essen, though, participating in the final alone was a historic triumph. On top, I was even rewarded with an invitation to the junior national team. Holger Osieck, who at the time was assistant to DFB coach-in-charge Berti Vogts, had seen me play. But my premiere in the famous national team kit was a disaster: I had screwed on thin studs, too thin, causing me to skid during goal kicks and also when we conceded the decisive goal. After that, I wasn't called up to the national team at junior level again.

Considering my reputation, some may now think that I grabbed Berti Vogts by the hair afterwards. But my anger was limited – among other things because I received another invitation: to a trial session at Schalke 04. That had become my favourite club, and my *mofa* was to blame for it because, with it, I was always able to drive to the Bundesliga matches, all the way up to the gates of the Parkstadion at Gelsenkirchen – if I was not going along in my cousin's car. And since the controls at the gates did not yet have that certain maximum-security atmosphere surrounding them, we would always blag our way into the stadium for free, walking all the way down onto the tartan track where those old benches for the photographers stood. That became my usual spot from which I would marvel at the legendary German keeper Jean-Marie Pfaff during the visit of Bayern Munich – from just five yards away. I learned one particular thing in my box seat: how much faster and tougher the professional game was. And those hard lads were now inviting me to a training session – yes, it was only the under-19s, but still.

Shortly before the summer holidays in 1986, I went – and could not believe my eyes. I might have been used to the fact that we were still playing on a cinder pitch at Schwarz-Weiß Essen. But our pitch was at least made of red cinder – Schalke were playing on a hard, grey-cinder pitch; it was the Trabant of football pitches. And to top it all off, they still had rectangular goalposts. I did my best, and at least impressed the Schalke youth coach enough that, shortly after, he phoned my parents' house: 'Michael Skibbe here. We would like to sign your son for our under-19s and make him a contract reserve player. This will also give him the opportunity of going professional later on.' So, only four years after my decision on the sofa, I had nearly reached my goal. Anyone else might have gone on a naked pilgrimage to Schalke in nothing but a pair of blue-and-white flip-flops but I said no. I was not going to commit to cinder and a reserves contract – no, thanks. I did have another offer from Wattenscheid 09, but I did not want to go there, either. I would rather have another great year of Schwarz-Weiß Essen than a bad time at Schalke.

Evidently, Schalke had taken offence at my rejection. By now, during the semi-finals of a youth tournament, I had driven Schalke mad with a few good saves, so they wanted me more than ever. As a result, they were now bringing out the big guns: the president himself, Günter Siebert. 'Mr Lehmann,' he said to my father on the phone, 'do come round with your son. *We would like to talk to you.*' As emerged during the conversation, Siebert had been raised in Kassel like my father; the two were getting along so well that my father forgot his 'health, school, sport' litany for a moment and promised to drive to Schalke with me.

# Conquering The Fear, Or, What It Means To Be A Goalkeeper

AS THE BALL CAME FLYING, I WAS STILL THINKING IT WAS GOING TO be okay – Emmanuel Eboué was there, my full-back; he would take care of it. He was already jumping towards the cross, but suddenly, he ducked his head. This could not be happening. Manchester United were on the attack; the ball came swooshing into my six-yard box like an artillery shell. Cristiano Ronaldo was just waiting for it, and Eboué, the only one who could help now, ducked his head. The ball bounced off the ground, eight yards in front of the goal. I ran out, spread my arms, simply standing there in anticipation of a mighty blow. Ronaldo, without hesitation, volleyed his shot. Still, I was staring at the ball shooting towards me at over 100mph, then felt the impact on my face. My brain flew backwards, and I went down. After such a hit, you cannot scream any more; all you do is moan. Ronaldo stood before me, bewildered. He could not believe he had hit my head either. For at least two minutes I lay groggily on the ground, then picked myself up. During the subsequent corner, as the ball came in, John O'Shea stood in front of me in order to obstruct me. I struck out my fist. With the ball out of the danger zone, the half-time whistle blew.

My first target during the break was my pal Eboué: 'You wimp!' I screamed, pretty much the worst thing you could say to a Premier League player. I kept ranting. The others urged me to calm down, but I did not want to. My brain hurt, everything hurt. 'Come on, it's not that bad,' Eboué said. Was he mental? What exactly was 'not that bad' about someone almost kicking my head from five yards? My manager asked if I could continue, and I went out again. This scene from Manchester United against Arsenal in the autumn of 2006 illustrates some of the obsession needed to be a good goalkeeper. It was one of my best ever games; I was in the form of my life after the World Cup in Germany. Shortly before the end, I stopped an Ole Gunnar Solskjaer shot from going into the far corner and thus secured our valuable 1–0 away win. In England, they sometimes called me 'Mad Jens' – it was above all a reference to my very aggressive style of play. Really, my way of playing was anything but mad. On the contrary, it was the result of coolly analysing probabilities.

I have no use either for the saying that goalkeepers are barmy. First and foremost, in modern football, the keeper should be an organiser. He must be able to give orders, particularly during risky situations in the box, as often the defenders no longer have a feeling for the ball or the opposing players. One moment, they are watching the ball; the next, they are looking for their opponent – in the process, they lose their view of the whole game. This view, however, needs to be preserved by the goalkeeper and be translated into pinpoint stage direction, especially if the ball is in motion and the game is in flow. Usually, defenders are well placed during dead balls, corners, or free kicks; the whole trick is to keep order as everything and everyone moves at top speed. To this end, it is not as important to watch the ball but rather the opposing players. If you know where they are or could be going, you also know where the ball is going and when it will be dangerous. This gets you that split-second advantage during which to shout at your defenders to take a step back, look to their right, or go left. I never needed to do much yelling: up until the penalty spot, my teammates would still hear me even above 50,000 spectators. I did have to shout, though, if my defenders needed to confront a counter-attack way ahead of my goal or simply did not want to hear me. The reason for this is that once a ball is on its way to the unmarked forward, the full-back can no longer react. The secret of a goalkeeper's success lies in his ability to anticipate not only individual shots but entire set-plays.

Most of my goalkeeping colleagues stare primarily at the ball. In an interview, Oliver Kahn once told of how, in order to focus during a game, he had begun to look only towards the ball. Only then did I really understand why Kahn did not see and mitigate many situations earlier: if you only look at the ball, all you know is where it is, not where it will be. For this reason, whenever the ball came from outside my box, I practically never stood head-on to it: otherwise, the segment of the game that I would be able to cover was going to be much too small. You only gain an overview if you free yourself from the fixation on the ball. Really, I always played like this, without anyone ever teaching me; I had already developed my style during my youth. My father created an archive in which he collected newspaper articles about me, and already in the very early clippings from my first games with the professionals, it said: 'Keeper Lehmann stood out by his good control of the penalty area.'

Maybe it was because I had originally started as an outfield player, a forward. I will never know whether, under different circumstances, I might have been a good pro outside of the box too. If anything, I would have probably played midfield, as I had never been the fastest – my legs are simply too long. But I could have found a spot in the centre of play because there too you have to be able to read the game, which had come naturally to me from the beginning.

The move into goal did mean, of course, that I was giving up something crucial: the feeling of fulfilment during the shot on goal. Scoring a goal is something definite, while every saved ball is just another step down the path – a path that never really finds an end. The strike cannot be taken from you by anyone, but the grand save is forgotten after the next conceded goal and often entirely worthless. Even the most average forward can note something positive to his credit: the goals he has scored. In contrast, the performance of the world's best keeper is recognised by mistakes, few as they may be. To this day, I still consider every single goal ever scored against me a humiliation, even those conceded during a warm-up before the match. Already before kick-off, I wanted and needed to deliver a top performance, which was why each ball the goalkeeping coach put past me was a real nuisance. You can imagine, then, how much goals against bothered me during a game. 'How stupid I am,' I would think to myself even before the ball had passed the goal-line. It would take ages until I was over a lost game. Some, I never managed to handle: for example, my defeats in the Champions League and European Championship finals, because such chances usually do not return. And since so much often hinges on a single ball, I too am in favour of video replays to decide on disputed goals. In football, a goal is the most precious thing. Occasionally, teams work for hours towards scoring one – or, from my perspective, towards preventing one. After all these efforts, it cannot be unclear whether or not a ball has crossed the line. Fortunately, goal line technology has now been introduced to many of Europe's top leagues, including the Bundesliga and the Premier League. But even when I had not conceded a goal, I would rarely leave the pitch a contented player. In at least 90 per cent of my games, I was not satisfied, because I had made a mistake. It might not have been important; it might have been one that no one had noticed, not even the manager. However, it still remained a mistake, and that meant I was still not perfect. I believe that only by consistent self-criticism can you develop to be a good player.

During my time in England, I started watching a video montage of each of my games together with my goalkeeping coach, Gerry Peyton. 'Plusses and minuses,' we called these sequences of my good and bad moments. Initially, Gerry, a funny Irishman, had not wanted to do this. At the start of our collaboration, he had been a real softie whom I had to teach more toughness in a typical German manner. 'Oh, no, no, you can't do that; you'll only hurt yourself,' he would say when during perfectly normal training, I had dived for even the trickiest balls. 'Sorry,' I replied, 'But I have to jump during the match too. And if I want to be good, I have to train as if it were a real game.' Gradually, he adopted my mentality in such a way that it eventually became too much even for me, and I had to slow him down: 'When I first arrived, you wanted me to jump onto a soft mat; now, you're doing things during which I almost dislocate my shoulder!'

Watching the videos went the same way. Initially, I had urged him to let me see where I went wrong. Later, he positively tormented me with the montages: 'Right, Jens, we'll need to take another look at that!' Facing your own mistakes in this manner can be agonising on occasion, but I was lucky throughout: the plus scenes were always more prominent than the minus moments, and this form of self-awareness certainly did not harm me. Gerry was very analytical with it and noticed even the smallest details; as a result, I was able to learn a bit more. Occasionally, after a conversation with a young player, I found myself thinking: the way he was talking, you would think he never made any mistakes. In the long run, though, you can wave goodbye to this artificially inflated self-assurance – a bunch of Michelin Men out of whom the air escapes with a squeak. He who is not willing to analyse and work on his weaknesses is eventually stopped by them, and another quickly takes his place.

Although mistakes define a keeper's life more than that of an outfield player, I have never regretted the walk into goal. I always perceived myself as the others' team-mate, and the development of modern football has accommodated this greatly: the steady increase in pace and the invention of the back four have made the *libero* redundant – the man who used to be responsible for organising the defence. Now, the goalkeeper is the *libero* too. This means a lot of work for him, created by his own defenders. The latter do not want and are not supposed to be man-to-man markers any more. Instead, they are zonal markers, with the result that they often stand in a completely wrong position to the forwards, granting them too many chances. I do not want to plead for the return to the old man-marking concept during which a defender of the Berti Vogts type used to pursue his opponent all the way to the loo – but defending means marking your man in the zone, because the latter alone does not score goals. While this may sound simple, many defenders do not understand it. Slavishly, they think of their own position on the pitch and, eventually, do not stand optimally to the opponent. This is where the goalkeeper comes into play as organiser, as *libero*: with your orders, you ensure the correct position. You control how far the back four stands on the field, how large the gaps are between players. Staying in one line, meanwhile, is something they need to organise themselves, but many of them have grown lazy. They move too slowly, especially forwards out of the defence. As a rule, if a ball is being played even a yard backwards by the other team, defenders need to move up a yard behind it; that is how they put the opposing forward under constant compulsion to move. The forward prefers to loiter on a level with the back four; it is convenient for him and makes him dangerous. If, however, the back four constantly pulses back and forth, he has to go with them, and that is when it becomes exhausting for him too. This is why I would try to set my back four in motion, shouting, 'Outwards, outwards, outwards!' – but not everyone listened to me, an issue which not even the managers press strongly enough.

Of course, I made mistakes over the course of my career, on and off the pitch – sometimes, you are simply off the mark about how a set-play will develop, and you are subsequently left to look a fool. I remember one of my first cup games with Schalke against Rot-Weiss Essen: shortly before the end, we were pushing for the equaliser; I was standing virtually alone at the halfway line as a long clearance came flying towards me. I wanted to stop it with the outside of my boot, but the ball jumped four, five yards away. An Essen player put it past me as cool as you please and ran with it into the empty goal – 0–2 and I was a complete laughing stock. 'A good keeper with potential, but he plays much too riskily at times' – such phrases became a kind of background music to me. A lot of it looked insanely easy, but every now and again, it would go wrong after all. Even in my final Bundesliga season in 2009/10 I was not beyond mistakes: during the home game against FC Köln with Stuttgart, we were trailing 0–1 when, just before the end, a long ball came sailing into my half. If I wanted to stand any chance at all, I had to go out. I was too late: Wilfried Sanou went through with the ball, and I had to fish the ball out of my goal for the second time that day.

In the beginning, this way of playing did not help me win my team-mates' trust. You might receive fewer head-on reproaches, but you know best what it is you have done wrong anyway. Once, during a second-tier game at the age of eighteen against Braunschweig, who at the time were still playing really good football under Uwe Rienders, I played over 89 minutes as if I had eight arms. But in the ninetieth minute, a wobbling ball slipped through my hands in the mud, and a Braunschweig player slid it in. What was the point of Uwe Rienders coming into the dressing room afterwards, saying: 'Great saves, sorry about the mistake'? Privately, he was might have been laughing to himself. It was one of my more bitter moments – and the only one after which I sat in the dressing room and cried.

But year after year, I learned more and more things you should not do – that way, I drew closer to an almost perfect technique and style of play. 'I knew that the best way to survive in goal was to optimize my technique to perfection'. What was becoming more and more important was making the right decisions at the right moment – something that young keepers, for example, do not know how to do yet because they lack experience and a grasp of the game. Arsène Wenger once remarked that I was improving the players around me – which is when you know the wheat has been sorted from the chaff.

No less important, however, is giving up all analytical distance in the moment and turning off rationality – in short: conquering your fear. Since the beginning, my basic emotion towards the goal, those three poles with a net, had been respect – simply based on the fact that I never wanted to smash into the post like my colleague Klaus Bagh had done back in the under-16s. His jaw fracture made me a starting keeper.

My style involved my frequently having to leave the safe harbour of my six-yard box in order to intercept crosses, through balls, and ricocheted shots. On the line, it is easy to look good; usually, you do not get hurt while you are there, either – but every excursion away from it can bring pain: the opponent can end up kicking or hitting you, whether on purpose or not. You might receive a ball in the face or your privates. Any normal person would now say, 'What am I, bonkers? I'm not doing that; I'm staying where I am.' As a keeper, however, you have to leave behind precisely these thoughts, all reason, and the entirely natural protective reflex. That was only possible for me if, during every game, I worked myself into that unique frenzy of adrenalin, extreme tension and maximum fixation on the match. One reason I set such great store by good, rational organisation was so that I might find myself in these situations as rarely as possible. The better the positions my defenders were standing in, the less the danger of me having to risk my neck. My centre-halves were constantly my best friends; if they were of high quality, they were virtually holy to me. Without their class, I would have been completely stranded: sometimes, even I am alarmed and angered by goalkeepers biting off more than they can chew whenever the fear reflex is turned off. Petr Čech, for example, was similarly uncompromising – until that very game in October 2006 when an opponent's knee shattered his skull. He might have returned to the game eventually, wearing a special helmet, but it took some time until he belonged to the best again. Surely, I would not have fared any differently; very rarely do you ever get over such an accident. I have simply been lucky: I could have broken everything. There are two scars on my scalp, something that will be interesting to see when my hairline recedes even more in future.

Ultimately, the absoluteness with which you are ready to conquer your fear separates the few very good goalkeepers from the many good ones. Once, I asked Michael Schumacher how many properly good Formula One drivers there really were. 'Including myself? Three,' he had replied, 'And you recognise them by their braking significantly later than the others.' With goalkeepers, it is similar. In 2006, when I was at the height of my performance, I believe there were only two or three others in the whole world who played at my level, willing to abandon all rationality and accept pain – all just to keep a clean sheet and win a match. Catching balls, being good with both feet, having a strong physique and proper acceleration – most goalkeepers nowadays are equipped with these things. Even reflexes are not crucial, because they cannot be trained. You can only train reactions, focusing on the awareness of an incoming object. But in a one-to-one situation, such as the Cristiano Ronaldo one described earlier, most keepers look away at the wrong moment. In some manner, they jump in the direction of ball and opponent, all the while hoping they will have a close shave.

Conquering fear is a matter of practice, too. Occasionally in training, I would have balls shot at me from a short distance, trying to stop them with either head or chest. In this respect, I have learned a lot from Toni Schumacher, my first teacher back at Schalke, and I am not talking about the famous Battiston scene from that semi-final which inspired me to go pro. I do not think Schumacher meant to injure the Frenchman on purpose as he jumped towards him; after all, he did not hit him with the outstretched leg but rather with his hip. It was a simple occupational hazard – for both of them. Schumacher showed me that the basis of all fearlessness is the confidence in your own body and that your body needs to be strong. At seventeen, I was still a pretty gangly lad, so I went into the weights room to gain more muscle. Schumacher had donated a multifunctional machine to the club and had it put into a tiny room at the upper end of the escalator leading into the Parkstadion. Add a photo wallpaper of the Caribbean to the windowless shack and *voilà* – a fitness centre *à la* Schalke. Barely anyone apart from Toni and me was using it at the time, but Schumacher was considered a special case anyway. After every game, on Sunday mornings, he would get into the dressing-room bathtub for an underwater massage during which he would empty a bottle of champagne. After one lost match, then manager Horst Franz went up to him and said, 'Toni, yesterday's match was so bad that we have to train today. Get out of your tub and put on some clothes. Oh, and we're on the cinder pitch today; the grass isn't playable because of the rain.' Schumacher simply looked across the rim of his tub and replied, 'Horst, I'll leave you a pair of keeper's gloves with your name on. This way, you can train on cinder every Sunday; I'm definitely not doing that.'

But on a normal training day, Schumacher was endlessly ambitious and disciplined, an attitude which taught me a lot. Everything else on the path to being a good keeper is routine. Ever since I had reached my definite physical stature at the beginning of my professional career, I kept leaving my goal and always got hit in return – but eventually, you get used to it. The penalty box is the keeper's territory, even if it lies directly in front of the opposition end, with everyone screaming 'arsehole' and 'wanker' at you. Of course, you hear all of that very clearly – in England, they had a fondness for shouting 'Nazi pig' in German – but you have to live with it. Assert yourself in these 792 square yards; the opposing forwards have to know that you will never pull back. Now, it was not that I regarded forwards as my enemies. I respected them, even when they were trying to impress me, often by less than fair means. There was the fair type such as Wayne Rooney; he would play and dish it out the way he was: always straightforward. But there were also old-school forwards like Alan Shearer, for example, who used his elbows a lot. That being said, I never injured someone intentionally. Once, I knocked out Newcastle's Scott Parker, but only because I was trying to protect myself: I had a safe hold of the ball, but he was still attempting to run through, so I turned away – he smashed into my elbow at full blast and did not return. I was always going to turn away before he rammed his knee into me or crunched my skull, as happened to my colleague Čech. When you are making a decision that involves potential pain, it is a matter of 'him or me', and so I would preferably decide for the opponent. I had to show people that they might well be hurt if they entered my box, and their being afraid of me made my job considerably easier.

In the ten years of my professional career, I always took pleasure in my job – because I always handled well the pressure to which a goalkeeper is constantly exposed. Not until my very last Bundesliga season did a tragic event force me to see my profession, even football as a whole, in a completely new light. Of all days, it happened on my fortieth birthday, 10 November 2009: Robert Enke took his own life. I remember it exactly: in the afternoon, I had celebrated my milestone birthday with my children and some friends from the neighbourhood; in the evening, I was sitting with a mate, when another friend congratulated me over the phone. Five minutes later, she called again, asking whether I had heard about Robert Enke. 'Nope, what's happened?' I asked, unsuspectingly. 'Robert's dead.' I was unable to believe it, probably like most other people that evening.

I had come to know him better during Euro 2008 when he was number two in goal behind me. In keeping with his calm nature, he had initially observed everything: considering everything he had heard about the rivalry between Oliver Kahn and me, he probably wanted to check what I was like as a colleague and competitor. He could not know that much of this duel was exaggerated. In training, he made a good, casual impression and was pleasant and likeable off the pitch, too. In public, he would never lay claim to being number one – but it was also clear that he was going to use every opportunity to pull ahead of me, just like every other rival.

Our families had met during the pre-Euros training camp in Mallorca. I still remember a boat tour, during which we saw a dead fish drifting in the sea. Robert's wife Teresa wanted to catch and bury it; her husband laughed and told us how she always pitied animals and would love to offer their home as a shelter to all stray creatures. We all admired the composed manner in which the two seemed to cope with the fate of their little daughter, who had been born severely ill and died only two years old. I always had the feeling that the experiences with his sick child had taught Robert to keep a certain distance from football and the hectic, sometimes superficial bustle around it. Of course, he was taking his sport seriously; otherwise, he wouldn't have come as far as he had – but he also seemed to know that there was more to life than 22 men running after a ball.

And now this inconceivable news. After checking the teletext to see whether my friend had perhaps got something mixed up, I called Oliver Bierhoff. He was with the national team, who were due to play Chile a few days later. But there was no doubt: Robert had thrown himself in front of a train. I told my wife Conny, who was just as stunned as I. Eventually, my children noticed that something was wrong, and I had to try to explain the inexplicable.

Why would a person like that kill themselves? But then, Teresa held a moving press conference during which she explained how long Robert had already been suffering from severe depression. Hardly anyone had suspected this; I for one had never noticed that he might be ill. Then again, I had only grown to know him closer within the national team – a pure performance society of thirty people or so, thrown together for a few days or weeks in order to achieve an extremely ambitious goal. Sure, you converse and laugh together – but in the end, you are first and foremost fixated on your own performance and are paying little attention to the others.

One parenthetical sentence spoken by Teresa during her press conference occupied my mind most: football had been Robert's one and only, she said. So perhaps my impression of the healthy distance he had seemed to keep from his profession had been false after all. Suddenly, some of the things we had experienced together appeared in a different light. For example, he would get into a fret over Werder Bremen's keeper Tim Wiese, who kept bringing up his own name for discussion regarding the national team. Because Wiese initially was not quite successful with this, he suddenly declared publicly that as far as he was concerned, the case was closed. Robert would sit next to me on the bus to training in Cologne and bluster, 'How can someone close a case that was never open to him?' Apparently, he was quite riled that Wiese had a strong lobby in Bremen bosses Klaus Allofs and Thomas Schaaf, while no one was throwing themselves into the breach for Robert, the inconspicuous Hanoverian. On the contrary, Bremen would not lose a single opportunity to take subtle digs at Robert: how it was wrong that someone who conceded two, three goals in every game and had not even won a single cap should be favoured over their keeper. On top of this, there were the so-called experts who advised Robert to move to a bigger club. The fact that no top club was found even though Hannover were willing to let him go did not make things any better. At the time, all I could tell him in response was that once I was no longer playing in the national team and Wiese actually made the cut, the two of them were going to have quite some fun.

After my farewell to the national team, Robert announced that he would not get involved with any public discussion regarding the keeper's position.

Apparently, he was expecting in return that every rival accept him as their number one and that no one doubt his status. Perhaps, in consideration of his illness, he also thought he needed to keep his stress levels as low as possible, so if he did not pick a quarrel himself, the others would leave him alone. From personal experience, I could have told him that things did not work this way, especially not in the national team. When you arrived there, the first thing on your mind was that this had to be what paradise was like: so many amenities, everything organised perfectly, respect at your club and in public rising rapidly – but suddenly, you realised that now, every little thing that before had been of no interest to anyone, was now being dissected in public. The pressure on the goalkeeper especially is immense, because he could no longer afford to make a mistake. In the national team, no one yielded the floor to a rival without a fight; there was a hailstorm of criticism coming from all sides, accompanied by hidden bits of malice. Those were the rules of the game, and Robert could not change them. Anyone who, for whatever reason, showed some sort of insecurity was going to be hassled and eventually ousted. I have often been accused of being, to put it lightly, too extroverted. Even for kids, this is one of the important aspects of football – having fun and getting rid of your aggressions. That does still apply to us pros: enjoying your profession because it feels good to be knackered after a game, but having vented our frustration too. Being professional also involves talking about your work in public, though. Robert was cherished by all as a reserved, congenial person – maybe it would have helped him to let out the anger he was bound to have felt.

There were plenty of opportunities: when he had finally worked his way up to being the German number one, a hand fracture set him back. Deputy René Adler was playing well, but Robert fought for his return; even the manager saw him as the front runner and wanted to start him in the decisive World Cup qualifier against Russia. That was when Robert caught a rare virus – suddenly, Adler, Neuer and even the disliked Wiese were ahead of him again. 'Why always me?' Robert is said to have asked a journalist friend shortly before his death. He was not even invited to the following, relatively trivial, internationals. Of course, Jogi Löw is not to blame for Robert's illness, let alone his tragic final step. But did Robert see it that way too? What leads to such a decision, which mood changes

THE MADNESS IS ON THE PITCH

turn the balance? In the end, those are questions no one can answer.

A few days after Robert's death, I read an interview with his friend and agent, Jörg Neblung, who said, 'Back when the failure in Barcelona was looming, with the aid of his father, Robert's illness was recognised as a depressive disorder.' I find that disastrous use of 'failure' entirely inappropriate, because for Robert to be signed by a club like Barcelona as a young keeper was a massive achievement. Even if things had not gone smoothly later, there had been positive aspects too. In the media's black-and-white scenarios with their superlatives, you have automatically 'failed' as soon as you are not at the very top; no one speaks any more of the efforts and hardships young players in particular take upon themselves.

After Robert's death and the vast expression of condolences by the entire country, a lot of thought was given to how people with depression could be helped in today's performance-obsessed society. Affected players should turn to those responsible at their clubs regarding their illness and ask for help. After a successful treatment, they should definitely be helped back into the team. Sounds good – but it does not work. Football teams have clear hierarchies; they are structured like a pack of wolves. Every day, the leader has to fight for his position; the next in line will not hesitate to attack at the slightest show of weakness. Should the ill person's substitute prove as good or even better, then no manager or club in the world will reinstate the convalescent out of pity, consideration, or duty of care. Fragile sportspeople can only be helped by showing them clearly what they can achieve realistically. Weaknesses in particular need to be highlighted, in order to remedy them with the help of managers and psychologists. Nowadays, it is common practice to praise even very young players to the skies, although they still have great weaknesses. If then a completely regular low occurs, the fall can be rapid and sometimes unstoppable. At the end of the day, each professional needs to make the decisions themselves: do I want to live like this, am I able to live and work in such an environment? You must not fool yourself; behind the supposedly golden gate leading into pro football paradise, dangers are lurking. Here, nothing is private any longer; consideration is an alien concept. Suppose a depressed player comes back 'healed' and makes a game-changing mistake: there will always be one in the team who thinks, 'Great, now we've lost because of this wuss!' After Robert's death, all the appeals to human sympathy, empathy and openness were ultimately soapbox speeches. Take my own humble example: not long after Robert's death, I made a mistake; I stamped on my opponent Aristide Bancé's foot and was sent off. Would the media, the public, have been as hard on me had I said, 'Sorry, I was having a difficult time; I'm a little fragile at the moment and need sympathy'? I do not think so.

Robert Enke's memorial was held in Hannover's stadium on the Sunday after his suicide, and of course I went. The coffin was laid out in the centre circle, 40,000 in the stands, even more outside the ground – almost a state ceremony. On the one hand, I was impressed by the vast show of condolences; on the other, I wondered whether Robert had wanted it this way. It was a deeply conflicting matter: for one thing, it was made clear with how many emotions we players and the whole of football were met, which for all the sadness, was an uplifting feeling. For another, must one then not wonder at the absurd excesses of the football business? It's a vicious circle: when the tragic fate of a player gains such significance – especially in its coverage – then no one who works in this world voluntarily may complain about some things outgrowing them. Evidently, our profession does not allow us to enjoy amenities without forcing its monstrosities upon us too.

Even the memorial brought with it such excesses: the TV channels covering the funeral were even making money with some sort of phone-call campaigns. Professional football is a ruthless, merciless business, and the significance attributed to it at times is definitely too great. After all, what is a lost match compared to the really horrible things that happen in life – accidents, wars, natural disasters? But apparently, certain excesses can no longer be curbed, things can no longer be reversed. I, however, have never had illusions about this, which is why Robert's death did not turn my understanding of my profession upside down entirely. I have experienced many disappointing moments during my professional career after which I asked myself what the point was any more and whether I should rather stop – but I have never been in a completely desperate situation, let alone one that might have been comparable to Robert's. The pressure under which he stood as the country's number one may have also been responsible for his illness and, as a healthy person, it's not my place to draw any kind of comparisons.

# Blue And White, How I Love You – My Years At Schalke 04

SCHOOL, HEALTH, SPORT – IN A SINGLE CONVERSATION, MY FATHER had thrown away the litany that had ruled my life for years, in exchange for 700 Deutschmarks, the amount I was supposed to get if I signed a contract with Schalke 04. Seven hundred a month, fourteen times my pocket money. On top of that, my driving lessons would be paid for and, for my eighteenth birthday, I would get my own car. All this was what Schalke president Günter Siebert told my father and me during that conversation which would be my first round of negotiations as a professional footballer. Officially, I was only supposed to belong to the under-19s, but I would be allowed to train with the pros, where my great idol Toni Schumacher had only just been signed as the new number one. The agreement was to be valid for two years, with a later wage of DM4,000, making me what they called a 'contract reserve player'. That appeared to be the sum at which my father was unable to contain himself any longer. We were still sitting in Siebert's office when he gave me a sign and said, 'okay, you're fine to do that.' Everything was secured in writing on the very same day; my father signed everything, and we drove home.

'So, how was it?' asked my mother. 'The boy's going to Schalke,' my father replied. 'What?' she gasped, 'That's impossible!' 'He's getting his driving licence, he's getting money, and he can do his *abitur* [high school],' my father explained, 'it's all been confirmed. He'll go to school in the morning and as he doesn't have his own car yet, he'll be picked up for training. Everything's staying within reason.'

I barely recognised my father any more; after all, Schalke was not known as the most solid of clubs at the time. But somehow, the background link to Siebert had mellowed my father, and so he was sold. I personally, of course, saw myself as first and foremost a member of the team to whose games I had made pilgrimages to on my *mofa*. Obviously, I knew all the big Schalke names – Klaus Fischer, Klaus Fichtel, Rüdiger Abramczik, the Kremers twins – but not until I became a member myself did I realise just how vast the club and its traditions really were.

My daily routine was as follows: 6.30 am, get up; 7.10 am, leave for school; 7.25 to 7.55 am, football on the school playground, played with a tennis ball; 8 am to 1 pm, lessons; 1.30 pm, lunch. At 2 pm, Schalke's head of youth came by in his VW bus and chauffeured me to training. During the drive, I did my maths homework until training with the pros began at 3 pm After two hours, I went into the youngsters' dressing room, finished the rest of my homework and went to train with the under-19s at 6 pm, before returning home at 9 pm During that time, I learned what work was and how a day was organised. When Horst Franz became new manager of the first team in the winter of 1987, he said to me, 'Boy, if you continue like this, you can forget about your professional contract. You're completely shattered!' And so, I trained a little less, became more alive again – things were looking up, on and off the pitch. And because I trained almost daily with the first team, I was able to bang my own drum among them a little. Eventually, three years sooner than envisaged in my masterplan, my time had come: during an indoor tournament in Dortmund, barely two months after my eighteenth birthday.

In the meantime, I had been given the contractually promised car – a brand-new BMW 3 Series. For someone who had only just come of age, this was like winning the lottery. In a somewhat naïve way, I was proud, and when I once recognised my history teacher on the way to school, I asked whether he would like a lift. It was raining and, as usual, he was walking from the train station. But there was not a trace of gratitude on his part. He merely looked at my nice car and said icily, 'No, I'll walk.' From that moment onwards, my history marks were doomed. But that did not bother me much, as I was finally allowed to start for the first team: Toni Schumacher had not wanted to play indoors due to his damaged knee, and Dieter Heimen, the number two, had been sidelined as well. Back then, indoor tournaments were still a regular feature during the winter break and were being taken rather seriously. After day one, I was accordingly euphoric, especially considering how well I had been playing. To this day, I can recall the song that was playing on the car radio on the way home: 'The Look of Love'.

'Nice song,' I was still thinking, while already losing control of the vehicle. The thought that black ice might have formed in Bredeney only came to me as I grazed the kerb and the car lifted off. Instinctively, I closed my eyes; the car kept flying and took down a garage wall. Opening my eyes, I saw the road directly next to my head. 'How strange,' I thought. Fumbling through the suddenly open window, my fingers touched tarmac. Only then did I realise that I had somersaulted and the car was standing upside down. With some effort, I pressed open the door and crawled out of the wreck. To this day, I do not quite know what happened afterwards.

Eventually, my mother would later tell me, the hospital phoned her. But because she did not have a driving licence and my father was on one of his genuinely rare pub crawls that evening, I had to manage by myself as best I could. Luckily, I was virtually uninjured – apparently, the football gods still had plans for me – and at least, in my euphoria, I had remembered to put on my seat belt. Long after midnight, I was brought home, where my mother appeared in the doorway wearing her white nightgown. 'The things you get up to, lad,' she said in a tearful voice.

The next morning, my father and I went to view the wreck. The passenger side was completely squashed, and heaven knows why the driver's side had not met the same fate. Only then did I realise that, in every sense, this could have been my final match day. My father cried when he saw how lucky I had been. I myself acted wholly unimpressed; in truth, I must have still been in shock. In any case, the very same afternoon, as if nothing had happened, I drove to the venue; after all, day two of the indoor tournament had to be played. Casually, I merely said to the masseur, 'I have some pain in my neck,' but before he could do anything, a team-mate told the room how he had heard about my accident on the radio. With that, I was unable to withdraw from a more thorough examination: the physiotherapist diagnosed whiplash; for me, match day was over. A little later, my father went up to Günter Siebert and put his foot down: 'He's not getting another BMW; he's getting a Golf diesel.'

My staying in the footballing fast lane nonetheless is something I owe to the clumsiness of Toni Schumacher, Klaus Fichtel, 'Pele' Wollitz, and everyone else who in May 1988 were relegated from the top flight after a catastrophic season, with 84 goals conceded. Suddenly, blue-and-white humble pie was on the menu and, being relatively inexpensive, I became the second-choice keeper behind Werner Vollack. While I knew the majority of my new team from training, I shared the lot of all novices and was suitcase carrier and apprentice for starters. That is until the misfortune of another colleague brought me luck yet again: on match day ten, Vollack was injured. So, on 30 September 1988, I was in goal in a proper pro game for the first time – at eighteen, five years sooner than I had actually planned. Granted, it was the second division rather than the Bundesliga, but players were professional in both league one and two, and the latter certainly was a good school. The opposing teams' preferred tool was a crowbar known as the high cross, but I had always been able to handle those well. After winning my first match 3–1 against Solingen, I – we – managed a small streak: four further games without defeat, three of those with a clean sheet. Suddenly, I was number one. We had started the season as one of the favourites for promotion, but streak or not, the team was weak. In the end, we came twelfth, and it was no longer Jens Lehmann in goal but Werner Vollack again, who had recovered from his injury.

While the team was knee-deep in relegation battles, I was knee-deep in my *abitur*. I made mistakes in a game or two, resulting in manager Diethelm Ferner telling me, 'Listen, Jens, we're in for a tight squeeze, and you've got your exams coming up, so I'm going to let Werner play for now. It'll be your turn next year.' As manager, I probably would have done it the same way – after all, you never know with an eighteen-year-old, and battling relegation is an experience of positively vital significance. Even for a young buck like me, the stakes were high: If we were relegated, my professional career might well be over before it had even started. And in my obsession, I had not wasted a single thought on a plan B. I had never asked myself whether I should be a banker or a lawyer, because I only wanted to be one thing: a footballer. The latter course was suddenly teetering on the brink, seeing as the third tier was non-professional at the time, and that teaches you quickly how to cope with pressure – something which would help me a lot in later years. Pressure does not mean that players are sitting in the dressing room with chattering teeth. On the contrary: hope dies last; players are encouraging each other. 'Let's hope he doesn't make a mistake today,' some probably thought about me. 'Pull yourself together,' I thought in turn about the defender who had recently dropped some appalling clangers. Then, it went wrong yet again. We lost, the thin varnish of optimism cracking, and the vocabulary of naked fear reared its ugly head. 'Oi, you stupid arsehole! I can't be arsed being relegated just because you don't know what you're doing!' One word provoked another. Nerves were raw: many of my teammates were grown men with a family to support; there was more on the line for them than for me, the young boy I was. However, such a situation also sorts the wheat from the chaff: the weak spots are revealed mercilessly, and no team in the world is exempt from that. No side is cast in a way for everyone to be of quality, neither on the pitch nor in their minds. Under pressure, the weak show themselves immediately, those who run scared and cannot keep up their standards. Even as a young bloke without much experience, you recognise them at once. On top of that, the pressure at Schalke was something else entirely, because for many fans, the club symbolises nothing less than the meaning of life. More than once after a defeat, our bus was pelted with stones – by our own fans. Without the police and their large shields, it probably would not have taken too long for the bus to look like my BMW after the crash. While I was the youngest on the team, I was by no means the worst; so luckily, I always got off cheaply.

When I was sent back to the bench during my exams, I did not rail against my fate, as my expectations had already been exceeded by a long shot – after all, I had not started the season thinking I would sweep Vollack out of the way. He was still a good keeper at almost 34: 150 Bundesliga appearances, even on standby during the 1986 World Cup. He was not a disliked rival, but rather a fatherly friend who trained intensely with me and from whom I wanted to learn something, especially in my first professional year. My last match before being benched was a 1-1 draw at home, against Rot-Weiss Essen of all teams, the flagship club from my home town.

At this point, we were standing fourteenth in the table, but it was to get worse: when Peter Neururer became manager on 11 April 1989, we were third from bottom. In the meantime, we had had three club presidents in less than half a year. One of them, senior lieutenant Michael Zylka, had only been in office three days. He had won over the members during the general assembly with a single flaming speech. Shortly after, *Bild* newspaper ran the headline 'Secret agent as president' in reference to the Ministry of Defence employee, and the shortest presidential era of all time came to an end – the Federal Criminal Police Office would not allow him to take up the post. As a player, you try not to be distracted by all of that, be it headlines or a brawl during a directors' board election meeting. 'Skint Schalke'; 'Can Schalke still pay the wages?'; 'Schalke – what is the club coming to?' During my first years there, this was what I would read in the papers again and again. Ultimately, however, the club paid us on time – as they had always done.

After the spy who was not allowed to love us, Günter Eichberg became president and brought in Peter Neururer to be our saviour. And what is the first thing you do when matters are not running smoothly? Book a training camp. And what do you do if there is no money for a training camp? You go to wherever the president has important friends and a holiday home. So, we went to the Eifel – Bad Bertrich, to be precise – where years later, the Swiss national team would prepare for the World Cup in Germany. The hotel designated for relegation candidates Schalke was of such poor quality that some beds did not even have mattresses, but frightened as we were due to our poor performances, no one dared complain about it – apart from Thomas Gassmann. 'I'm not staying in a hole like this!' he said, a man who had not made a single appearance by that point and who would always drive his little red convertible with the top down, even after showering in cold weather. The fact that he was sidelined the following week due to acute frontal sinusitis did not matter; the main point was that he had thrown his weight about. I, who after all had played quite a few games, stood marvelling at such chutzpah. But it proved successful: slatted frames where brought in from somewhere, and we stayed for three days. Gassmann, by the way, went on to be a journalist and sports editor – quite the career for such a delicate player.

40

The camp must have achieved something, however, because slowly but surely, we were climbing out of the deep end towards the pale light of the lower mid-table. The penultimate match day saw us face Blau-Weiß 90 Berlin, fifth in the table. If we won, we were saved. If we lost – well, best not to think about that. Sixty thousand were in attendance, a second-tier game. Only then, sitting on the bench as a substitute in this lion's den, did I comprehend just how important a club Schalke really was.

Eventually, we won 4–1, stayed up, and I was looking forward to my second season for which, after all, Diethelm Ferner had presented me the prospect of a place in goal. But now the manager's name was Peter Neururer, and he was still impressed by old soldier Vollack. The latter might have constantly had a stiff knee, but he grafted mightily in the weights room, suggesting a will to give everything one last time. Meanwhile, I no longer had to struggle with school, was in high spirits and trained a lot more than Vollack – in vain, at first.

But after match day nine of the new season, with the team stuck in fourteenth place again, there was need for change. A switch in goal is always highly symbolic, for it makes the manager appear as someone who makes brave decisions, so I came in. On 19 September 1989, almost exactly a year after my debut, I was in goal for Schalke again. I stood there too on 17 May 1990, the last game of the season, after which we still did not get promoted but at least finished fifth. If anyone now believed that better, more reasonable, more comprehensible days were to dawn, they did not know that 'Schalke' was merely another term for 'insanity'. In mid-November 1990, Günter Eichberg all of a sudden gave Peter Neururer the boot. Okay, the preceding draw against Fortuna Köln had not been great, but at least Schalke were in second place. Second! And yet, apparently, a new manager was needed. Initially, this was Klaus Fischer, bicycle-kicking legend at Schalke, but he was only an interim solution until the end of the year. On 1 January 1991, my new manager was called Aleksandar Ristić, a man who understood football, but knew of psychology and leadership what a well-dwelling frog knows of the ocean. 'Boy, if you save as badly as last week one more time, you're gone. I promise you, you're gone!' he once told me before a game – in front of the whole side, when really, the purpose of a team meeting is to fire up everyone through positivity.

To top it off, Günter Netzer was on Schalke's payroll at this time, officially as advisor to both club and president. He seemed to be of the opinion that I was still too young to be number one. Ristić agreed, wanting to bring in his own keeper from Düsseldorf, Jörg Schmadtke. Although I was only 21 years old at this point, I refused to be conned into having self-doubts, neither by Netzer nor Ristić. If they preferred the four-inch-shorter Schmadtke to me, then they had absolutely no idea. That was my first thought, and I clung to it – successfully, too. I played well, was not sold, and on Sunday, 2 June 1991 I arrived where I had wanted to be since the 1982 World Cup semi-finals: in Germany's top division.

Technically, we had already been promoted a day before, on the team bus: we were on our way to the hotel, where we would be preparing for the Sunday game against Fortuna Köln. Around 5 pm, we learned from the radio that Stuttgarter Kickers, our promotion rivals, had only drawn; this meant we were five points ahead with only two games left. Bearing in mind that three points for a win had not yet been implemented, it was top flight, here we come. Still, if now you think that all hell broke loose on the bus, you still do not know Schalke, – because sitting at the front of the bus was Aleksandar Ristić, the Bosnian mood-killer, and in his presence, no one dared utter even a small 'huzzah', let alone dance a polonaise down the aisle. 'Hey, Lehmann, what are you doing?' he would have surely shouted, 'Sit down. We have a game tomorrow.' True, we had been top of the league for many weeks, and everyone was expecting promotion, but reaching the goal of my dreams in such a frozen manner was not something I had been expecting. At least everyone was given a glass of sparkling wine in the evening – followed by Ristić's typical motivational fireworks. 'Well done, men,' he said. 'We've been promoted; the goal's been reached. But tomorrow, I still want us to play well, because tomorrow is Gittler's party.' Günter Güttler, who Ristić insisted on calling 'Gittler', was a Schalke midfielder. He had planned a promotion party. And yet Ristić, tried nonetheless. 'We want to have a good party, so we must win the game.' Spurred on in such a wooden manner, we were trailing 1–0 come half-time. Ristić stormed into the dressing room as if someone had stolen his dearly beloved camomile tea, kicked the kit manager's drinks trolley across the room, and yelled, 'Jebotewo! Jebotewo!' All that Bosnian 'bloody hell' caused his hard-boiled sweet to fly out of his mouth and stick to a player's cheek.

He cared not but rather continued his tirade: 'If we lose match, party at Gittler's is off!' Poor Günter's heart sunk to his boots; he was already envisaging himself sitting alone in his garden with 110 gallons of beer, eight stone of potato salad and eighty meatballs, until Alexander Borodjuk and Peter Sendscheid saved him with their goals to win us the game 2–1.

My first top-flight match took place on 3 August 1991 – a goalless draw in Hamburg. Afterwards, I was positively pestered as to just how great the gap was between the two divisions and how I had experienced my top-flight debut. 'Eh, pretty boring,' I replied, naïve as I was. The next game was against Eintracht Frankfurt, at the time including Uwe Bein and Andi Möller – and lo and behold, my boredom disappeared: five times I had to collect the ball out of my net. Luckily, we would never concede more than that, but that was not to mean that there were any prizes to be won playing away. And so it came in a way to which I had been accustomed by then: relegation battles, quarrels, wars of nerves. I still recall the bust-up before the away game in Nuremberg: I was taking my midday nap when pandemonium woke me up; a short time later, a special meeting was called. Ristić had caught two players at a game of backgammon and hurled the board along with the pieces across the room – that had been the noise that caused me to wake. 'Yes, players Schlipper and Flad, they're not playing,' Ristić said in the meeting. '[I] have told them if we can't win the game today, they can go look for new club. And can come with lawyer, I don't care. Is no discipline, is out. And you, Luginger, you paying five thouand Deutschmark.' The poor bloke looked as if he had been kicked by an elephant – after all, he was merely Flad's bunkmate and had been lying dutifully in bed as the other two were playing. We had not yet won a single away game, but this time we did achieve a 1–0 win by the skin of our teeth.

Eventually, Ristić's brutish methods no longer bore any fruit, and after an embarrassing 1–2 home defeat to Stuttgarter Kickers in the spring of 1992, it was that time again: a change of manager. We were a point away from the relegation zone with four games still to play, and again Klaus Fischer had to come in as a stopgap. Under him, we cooked up two defeats and two wins – enough for eleventh place, which does not sound as bad as it was, seeing as we would have been relegated with only three fewer points. As a young newcomer to the Bundesliga, I could actually be quite content with my performance: I had only missed two games, and just 45 goals conceded saw me in eighth place among the keepers.

For the following season, of course, I raised the bar. Udo Lattek, a manager with multiple titles under his belt, had been signed as new manager, and things did not start out badly under him: while we lost the opening game 3–4 at home to Wattenscheid, we did win 2–0 in Dortmund the very next match day – and anyone who knows even a little about how blue-and-white and black-and-yellow hate each other can guess that afterwards, Lattek was worth his weight in gold. At the time, if you led Schalke to a win against Dortmund, the Royal Blues would immediately initiate a beatification with Pope John Paul II, who himself was an honorary member of Schalke. The following games were somewhat chequered, until we had to go to Leverkusen on match day eight. It was 26 September 1992, a day I will never forget – not because we ended up losing 1–6, but because I spent the end of the game in hospital.

We were already trailing 0–3. I was completely pissed off and feeling aggressive as a cross came sailing into our area once again. I went out, was too late, and as the opposing forward headed the ball onto the crossbar, gravity slowly pulled me back to the ground. Shortly before the landing, I hit my colleague Andreas Müller's calf; the entire motion sequence was all over the place and, aiming for an emergency landing, I needed to rely on my right leg – which, in turn, was not prepared for this and revolved around itself. Upon contact with the ground, I immediately had a light, buttery feeling in my knee. And then there was a crack. A crack which sounded as if a crustacean was being dissected. Although the pain kept within a limit, I knew at once that something was badly wrong. Cruciate ligament, intra-articular ligament, meniscus: all torn, such was the diagnosis later on – and the joint capsule had blown up too. Somehow, I made it into the dressing room, in front of which my brother was already waiting. He had been at the match and realised at once my need for help. We drove to Essen, to a hospital, where my initial feeling was confirmed: total loss. At 21.

Luckily, new technology for cruciate ligament surgery had been invented recently. Lothar Matthäus was the first celebrity colleague to try it out in Vail, Colorado, with the subsequently famous Dr. Steadman. 'Here, we use the same technique,' said the doctor at Essen's clinical centre. 'Of course, you can fly to America, but you will have to wait a week before getting started at all. We would do it here straight away.' I did not hesitate for long: here, I had support, my friends, my parents – and why should German doctors not be just as good at it as the Yank? The very next day, I underwent surgery in Essen and virtually reloaded my footballing life. 'We hope you will be healed entirely,' the doctor said, 'But the technology is still new; we shall see how things develop. In any case, for all of your footballing life, you will need to tend to your muscles.'

And I went to work on that as soon as I had been discharged. I did the rehab in Düsseldorf, where I had regained my form once before, after a comparatively harmless ligament rupture. This time, however, something was different. Every day for more than four months, I toiled away with therapist Michael Stahl. He had been a keeper himself once, and for the first time, thanks to him and his knowledge, the work on my body had something of a scientific basis.

Jumps all the way up to my bedroom ceiling were no longer on the agenda; they had been replaced by targeted muscle development coupled with both coordination and reaction training. Each weight training was followed by a portion of egg-white protein, until I eventually weighed 87kg instead of 81. Actually, it was not until this rehab that I became the athlete I would be for the next few years.

Thanks to this injury, I learned the hard way just how quickly things could end for sportspeople, so I decided to challenge my mind more. Already before the injury, I had enrolled at the Hagen Distance University, with business administration as my speciality. True, it was not a proper degree course yet; I simply did not have the time at first. I did have some time after the injury, though, so I began to cram for my maths credit. The corresponding four-hour exam the year after wore me out more than most of my matches. Sitting staunchly on my chair, my knees were bent and tense as if during a penalty shoot-out. 'Bugger,' I thought, when I finally put down my fountain pen and made to get up. The injured knee was as if rusted; I simply could not stretch it any more. It took me an hour to even gain momentum, but at least the whole ordeal turned out to be worth it: I won the credit. Later, I enrolled at the University of Münster, where I lived in halls. Perhaps I should claim to have moved there for the study opportunities, but first and foremost, I had been attracted to the Münster lifestyle: pretty female students and a casual atmosphere in a beautiful bicycle town. My decision to move there prompted my parents to ask, 'What on earth do you want in Münster? Is football not as important to you any more?' But I merely wanted something different: different people, a different environment. Six years I lived there, in a flat of a pre-WWII building. Just the right thing to get your mind occupied with something other than football. Admittedly, every day, I drove the forty minutes across the A43 to Schalke for training, but there was enough time left for some student life – even though I had to leave the parties early before they had started properly. In this regard, sincere professionals never grow up; 11 pm is last orders. In time, though, due to the UEFA Cup games that Schalke would come to enjoy, I was short of time to study properly, resulting in me failing the degree. In all except knowledge, however, the course had furthered me most as a school for learning, aptitude and power of concentration: picking up new things and reproducing them during the pressure situation of an exam is perfect training for a professional footballer who wants to advance.

But from the mind back to the knee: after only four and a half months, I was fit again – to this day, possibly record-breaking time. Out of gratitude but also self-interest, I talked Rudi Assauer into signing Michael Stahl, my therapist, as goalkeeping coach for Schalke. Up to that point, he might have been unknown to many, but fixing me in such a short space of time had to be enough proof of his ability. This way, my injury and the agonising rehab had at least had a happy ending, namely a qualified goalkeeping coach coming in for Schalke.

I did not play again that season, though. By now, Holger Gehrke stood between the posts, a seasoned colleague who was doing well and did not give the manager a reason to change keepers again – not even when the manager was no longer called Udo Lattek but Helmut Schulte. Granted, under Lattek, we won in Dortmund, but as the first half of the season drew to a close, Schalke were only eleventh again: not good enough. It was time, then, for Schalke to roll the managerial dice once more. Helmut Schulte was the sixth coach in two years; again, I had to convince someone new of my ability, which meant training more – and harder.

'Jupp, what's the deal; am I playing or what?' I asked assistant goalkeeping coach Jupp Koitka at the beginning of the 1993/94 season. 'Well, Jens,' he replied, 'If it were up to me, you would be; I've told the boss the same thing.' That gave me absolute confidence – until Helmut Schulte called me up before the opening match: 'Jens, after consulting with Jupp Koitka, the coaching team has just decided to let Holger Gehrke play.' I was shocked. 'Jupp, didn't you tell me you were going to come through for me?' Koitka merely bowed his head and did not say a word. Schulte was looking almost as baffled as I felt but could not reverse his decision. And so, my fate was once again the bench. If I genuinely want to advance, I thought, I cannot stay here much longer. But what was I to do? I had not played a match in nearly a year – who would want to sign me? Resigned to my fate, I continued, and when we found ourselves in the relegation zone after five games, it was time for another demonstration of authority by the manager: Gehrke off, Lehmann on. It did not help him much; six weeks later, Helmut Schulte too was merely a piece of blue-and-white history.

The new coach, Jörg Berger, had greeted me pleasantly on his first day, and so I travelled to Leverkusen rather confidently. It was not going to be an easy match; after all, it was my return to the stadium where almost exactly a year ago, the knee catastrophe had nearly ended my career. As if a curse lay on the Leverkusen ground, I would never forget 16 October 1993 either. Health-wise, everything might have been running smoothly, but I was forced to learn a new way of getting home. It was already 0–2 after 27 minutes, when Ulf Kirsten took a harmless shot from the edge of the box. And because things always go worse than one thinks at first, the ball slid through my fingers – a clear keeper's error, making it 0–3. At half-time, Jörg Berger told me in his always proper manner that he was taking me off for now and that he would see me in his office the next day.

I could understand him taking me off, even if it was a humiliation to the power of ten. But what did 'See you tomorrow' imply? A year earlier, my brother had driven me, and was in the stadium now too, but of course he had no way of knowing what had happened in the dressing room. He was expecting me to be back on the pitch, while I was already dressed and standing at the exit. Mobile phones had not been invented yet, so I had to ask some random people where the nearest station was. It was only 500 yards away, but as I stood on the platform with my kit bag, I remembered not having any money for a ticket. I was lucky under the circumstances, though: next to me stood an elderly gent whom I recognised as a spectator from training at Schalke. 'What are you doing here?' he asked, perplexed. 'Been subbed off,' I replied. 'Ah, geez, that's bitter,' he said, 'Don't take it too hard.' 'Could you maybe lend me a fiver for a ticket?' I asked; he obliged at once. The train pulled up before long: nonstop to Essen, getting me home on borrowed money. I arrived just in time for *Sportschau* and just about heard the commentator telling viewers of my departure. We had lost the game 6–1.

The next morning, I walked dutifully into the manager's office. 'Right, Jens, have a seat,' he said. 'That was all a bit daft yesterday, of course. What I am to do with you now? I think it best for you to look for a new club.' Great – I had played a mere 45 minutes under the man, and he was already sick of me. Searching for advice, I went to see Rudi Assauer: 'The coach says I'm to look for a new club.' 'Rubbish,' he retorted. 'Rubbish, rubbish, you're staying put!' And when Rolf Rüssmann wanted to sign me for Borussia Mönchengladbach during the winter break, he was told the same. Hence, because professional footballers are the property of their clubs just like office chairs and coffee machines, I had to stay. But every cloud has a silver lining and, as is so often the case in a keeper's life, a colleague's injury gave me the chance to shine especially brightly: after Holger Gehrke had copped it during the winter break, I was back in goal as the second half of the season kicked off – a place I would vacate only twice over the following four and a half years.

When I returned between the posts, we were second from the bottom, and I knew that there had come another one of those times when my career would decide to go up or down. If I did not surpass myself now, I would be out of the picture entirely. However, I had always coped well with such situations, and so I saved every ball there was, and then some. I particularly remember the match against Werder Bremen, who at the time were the uncrowned kings of Friday evenings. Up to that point, no one could get to them – until we travelled to the Weser. I ran out of my goal maybe a thousand times to catch the hail of green-and-white crosses, and in the end we won 1–0. Twenty points we got out of the first nine games after my return; during those, I only conceded five goals. It was the beginning of a phase that three years later would culminate in my being voted

Best European Goalkeeper and in the most important match of my life, which ended in UEFA Cup victory. In between, there lay the best Schalke season in twenty years, during which we came third with the least goals conceded across the league. The following season saw us improve on this record by four goals: in 1997/98, I conceded a mere 32 goals in 34 games. During that season, I also achieved the feat of not only keeping many clean sheets, but also adding something to the credit side of my account: a goal. A full-value hit, scored from open play – and in Dortmund, no less.

It was an early Christmas present, unwrapped five days before Christmas Eve in the Westfalenstadion. For 85 minutes, the match had been swaying to and fro like the mass of people in the South Stand, when I decided to flip fate. We were trailing Dortmund 1–2 at this point; Andi Möller had put a ball past me five minutes previously. For all the adrenalin, I was not watching the clock properly, thinking there were only one or two minutes left to play – and I decided to run forward during a corner. An elbow check took me to the ground; the ball got lost and, panicking, I ran back into my goal. No sooner was the situation back under control than I shifted back into forward gear and was already thirty yards away from goal as Michael Zorc suddenly grabbed the ball for Dortmund, recognised my precarious situation between goal and attack at a single glance and lobbed the ball from fifty yards. I sprinted towards it at high speed, catching it with a mighty jump and slamming it over the crossbar and out of play – corner for Dortmund. Intercepted. Forward again. I had been running more in these five minutes than I normally did in an entire season. Completely shattered, I was still lurking in the Dortmund box as our very last corner came flying in. Thomas Linke went to meet it, I zipped from the penalty spot to the far post. Somehow, Linke sent the ball my way, I approached, and before I had even touched the ball, I knew it had gone in. I did not even have to jump, merely hold up my head – nothing could go wrong now. And it did not: 2–2, final whistle. Again, the Schalke fans were singing what they had been previously after each of my flying visits into the opposition box: 'Make Lehmann a forward!' What a feeling. A goal is different, much more definite than a save, after which the next move needs to follow at once. Here, all emotion can be let loose without having to focus on what happens next. Oh, to be a forward.

Certainly, had I known that only a year later, I would return to Dortmund as Borussia's new number one, and had I suspected how resentful some Dortmund fans could be, I probably would have missed the ball. But that is a different chapter.

# My (Short)
# Italian Adventure

FOLLOWING OUR SURPRISE UEFA CUP WIN IN 1997, I NEEDED A fresh challenge after eleven years at Schalke. Given AC Milan's persistent interest, and the fact that we had triumphed at the San Siro for that historic victory, a move to the land of calcio made sense. After all, at the time it was the home of some of the biggest and best clubs in the world. Today, I believe I know why my Italian journey did not last much longer than six weeks: I was too impatient. But one thing at a time.

Everything started with a phone call shortly after the UEFA Cup win of May 1997. It was an Italian on the other end, who had been observing the Bundesliga as a scout for Milan. 'We would like to sign you,' he said soon after the usual pleasantries. 'We're not as convinced by our current goalkeeper any more; we need a new one.' I, however, had a valid contract at Schalke, and apparently the Milanese were not quite unhappy enough with their keeper to buy me out after all. In any case, the scout put me off until the following year: 'We cannot do this now, but it will happen in 1998.' And with that, I had a new incentive not to get too comfortable straight after that UEFA Cup win. Throughout the entire season, I was under pressure: if I wanted to move to Milan, I had to do well, and that meant no mistakes. As I always performed well under pressure, I finished the season as best Bundesliga keeper – only 32 goals conceded in 34 games. Yet, we only came fifth; the balance of preventing goals and scoring them had not been perfected, but it was enough to qualify for the UEFA Cup again.

The Milanese scout must have watched this season closely too, because he phoned again in spring 1998, saying, 'They want to meet with you. Could you come to Milan?' Of course I could, but not alone. I knew instantly that this would be a complicated foreign transfer abroad, and based on the fact that I did not know a single word of Italian, I knew I was going to need a good lawyer. Up to that point, I had agreed all my contracts on my own, without an agent; it was how things were done at the time – the stakes were not as high, it was all done in a few minutes. But Milan? I was going to need an expert for that. So, I phoned Jürgen Klinsmann, who had played in Milan for Internazionale for three years, and he recommended a Swiss lawyer, Andy Groß. We arranged to meet at Düsseldorf airport for a preliminary talk, and when the advocate emerged at arrivals, I could hardly believe my eyes: cowboy boots, leather jacket, ponytail, goatee – this was supposed to be the stone-cold solicitor? 'You're a lawyer?' Rudi Assauer asked, perplexed, when we appeared at his Schalke office later on to discuss the terms of the transfer. 'Yeah, I am,' replied Groß, who was good for a laugh, 'Even if it doesn't look like it much.' Assauer was still murmuring, 'Groß, Groß, Groß – I'm sure I know you from somewhere,' when negotiations were already in full flow. Eventually, it came to him: three years previously, Groß had set up striker Jürgen Klinsmann's contract at Bayern, a gold-plated deal about which even the hardened Uli Hoeneß had been furious. Anyway, Rudi Assauer showed a healthy portion of respect, which might have contributed to the proceedings with Schalke being fairly pleasant. Finally, for a sum never precisely determined, I was free to leave in the summer.

Shortly afterwards, Groß and I flew to Milan. The vice president, Adriano Galliani, had invited us to his flat and made a lovely dinner. I cannot remember the dishes, but the main course for me was the following sentence: 'Okay, we want you.' At least, that was how my lawyer translated it; I did not speak any Italian at the time. My wages, too, were cited in German – a figure I thought superb, and so we came to an agreement rather quickly. Once I had taken a thorough look at the city on a second trip there with my then girlfriend, it was clear that this was happening. I had already begun to learn Italian when, four weeks before the end of the Bundesliga season, a middleman from Madrid phoned, saying Real wanted me. Suddenly, two hearts were beating in my chest: granted, Milan was great, one of the biggest clubs in the world, but Madrid? They were not only big, they were legendary. 'What do I do now, Andy?' I asked my lawyer in the hope that the ponytailed man had some good advice for me. 'Jens, you've accepted that Milan offer,' he replied, 'The contract is ready for signing too – you're not getting out of that one.' In the meantime, Bodo Illgner had got wind of the offer and gave me a nervous call. He had only moved to Madrid two years previously, immediately winning the league, and he was suddenly worried that I could come in and replace him. But I was able to reassure him. Unlike Andi Möller with his phrase of 'Be it Milan or Madrid – just as long as it's Italy', I knew my geography and knew what I wanted: Milano, Italia.

My attic flat on Piazza del Carmine in Brera belonged to the same residential complex as the one in which we had met with Galliani. Brera was the city's entertainment district, but also, as I know today, a mafia stronghold – drug-trade centre included. Luckily, I did not notice any of it. I cannot remember whether the flat was owned by the club; in any case, I did not pay rent, and the furniture was free too. In that regard, Milan, to this day, is the greatest club for whom I ever played. They had style, class, magnitude – just like the city itself. At Schalke, I had occasionally still trained on cinder pitches, even as a professional; at Milan, this was unthinkable. The training ground was impressive, with many describing it as the most beautiful in the world: a complex outside town with countless pitches and a separate building, where players not only got changed but received medical care and did their fitness training, with rooms for lunch and even overnight stays. When I saw all this on my first Milan trip, I knew it was the place to be. Everything was two, three, hell, ten times bigger than at Schalke. There were several doctors just for the players; one of them, Dr Meerssemann, a trained osteopath, did tests on me I could never have imagined. Afterwards, he was able to tell me precisely when my body had once gone through something awful.

Although everything was so big and new for the boy from the Kohlenpott, the coal-mining area of the Ruhr, I was not nervous or frightened for even a second. I had set myself three goals: learning Italian, winning the league, and becoming so good that the national team would no longer be able to see past me. The side had it in them: Alessandro Costacurta, Roberto Donadoni, Paolo Maldini, along with the Croat Zvonimir Boban and the Brazilian World Cup winner Leonardo – illustrious names, the lot. Not to mention my German colleague Christian Ziege alongside Oliver Bierhoff, who had scored 27 goals for Udinese in the previous season, becoming the league's top scorer. The greatest, however, was George Weah from Liberia: Africa's Player of the Century, World Player of the Year 1995, an absolute machine. Initially, I felt a little lonely in this star ensemble, but I settled in quickly – not least because I had been learning Italian for half a year already, and because I knew I had by my side a German friend in Oliver Bierhoff. After I had become acquainted with the local rhythm of speech, things became simpler. Mind you, this did not apply to my private life, where new women soon arrived – for whom, incidentally, I did not need to speak a word of Italian: one was Danish, another from the US. In my professional life, however, those language skills helped me a great deal. For one thing, teammates and officials respected the fact that someone threw themselves into something; for another, it facilitated team play, and that was vital. As they say, no matter where you are, it is what you do on the pitch that is important. After all, the game runs more smoothly if you have something to say to each other – and know how to say it, too. I kept cramming with an Italian teacher, who could not speak any German, only English. This way, I practised two foreign languages in one go.

Unfortunately, the only one with whom communication remained difficult, no matter the language, was my goalkeeping coach, Maurizio Guido. He was certainly one of the reasons my Italian journey only turned out to be a short trip. Guido was not actually unlikeable, but he had never played in the higher leagues himself and represented a completely different goalkeeping school compared to me. He wanted to show me an entirely new technique, but it did not convince me. For Guido – as for most Italians, footballer or not – dramatics played a large role. Transferred to goalkeeping, this meant flying for flying's sake. In training, I had to do exercises without the ball during which I was supposed to throw myself somewhere based on speculation; it was more acting school than goalkeeper training. Eventually, I revolted. 'This is utter rubbish,' I said. After all, it was important to remember that just because Milan had a better training ground and a more modern arena than the Parkstadion, they were not automatically playing football from another planet. With Schalke, we had played Inter in the two previous years, who had always been level with Milan. We won one of those fixtures (the 1997 final, on penalties), and we lost the other only after extra time. Hence, the footballing difference had not been as vast, even if every single Italian had been technically superior to his German counterpart and the tactical instructions had been much better.

My Milan manager, Alberto Zaccheroni, placed quite a lot of importance on tactics: under him, I understood for the first time what was important in zonal marking, and how the sequences had to be coordinated. He would explain it again and again, sometimes on a flipchart, sometimes on the pitch. He would grab his players like a mannequin, put them in position, and issue orders: 'okay, let's attack. You pass here, we others move like this.' Step by step, he would walk down the paths with us. The next scenario would follow: defence – and so on and so forth. Once that is done a hundred times, it eventually works automatically. Of course, in a match there is seldom, if ever, a situation that matches the training exercise 100 per cent, but the routines help as soon as things get tight. In that case, I would pass to where my team-mate almost always stood, because we had practised it this way. In a match, this might only work three times out of ten, but that is a lot already, considering that it does not work at all for less tactically trained teams. It was here that German football's central problem lay: in these parts, they only trained against the ball. The expression in itself was silly enough – the game rotates around the ball; you play with it, not against it. Spectators were not swarming into the stadiums to watch a great match 'against the ball', were they? The question at the centre, then, is that of how to line up when the opponent is in possession. Very few managers in world football, however, have an answer to what I think is the more important question of how to play when their own side is in possession. Now, Zaccheroni had a lot of answers ready – perhaps not as many as Arsène Wenger at Arsenal, who for me is untouchable in this field. In the matter of psychology, however, there was much room for improvement for Zaccheroni. At times, it seemed as if for him, players did not carry names but merely numbers: 'When the ball is played like this, number so-and-so needs to go here,' he would say. His dryness on that front was almost comical: 'Which player was that again? Ah, yes, number twenty-two. Run, twenty-two, run!'

We won my first Serie A match with a clean sheet against Bologna on 12 September 1998, but when we went down 3–1 to Fiorentina at home, the permanent place in goal that I believed secure was already in danger. My deputy, Sebastiano Rossi, had been number one during the previous season, which was why, of course, he was cross with me. Despite the fact that he was not actually a very good keeper – too stiff and barely any understanding of the game – he was piling on the pressure. And after having profited on and off from my rivals' injuries over the years, I suddenly became the victim myself: precisely 27 minutes into the match against Cagliari on 25 October 1998.

Before the game, I had been plagued by some back pain, so a young junior doctor placed a small wedge into my boot, underneath the arch of my foot. It suddenly changed the entire static of my body, and with a swift movement, I tore a muscle in my right hip. Never before had I had a strain, let alone a fibre tear, and definitely not in such a strange place. It was my turn now to be stiff and immobile, and when the ball came towards me in that ominous 27th minute, I limped forwards, came too late, and hit the man – penalty. At this point, we were already trailing by a goal. Naturally, I wanted to make good my error myself, but there was no way: I had to come off. Rossi came on, stood on the line, saved the penalty, and in the end we won 3–2. I did not suspect, of course, that in this moment, after only seven match days, my Italian adventure was over already.

No sooner was I fit again than I went to see Zaccheroni: 'Coach, I would like to play now.' 'I know, I know,' he replied, 'but number twelve plays quite well; I would like to give him another opportunity.' 'Coach, if I don't play, I have to change clubs.' 'I know,' he retorted again, 'but what do you want me to do?' This is the way of the tactics freak: number one is not fit to play, so number twelve plays. And things were to stay this way even as Rossi's performances went further and further downhill. By now, even Erich Ribbeck, the national coach, had got in touch: 'Jens, if you're not playing any more now, I can no longer call you up for the national team.' Half a year earlier, I had earned my first full cap – granted, only against Oman in Muscat – but I had been playing my part and had even sat on the bench during the World Cup in France over the summer. And now, already, there was to be an end to it all, after I had taken so many years to come this far? I called again upon the manager and the board: 'I need to play; otherwise, I'll get kicked off the national team, and I don't want that.' 'Ah, Jens, you'll be fine,' came the reply, 'stay here, you have a steady perspective.'

But I was suspicious and thought it might be time for a phone call to the man in the cowboy boots. 'Andy, it might be better if we tried to find another club after all.' My lawyer phoned Michael Meier, manager of Borussia Dortmund; eventually, a transfer rumour made the rounds in the papers; and suddenly, Gerard Houllier, who was in charge of Liverpool. Another one of those legendary clubs, who were now suggesting a wage high enough to prevent me from questioning my sense of self-worth. Of course, this was good for my ego, and since I had no noteworthy social ties in Milan anyway, I boarded a plane to Liverpool to take a closer look. On the way, however, doubts began to emerge already: was I really leaving behind a charming city with pretty people full of good taste and style, only to move to some grey industrial town in the north of England? Upon my arrival, the weather performed for me a caricature of itself: torrential rain from all sides. The club hosted me in one of those hotels in which every step on the old wood flooring creaked and where a draught came through every nook and cranny – true English construction quality, then. When, on top of that, I came to see the training ground, which stood in proportion to Milan like a Mini to a Ferrari, my decision was made: money was not everything. I was not moving. I had grown up in industrial Germany but in England, I would be on my own – just like in Milan. Another German colleague was being less squeamish, and with it, would bring me the next important turn in my life. Stefan Klos, number one at Borussia Dortmund and my old rival from days with the under-21s, was going to Glasgow Rangers after the winter break. Suddenly, Dortmund needed a keeper. Contact had been made already via Andy Groß, and barely half a year after my departure from Schalke, I signed for their arch-rivals.

On my last evening in Milan, I went for one more dinner with vice president Galliani and Ariedo Braida, the Director of Football. 'Jens, what is it you want?' they asked. 'Why are you leaving? It is nice here in Milan: good food, pretty women . . .' 'But I want to play football,' I replied. 'Pah, football. Football is not that important. Things will sort themselves out.' Oliver Bierhoff, too, tried to convince me to stay, but when God had issued the gift of patience, I had already left the room – which is why I was on a plane to Turkey shortly after. There, Borussia

Dortmund, my new club, were preparing for the second half of the season.

Belek was a horrible place I had hated ever since we had been there several times for a winter training camp with Schalke. And as if the whole world wanted to mock me for my hurried flight from paradise, it was raining heavily enough for Noah to set up his ark again, in which, after all, he is said to have run aground on some Turkish mountain. I was staring out of the window into this doomsday, when the phone rang: a call from Oliver Bierhoff in Italy. 'Listen, Rossi got sent off today. Five-game suspension.'

Was there a greater idiot out there than me? It was a bitter lesson I learned on this day in Belek, but one which would help me in future crisis situations. For all my ambition, I could not think in the short term – chances were going to come, just like Galliani said. Really, things had been going well for me in Milan: a good club, a great city, and a place that had taught me a lot about football. Back then, football in Italy was bigger, greater – unlike today, when the stadiums are ramshackle, the spectators stay away, and there are too many hooligans in the stands. My consolation was a bonus and a watch from Milan, sent to me half a year after my departure, because the club – and therefore I – had finished as Serie A champions. My part in it might have been only small, but because it was my first league title, I was still a little proud of it.

# Royal Blue Vs Black And Yellow – My Risky Dortmund Transfer

'WHAT KIND OF IDIOT AM I?' WAS MY FIRST THOUGHT AS I FINISHED the phone call with Oliver Bierhoff and stared into the Turkish rain. If only I had been a little more patient in Milan, I would be playing there instead – and certainly not just the five games during which Sebastiano Rossi was suspended: no, when I got a chance, I took it. Zaccheroni would not have been able to look past me.

It was a simple fact, however, that I was no longer sitting in my magnificent flat on Piazza del Carmine but in a Belek hotel; I was no longer substitute goalkeeper at AC Milan but Borussia Dortmund's number one. Was that really me, though? In a sudden rush of hope, I called my lawyer. 'Andy, are we still able to reverse the Dortmund contract?' 'Give me some time,' he requested, 'I need to call Milan.' When my phone rang shortly after, I practically tumbled towards it. Did I perhaps have a future in Italy after all? 'Galliani signed this morning,' Groß said in a quiet voice, 'And UEFA's transfer confirmation has come in already, too – the sale is completed.' A new low, then – and what a low it was. And others were to follow.

Of course, in retrospect, one could question whether it had been such a bright idea to move to Dortmund of all places – after eleven years at Schalke, no less. After all, if you have never heard of the resentment – the hatred, even – between the two clubs, you must have been living on Mars for the past hundred years. Then again, a fairly great portion of spite must have played a certain role in my decision – the manner in which they had said goodbye to me at Schalke prior to my Milan transfer had quite annoyed me. Eleven years I had risked my neck for Schalke, helping them to achieve the greatest success in the club's history – and yet, I had my goodbye said to me practically at the back door. Over the previous year, Rudi Assauer had been saying, 'No, no, no, he's staying!' to everyone who would listen (and to those who would not) – even after the contracts with Milan had long been signed. Allegedly, he had to do so for tax-related reasons, in order to disguise the flow of transfer monies or something or other. The only thing I know for certain is that I was not given an appropriate farewell. Eventually, in May 1998, in Billerbeck, Münster, I had thrown a party myself: a great celebration for all my friends, my family, the majority of my team – but no one on the part of the club or the fans had bothered with anything, which I found rather disappointing. When Dortmund then made their offer, Schalke officials somehow got wind of it and even called me to negotiate: 'Would you like to return to us?' they asked. 'If you're sincere about this, I will come back to you if I return to Germany,' I replied. Afterwards, though, no Schalke official got in touch again. Sod you, I thought; the way you have been behaving, I do not owe you anything: no loyalty, no sentimentality, nothing. There is no room for that in the professional game in any case. I wanted to play, Dortmund wanted to sign me, so that was where I would go. Had I known how much of a fateful decision that would turn out to be, there would certainly have been more emotions involved: I might have experienced things on the pitch that I would never have thought possible, but off it, I met my wife, my true love. For that alone, I am grateful to Dortmund, and I see my ending up there as a change of fortune.

It was clear from the beginning that I was going to have my work cut out. Already in the first game of the season, a campaign against me began to rage, which I can only recall with a shudder, even to this very day. At the centre, there was a group of perhaps fifty people, hardcore Dortmund fans, who simply did not want to make peace with my past. Or perhaps they considered the transfer fee of DM7,000,000 [around £2.5million] too high. Whatever the reason, they were already chanting, 'Lehmann out, Schalke pig', during an entirely irrelevant friendly in Osnabrück, where they had driven to for that single purpose. And it continued this way when the second half of the season began. Granted, during my first match for Borussia, I had not exactly covered myself in glory, seeing as we lost 0–3 in Berlin. My first home game a week later, however, we won 3–0 against Nuremberg – and yet, those chants were still audible: 'Lehmann out, Schalke pig'. The majority of Dortmund fans were nice to me, the more so as I was keeping quite well during the following few games, but those calls could be heard again and again. I do not know whether the constant insults wore me down at some point; the fact is that I eventually did something during the game in Rostock on 10 April 1999 that did not exactly improve my position.

We were trailing 2–0 when Rostock's forward Timo Lange went down in the box. I marched up to him, shouting, 'Don't dive, you actor!' and tried to pull his short and wet hair with my rain-soaked gloves. He fell down, the referee came running, already fumbling in his back pocket – and there it was, the first red card in my career. Lange receiving a second yellow for diving was of little comfort to me. During the trial before the DFB sports tribunal, the judge himself had to admit that the plucking attempt was no big deal. During the hearing, he prompted me to pull his hair with gloved hands. 'It doesn't hurt that badly; you're right there,' he said, giving me the opportunity to vindicate myself once more: 'Listen, he did dive! Yes, I tried to grab him, but think of the massive gloves and the rain – you don't collapse with pain in that situation!' But the verdict was inescapable: violent conduct, three-game ban.

Barely back in goal, I already had to embark upon my most difficult passage: match day thirty, away at Schalke. Of the 61,700 spectators, 61,699 seemed to be whistling and booing whenever I got the ball – over the entire course of the match. Really, keeping up that kind of anger over an hour and a half was quite an achievement. But it was also the point at which I noticed what I had gambled away with my departure from Schalke: I had left a hero, one of the heroes of 1997. No one there had ever found any fault in the way I played. Sure, I had made mistakes, ridiculous ones even. But one thing that had been clear to everyone at Schalke was the fact that I had been throwing myself into the game, always giving 100 per cent, and that usually, the fans appreciated that. Their calling, 'Make Lehmann a forward!' during my occasional trips into the opposition's box were proof of great affection. That was probably why they were so angry and disappointed to see me returning in a Dortmund shirt. This was not necessarily the best move you have ever made, I thought, standing in my goal with a chorus of whistling roaring around me. I had not exactly found friends in Dortmund, and I appeared to have lost all those I'd had at Schalke. The match itself went by unspectacularly. In the end, we parted 1–1, and perhaps the fact that I should not win a single game against the Schalke during all my four years with Dortmund was to be an additional lesson for me.

On the field, things were not going too badly during my first half-season at Borussia: on the very last match day, we even managed the leap into fourth place, allowing us to be part of Champions League qualification. With this, then, I had finally arrived in Europe's highest class, albeit there was not too great a difference in levels between the initial Champions League stages and the old UEFA Cup. In qualification, we had to go to Teplice in the Czech Republic. It was a side trip into football's nether land, where the domestic quarrels were to catch up with me with a force I would never, ever have thought possible.

As I walked onto the pitch to warm up, my special Dortmund friends unfolded a huge banner in their block badly insulting my girlfriend. I went straight back to the dressing room, telling manager Michael Skibbe and DoF Michael Zorc I was not going to play here. Hectically, some stewards were sent off to remove the banner, while the officials tried to persuade me: 'Come on, Jens. You have to play; today is important for us! Maybe warm up on the pitch next door.' Eventually, I allowed myself to be persuaded into playing – after all, I did not want to give those idiots in the crowd any satisfaction. We won 1–0, but things were not over yet: of course, the papers covered the incident and the fact that I almost ended up not playing. But while most of the reporters left it at the vague observation that I had been insulted by our own fans, *Bild* printed a picture of the banner, describing down to the last detail what it was all about. It is relevant to note that Benno Weber, the sports editor-in-chief for the west of Germany, was an ardent Schalke fan, who had commentated on my move with the words, 'Lehmann, you're a Schalke idol, and you're going to Dortmund? Surely you don't think you'll get away with that!' A war had definitely broken out between us now, and I decided not to speak to *Bild* journalists any longer. For payback, they wrote that while I might be a good goalkeeper, I was a difficult person of very, very questionable character.

I tried not to get wound up by all this and to get on with my work instead:

preventing goals against the club who was paying me. In the group phase of the Champions League, however, reached via the Teplice victory, this was going rather poorly: after only one win, three draws and two defeats, my debut in Europe's premier competition was over. The wooden spoon was to continue playing in the third round of the UEFA Cup against Glasgow Rangers shortly before the winter break. Before the first leg at Ibrox, president Gerd Niebaum came into the dressing room to wish us good luck, and because the big boss was present, Andi Möller felt inspired to say a few pithy words too, although he was not one for toughness at all out on the pitch. Without a doubt, he was a great player, but as soon as things got a little rougher, there would be little to see or hear of Andi. In the warm dressing room, however, he used the opportunity to present his image differently. 'Men, we'll give it our all today; we'll throw ourselves into this. Everyone is running for the others!' I simply could not help myself. 'Yeah, Andi, but don't just talk about it in here, do it out there!' I blurted out. What followed that night was as I had expected: Möller had to play outside left, did not enter into a single challenge, and we ended up losing 0–2. But instead of taking the braggart to task, the coach rounded on me. 'Jens, I'm losing it here,' Skibbe said during the next team meeting. 'Andi's trying to rouse us, help us, and you contradict him in such a daft way – just how stupid are you?'

The return leg saw us take the lead after 28 minutes, but the second goal, which would have taken us into extra time at least, simply would not come. Hence, it was time for me to remember my early forward days: on a corner in the last minute, I moved forwards, and promptly, the ball hit my left foot after a flick-on. I took aim, and – luckily – I missed: two Rangers players threw themselves towards me, sure they had blocked my shot, only to be crawling on the floor uselessly as my ricochet trundled towards Fredi Bobic – who could now slide it home, cool as you please. Nothing happened in extra time, which was why I received once again the opportunity to work on my reputation as a saver of penalty kicks. Having failed to stop the first Scottish effort, I saved the next three – making Christian Nerlinger's miss somewhat irrelevant. And as things go in football: success allows all strife to be forgotten. The fans were even chanting the manager's name euphorically, even though he had been on the rocks in the weeks before. He had attained some doubters in the team, but now, precisely those players who had been trying to get rid of him were carrying him towards the stands on their shoulders.

Despite the virtually last-minute success, there was something already very wrong with this Dortmund side: the manager was struggling to get the right results with this disunited team, and again and again, internal matters – especially about me – were passed on to the press. At one point, Stefan Reuter assembled the squad. 'We need to find a common line,' he said. 'We can't constantly have internal matters being splashed across the papers. It's not good for us, and it doesn't make us any healthier.' Subsequently, defender Alfred Nijhuis said we should follow the example of players like Jürgen Kohler, the World Cup winner, who was an absolute asset due to his experience. I was flabbergasted: just before the meeting, that very same Alfred Nijhuis had told me how much he hated Kohler, because he was taking liberties based on his achievements and did not have to fear consequences after poor performances. I should do something about him, Nijhuis said. That was when I realised that it was the latter who had been feeding internal details to the media, details that were none of their business whatsoever. I came across a second traitor with the help of my future father-in-law, a seasoned Dortmund resident, who knew many sports journalists in town well. 'Whenever they want to know something that's going on inside the team,' he said, 'They call Miki Stević. He tells them everything.' I had always had quite a good relationship with Stević, but it was now becoming apparent that he had been nice to my face while playing his own game behind my back.

We got our comeuppance for our lack of unity straight after the winter break: a 0–1 defeat at home to Kaiserslautern. Although we were still in sixth place, the board had their doubts about Michael Skibbe, and the manager was sacked. He was succeeded by former Dortmund defender Bernd Krauss; no one really knew why. He had won the DFB-Pokal with Mönchengladbach once and was publicly compatible – a very important quality in decision makers. Now, he was returning to his native city, something that, in hindsight, he probably should not have done. He was granted eleven matches as our coach; we did not win a single one of them, and after a 1–3 home defeat to Unterhaching, we were once again without a manager and Krauss without a job.

There were only five games left to play by now and, standing in thirteenth place in the table, we were close to the abyss, only two points away from a relegation place. Time to call the fire brigade, then, and this time it came by the name of Udo Lattek. In a way, it was as if Helmut Schmidt had been made chancellor again: Lattek's last job dated back seven years; he had been my manager at Schalke at the time. Whether it was this reminiscence or the fight against relegation that was making me nervous, I began to make mistakes both on and off the pitch. On Easter Sunday, we played Bayern Munich; because, now, every game was a final, we had travelled to the hotel a day early, with a light warming-up session scheduled for the next morning. That fits nicely, I thought, this way I can take a short trip to see my family and hunt for Easter eggs. At 10.30 am, I drove to our meeting point with a cheerful heart, only to find that the squad had left at 10.30 am instead of the usual 11 am, and I had missed it. 'I don't want to see you,' Udo Lattek jumped down my throat when I finally turned up. 'Before such an important game, too – unbelievable!' On top of it all, I messed up the match in the evening, allowing a free kick to rebound, so that Hasan Salihamidzic was able to slide home.

Lattek would not speak to me over the next three or four days, and so it was my luck that substitute keeper Teddy de Beer was not in the form of his life either. I continued, therefore, to trudge around between the posts, toiling for yet another 1–1 against Schalke, and I did not cut the best figure during the international against Switzerland in Kaiserslautern either: I allowed a harmless ball to slip through my fingers from thirty yards. 'Lehmann can't hack it' said one paper; 'Erroneous purchase' said another, with *Bild* leading the way. We were up to our necks in it, when *Bild*'s Benno Weber turned up with something he called 'a peace offer'. Our press officer brokered a meeting: 'Listen, I'm sorry about what we wrote about you back then,' Weber said. 'We wouldn't do that again. But at this point, we all take great interest in Borussia's survival, or the ground might fall out from underneath our feet. That's why we should treat each other fairly from now. We'll write nicely about you, and in turn, you'll play well and talk to us again.' As a result, I ended my entirely private *Bild* boycott – since, had we actually been relegated, they were likely to have chased me out of town in capital letters. Weber had been right in one aspect: in Dortmund, you are not only playing for a single club but for the mood of the entire city. At Dortmund, as at Schalke, the self-assurance of the whole place depends on how you are playing the game. You learn to cope with this responsibility, and I always allowed these expectations to get close to me, because they helped me to be that little bit more concentrated, more focused. We saved ourselves with a 2-1 win against Stuttgart at the end of April, without which we probably would have been relegated. In the end, after all the hassle, I was at least able to register some solace: although we had almost been done for, our defence was third-best in the league; only five teams conceded fewer goals than us, including the top three.

Immediately at the start of the following campaign, however, during our pre-season tour, I learned that this record would not win us anything, much less any sympathies. 'Lehmann out, Schalke pig, you arsehole' – the calls ringing out to me from the halfway line of the stadium in Arnsberg sounded all too familiar. Later on, this bloke whom I do not even want to call a fan planted himself behind my goal, and when I failed to save a penalty just before full time, he positively rejoiced: 'Yeah, Lehmann, you muppet, you're useless!' In this ground with an atmosphere like someone's front room, everyone heard every single word; the insults hit you more directly than they would in a huge arena. And in front of your own supporters, no less. I turned to move behind my goal and seized my tormenter by the scruff of the neck: 'If you don't stop this now, I'll thump you!' At once, a commotion arose, with ten other Dortmund fans coming to aid their colleague. I received a heavy blow from one side. A scramble followed, out of which Christoph Metzelder and Ahmed Madouni only managed to free me with some effort. We took shelter in the dressing room, where a little later, my adversary turned up with police in tow. 'I didn't do anything,' he protested, 'but you hit me so hard that I lost my hearing aid. I'm reporting you!' That was all I needed. Had I, in my rage, really grabbed hold of the wrong man, a completely harmless one who could not even hear properly? I apologised, while the DoF presented him with a shirt in order to make peace. Later, though, our physio said, 'Of course it was him! I was watching him the whole time; he was the one who kept provoking you.' This sanctimonious pest received a stadium ban in Dortmund, as did many others from that anti-Lehmann clique. Initially, this did not actually help me, since they were still granted entry in other grounds across the country.

The inglorious peak of this battle of nerves occurred during another friendly match, this time in Belgium. I only played the first half; during the second, I sat on the bench directly in front of the small stand where my special friends had assembled again – how well I knew them by now. At first, they only chanted the usual tirades, but then I heard: 'Hope your son snuffs it!' My first child, Mats, was only two weeks old at that point; I was still in a state after the birth and would have much preferred to be standing by his cot than being verbally abused somewhere in Belgium. 'May your son get the plague! Piss off! We don't want you here!' If there had not been a solid fence between them and me, I swear I would have grabbed one of them and vented my spleen at him. Dragging a baby into such a mud fight was disgusting. It simply could not get any worse – and it did not, because eventually, I had a grand meeting with Dortmund fan clubs, to whom some of my foes belonged. Where this would have been a home game for every other professional, received with chants and applause, to me it was like running the gauntlet, as if I had been forced to play Schalke by myself in nothing but a pair of black-and-yellow underpants. I had anticipated this and organised an escort – our physiotherapist, a wrestler of impressive build. It was perfectly quiet when we arrived, so I tried a diplomatic approach: 'Listen, I haven't done you any harm. What I have done, with which you may not agree, is play for Schalke—' I was interrupted. 'But you said you'd rather die than go to Dortmund!' 'I never said that,' I replied, 'I don't know everything the media write, but that is definitely not true.' It went on like this for a while, back and forth, until the greater misunderstandings were eliminated. But as things go in football, ultimately, all that counts is success; even the most hard-core supporters would rather win with a hated keeper than be relegated with a nice, native fool. Hence, by summer 2002, it was all love, peace and harmony: we had become German champions and nearly won the UEFA Cup, too.

No one had been expecting this. Four or five matches before the end of the season, our president had already set the bar: 'We won't win the league any more, but maybe it'll be enough for second or third place.' Since the Champions League played such a towering role financially, qualifying for it was almost more important than winning the title. For the club – and the treasurer especially – third place was of just as much value as the championship. I, however, was rubbed up the wrong way by this attitude. 'Mr Meier, how can you say something like that?' I asked our DoF. 'We can still win the league: if we win everything and those above us lose two, we're first!' Michael Meier listened intently; he approved of my optimism. Despite numerous arguments, I had always had great respect for him, as his manner resembled mine: strictly separating professional life from private. On match day 31, we were still five points behind Leverkusen. They were the superior team that season, not only topping the league but reaching the final of both the Champions League and the DFB-Pokal. While the interviews with Jens Nowotny and others were centred around whatever they would do after they had won the title, I merely thought: hang on, there are still three games left to play. They should be quiet until even theoretically, nothing could go wrong any more. And as if I had anticipated something, Leverkusen became flustered: 1–2 against Bremen, 0–1 against Nuremberg, and suddenly, with one match left, we were top of the league after a spectacular 4–3 win in Hamburg. Now, we just had to win our final home game against Bremen in order to win the title.

That, of course, was easier said than done, and we ended up trailing 0–1 with heavy legs shortly before the end of the first period, in front of nearly 70,000 people. Luckily, Jan Koller managed to level just before half-time, and after Ewerthon scored our second after 74 minutes, we stayed in front, despite nearly being relegated the year before. It was my first full-value domestic title, even though I was officially allowed to call myself Italian champion. But those few minutes I played for Milan had been nothing compared to what I had achieved in Dortmund. Finally grasping that piece of silverware was an amazing feeling – the trophy was very heavy, as if its sheer weight was supposed to spell out once and for all the fact that you had lifted the toughest prize in German football. Nevertheless, I did not want to take it home to bed with me. For one thing, I was not quite that type, for another, the euphoria I felt simply would not reach its peak, even though such a triumph in the nick of time should have released all emotions. Some players, for that matter, had already won the league elsewhere: Kohler, Reuter, Tomáš Rosický, Koller, Márcio Amoroso, Dede, Christoph Metzelder, and Sebastian Kehl were some of our stars and starlets. Besides, the season was not yet over for us: four days later, we were in the UEFA Cup final against Feyenoord.

Again, to us, this was the proverbial losers' cup, which we had only reached after yet another exit from the Champions League. Nonetheless, there were big sides here too: my old employer, for example, AC Milan, whom we were set to meet in the semi-final after lacklustre rounds against Copenhagen, Lille, and Liberec. Of course, we were stark underdogs, but the first leg became one of those days on which everything goes your way, and we won 4–0. Yet that was nearly not enough: the return leg saw us trailing 0–2 quickly, and when Serginho made it 3–0 just before the end, we were already picturing the ridicule we would have to endure if we were eliminated. But almost immediately, Lars Ricken made it 3–1, sending us to the ultimate underdogs' final, since no one had expected Feyenoord to make it through either. After all, the Dutch had had to struggle with the other Milan, Inter, during their semi-finals. Their qualification spoke volumes for the side's class – but at the end of the day, they were still 'only' Feyenoord, so we figured we stood a good chance indeed on 8 May 2002.

It had to be said that we were rather struggling with this emotional state of having only just won the league and now having to give it our all once more. Matthias Sammer, who together with Udo Lattek had saved us from relegation and then led us to the championship as boss on his own, appeared to be positively content with the situation. Celebrating was not his cup of tea anyway, and so he took the opportunity to prevent all title celebrations: no parade, no party. After the decisive victory against Bremen, we were sitting together at an Italian restaurant for a while, but everyone went home by midnight, as the coach had decreed. Even Sebastian Kehl and Christoph Metzelder, who had both been suspended for the final, were forbidden to continue the celebrations. Jürgen Kohler did not even turn up at the Italian place, writing in *Bild* the next day that he had stayed at home to prepare for the big game on Wednesday. Then it transpired that he had been in town, where he had downed a few tequilas. The upshot was a professional foul in the final, Kohler being sent off, and Feyenoord being 2–1 ahead ten minutes later. In the end, we lost 2–3, even though I nearly managed to score the leveller shortly before full time. For a footballer, there are small and big defeats, and the one against Feyenoord did not count towards my spectacular losses, after which I would be disconsolate for days and weeks at a time. We were German champions and, a few days later, preparation for the Japan and South Korea World Cup was due to begin. This left little time for gloom, even if a European final did not come round every day. What annoyed me most was the fact that we had not gone for proper drinks after winning the title, since in the end, our asceticism had not

THIS IS NOT USED

been of any use to us at all. Meanwhile, I had extended my contract by two years, as it had been going perfectly on the sports side of things, bar the quarrels with the fans. The next season started off promisingly: by the begin of the winter break, we stood in second place despite many injury concerns. Nevertheless, it was to be my last season in Dortmund, partly because of the club's signing of a real nuisance as my deputy in the summer: Roman Weidenfeller.

I had not yet returned from the World Cup when he was already giving it large during the training camp. 'Ah, Lehmann,' he said to Philipp Laux, our third keeper, 'I'll get him out of the way, no problem. I'm here to play.' During our first session, together he immediately grabbed my training gear and put it on. 'Lad,' I said to him, 'that's my stuff, and I would like to wear it. Get the kit manager to sort you out with your own.' 'I'm not doing that,' he retorted. 'But the problem is yours,' I replied. 'I mean, it's you who needs an overall, not I.' 'Well then, you go and get yourself a new one.' It went on in this manner for a while, prompting me to think that Weidenfeller was a bit of a special case. He kept taunting me, trying to fight in his own way. My answer was – nothing. I simply stopped talking to him; three-quarters of a year did not see a single word exchanged, not even 'good morning' or 'goodbye' – nothing. That may sound childish, but such a rivalry must not be underestimated – if you are too nice, you will be punished for it in the end. The silence did not burden me in any way, as I was playing unchallenged. Weidenfeller was being eaten up by ambition and, as a young keeper, could have learned something from an old hand like me. But he wanted to play at all costs and seemed to think that this little psychological warfare would lead him to success. 'My role model is Oliver Kahn,' he would announce to everyone, simply to provoke me. 'Of course I'm better than Lehmann,' he would go on, 'I just need to be given the opportunity to prove it.' Eventually, he received it after all – as often happens in goalkeeping, not on his own merits but due to the injury of a rival. Unfortunately, in this case, it was mine.

The misery began with a great win – in Milan. We were playing in the second group stage of the Champions League and had to win if we wanted to have even a slight chance of progressing. Winning in Milan was easier said than done, but we were heading in the right direction, leading 1–0, when I had to leave my goal from a corner, which resulted in me receiving a dead leg from Paolo Maldini.

I continued despite being in pain – a mistake, as it would turn out in hindsight. Although I was being treated during the week by Klaus Eder, the national team's physiotherapist, something was brewing in my leg. At the following game in Bielefeld, I could barely move any more and forced myself through a goalless draw – it would be my last game for Borussia. Initially, the doctors still said reassuringly, 'That's only going to take a week or two,' but the bruise in my upper thigh simply would not dissolve. Eventually, the blood in the leg calcified, a so-called myositis. With this, the season was over for me; for the final eight games, my favourite conversational partner, Weidenfeller, was given the chance to show his skills. The fate of so many novices befell him: all of a sudden, the confidence was gone, and mistakes began to happen. You think about one and, before you know it, you make the next, and the points are gone. In a flash, the Champions League qualification we thought was secured was in danger. After I left Dortmund, however, I came to develop a good relationship with Weidenfeller. Impressively, he fought his way back into the team after having lost his place temporarily. Now, he is still playing at the age of 37 and has since represented the German national team.

In order to speed up my recovery, I went to Sardinia with Conny in April and stood in the cold seawater for half an hour, twice a day. Saltwater was supposed to accelerate the healing process, the doctors had said. But it was no use; I did not play another game for Dortmund that season . . . or ever.

We could still have made it directly into the next season's Champions League with a win at home against Cottbus. The side in second place against the one who was relegated already, with 68,000 spectators in the background – it sounded like child's play, especially with Rosický making it 1–0 after 25 minutes. But in the 74th minute, we conceded a silly goal out of nowhere, and at the end of that match day, we were only in third place. Champions League qualification again, then, and out comes the atlas: just where were Žilina, Trebinje, and Tiraspol? At this point, I had no idea that I was to be cast away to somewhere entirely different. I went on holiday, began my pre-season preparation, and during the League Cup semi-final against Stuttgart on 21 July 2003 at Waldstadion in Aalen, I stood between the posts as starting keeper – for only sixteen minutes, mind. Kevin Kuranyi came running into my box on his own; I clutched him a little; he fell, and the last thing I saw while in Dortmund's service was a red card.

# Showing Strength
# – A Rule Of The Game

THE FACT THAT MY TIME IN DORTMUND ENDED WITH A DISMISSAL of all things is particularly apt, since the red card had been something of a guiding theme during my Borussia existence – five times I had been sent off in those four years: three due to two yellow cards, and two straight reds. I do not want to discuss whether or not those sendings-off were justified. This last professional foul against Kurányi seemed to be, although I only held on to him slightly, but the four other ones were all a joke. I am probably the only one of that opinion, but those dismissals shaped my public image decisively: until the very end of my career, after every trivial yellow card, my catalogue of sins was enumerated to me.

Over the years, the impression was created that I was unrestrained, if not a madman. I was 'the mad German' during my time with Arsenal, although that nickname was rooted in my attacking and risky way of play. For that reason, I was often involved in rough tackles. I always left all my aggressions on the pitch, as does every player who plays football as a hobby. Every single kick-about on a field with jumpers for goalposts is the setting of a yelling match as if the game were deciding life or death. In the lower leagues, where sport is chiefly meant to be fun, loving family men are kicking lumps out of each other, making a Bundesliga match day look like the bingo round at the nursing home. It is one of sport's purposes: venting your aggressions within the scope of the rules. As a professional footballer, I essentially did just that; I was merely lucky to have been able to turn a hobby into my profession. This, however, also meant that the recreation ground dweller from back then was embedded inside me. Of course, over the course of your career, you learn better to channel your emotions, with one decisive difference: we pros had every single stir registered, recorded, repeated five times over in super-slow-motion, commentated on, and flogged to death – across the globe. My red card in the 2006 Champions League final happened on the biggest-possible stage, but at the end of the day, things like that occur every day on every recreation ground in the world: the keeper comes out of his goal a tad too late, hitting the striker instead of the ball.

Yet I actually consider myself to have been a quiet, sober goalkeeper. I have already tried to explain how important control and organisational skills are for a modern keeper: if I wanted to be good, I could not afford any kind of lunacy. And it was not as if I ever lost control properly. I normally always knew when to stop. My resting heart rate of 36 was certainly helpful, as it meant that I recovered very quickly from stressful situations. Over the years, I learned to better understand and read the game – a quality which not many other players hold. Ultimately, even some situations in which I was made to look a fool had their purpose. Take the red card after the dispute with my Dortmund colleague Márcio Amoroso in February 2003, for example – at Schalke, of all places. Having come back from conceding two early goals, we were fighting our way towards a laboured 2-2 when Amoroso gambled away the ball at the halfway line again and did not pursue it, as always. Seconds later, the ball hit my net: 2-3, with only ten minutes left to play. In order to vent my anger, I left my goal and ran thirty yards towards Amoroso, but before I could get hold of him, he pushed me back. Yet, ever since, it was claimed that I had run out of my goal to shove him, when the only one shoving had been my Brazilian colleague. All I could was to yell at him to finally move, to come back, to pursue the ball, before the referee was standing next to me – Mr Fandel showed me the yellow card for unsportsmanlike conduct against my own team-mate. And since I had been booked in the first half already due to a minor trifle – complaining about a tough challenge on Rosický – Fandel reached for the red card in his back pocket. The stadium, of course, was clamouring: Lehmann, the traitor who had gone to Dortmund, was being sent off at Schalke – for attacking his own man. But there was even more to come: too late, I finally registered that the goal for which Amoroso had been to blame had been disallowed, meaning that I could have saved myself the sprint and the sending-off. And yet, the move had not been a mistake, as it had an effect on Amoroso. I do not know whether he was afraid of me when I leaped towards him like that; in any case, he handled his task more responsibly afterwards and did more defensive work, too. Perhaps it was also due to the fact that the manager imposed the highest of penalties, substituting him after our little dialogue to bring on the reserve keeper, even though Amoroso had only come on after half-time.

I would become unpleasant too whenever things did not go all that well from a sporting perspective. Based on my conservative upbringing in football, results and success stood above all else. If they did not occur, naturally, my fury over some accompanying symptoms of the modern entertainment industry that is football unloaded itself. For instance, the fact that nowadays, before games and even during half-time, many players stand in front of the mirror to do their hair, applying gel and straightening things until the referee calls for the second half. Hairbands and headbands are now being employed as well. My Stuttgart colleague Khalid Boulahrouz once played a very awkward game in St Petersburg while wearing the latter. I had the feeling that he could not hear me, reinforced by the fact he was not winning a single header. After a huge chance for the Russians, out of annoyance, I ripped the piece of material off his head. He was the first player I had ever seen wear such a thing.

There was a version of Lehmann the footballer who would fly off the handle if he thought his goals – or indeed his goal – were in danger. After all, I did describe, did I not, how I became a professional, how my career had not been a simple no-brainer during which I received support from an incredible number of people? It was a tough fight, and winning games did not become easier, on the contrary: you had to give your all and devote yourself to the sport entirely. This aim – winning – for which I had been living and working in discipline for years, was not something I wanted to destroy through recklessness, bumbling, convenience, vanity of colleagues, or strange refereeing decisions. Perhaps that is why I became a little more unpleasant over the years, as I still had to account for my own mistakes. Often, ensuing public discussions were accompanied by the claim that Lehmann carried two faces: one on the pitch and one in his private life. I no longer want to comment on this, since it does not really matter to me and I do not see a reason to justify myself. After all, when things are going well, I am not asked for justification, am I?

During my last year in Stuttgart at the end of my career, I took extra care to associate well with the referees, but in some cases, this was a very difficult thing to do. Alongside really good and relaxed people, there was also Wolfgang Stark from Bavaria, who was notorious for being terribly arrogant: he would brandish yellow cards whenever players called attention to an error in a normal tone of voice. He sent me off immediately in a match against Mainz once, even though he had not even seen whether or not I had stepped on that player's foot. He had merely seen the actor lying on the ground and me standing up. Upon Sami Khedira's question as to why Stark had shown me the red card, the ref explained that I had shoved my opponent. 'But he's clutching his foot,' Khedira wondered. 'You can twist your ankle being shoved,' came Stark's retort. After watching official TV footage, he wrote in his report that I had stepped on the man's foot. The fact that we players did not have any respect for such a referee went without saying. How he was allowed to call himself a FIFA referee I will never understand.

However, it is not only dealing with referees that required simply too much self-control of us players. On the one hand, everyone who has a stake in the football industry – fans, officials, TV – were all complaining. They would whinge about there not being any proper showmen among footballers any more. The subscription channels Premiere and later *Sky*, as well as shows like *Sportschau, Deutsches Sportfernsehen* – they all paid good money to be allowed to show great emotions. Like vultures, they lay in wait with their microphones to fish for some emotional, unadvised utterances from players and managers after the match. But then, if you did them a favour by saying what you were really thinking, the DFB would immediately initiate investigation proceedings or chair a round table to improve people's ways. At the same time, they occasionally contribute to unnecessary escalations. Take, for example, the incidents at the Westfalenstadion in the summer of 2009, which the media would later term the 'elbow affair': we were playing against Borussia for Stuttgart and, shortly before half-time, Dortmund's Neven Subotić brandished his arms in front of my face, trying to push me away. A foul, actually, but referee Dr Fleischer disagreed. So, I too raised my arms in order to get some space and be able to catch the wide throw-in. When I took them down again, without realising I struck Subotić slightly on the back of the head. He pulled up his elbow, hitting me in the mouth in such a way that, for the first time in 22 years of professional football, I feared for my front teeth. I was awarded a free kick, and after the game I loudly complained in public that, surely, I would have been suspended after such an elbow-check.

Initially, Dr Fleischer defended his claim of having seen the incident clearly, which was why he had awarded me the free kick. A few hours later, he suddenly announced something entirely different via the DFB: he had not seen the scene properly at all but merely noticed how I walked away in pain, hence the free kick. Had he had the full view, both Subotić and I should have been shown the red card. To me, that meant only one thing: Fleischer must have been put under pressure from outside, maybe by the control commission or the DFB's referee supervisor, to retract his original statement – a unique procedure, with its only aim being my suspension. And that is how it came that, on the morning of the season's most important game, the second leg of the Champions League qualification against Timisoara, I had to brood over a statement for the control commission, as if I did not have anything better to do with my time. Following the objection of sporting director Horst Heldt saying that I had an important game coming up in the evening, the chief prosecutor Mr Nachreiner merely retorted that he did not know of this. Apparently, my explanation, eventually recited in Frankfurt by a sports lawyer, was so plausible that Nachreiner could no longer pursue his case. He would have got into dire trouble with it, too: if he had overturned this factual refereeing decision, any further decision on the pitch would have been contestable. After all the squabbling, my lawyer pointed out to me that this attempt at subsequent match-fixing would constitute a criminal offence. I also spoke to DFB officials about it; they recommended I refrain from pressing charges.

Only a few things embarrassed me over the course of my career and, most of the time, it was whenever I made mistakes off the pitch. Take the stupid thing I did after that red card in Mainz, for instance: I wanted to go to Frankfurt after the match, as I was catching a flight to Munich. Leaving the dressing room in this small stadium, I did not know where the exit was and so was pursued by television cameras. Finally outside, I found myself among a throng of fans, one of whom recognised me, came close and reproached me for the sending-off. Made to feel terribly uncomfortable and wishing he would shut up, I took his glasses off him. He did in fact fall silent, asking me for his glasses back while running after me. I returned them to him, apologising for the incident later on Johannes B. Kerner's talk show.

Do I have a logical explanation for all this? I would not want to create the impression that I consider all these episodes mere misunderstandings. There is indeed an explanation for the fact that, in my time, I was probably the keeper with the highest number of bookings: my way of playing. According to statistics, I was involved in challenges twice as often as other goalkeepers, which makes sense, since my game thrived on intercepting crosses and through balls. Again and again, I left my goal-line, my six-yard box, even my area. That meant I was more often in contact with an opposing player than a keeper who preferred to stay between his posts. As a rule, in these situations far away outside my goal, I had to be aggressive or else I might as well not have been there in the first place. Often enough, I received an elbow to the head or a hand to the eye. It might seem, therefore, that all these attacks and counter-attacks led to my appearing more aggressive on the pitch than many of my colleagues.

In principle, exaggerated aggression on the pitch is no good way of deciding a game in your favour, which is something that even many of the perceived football experts on TV do not understand properly. If things are not going well by half-time, they often demand in pithy terms that someone lay down a marker, simply commit a foul in order to wake their teammates from lethargy. But what kind of marker is flooring someone and being sent off for it? This was the seemingly ineradicable German myth of the leading player carrying away his teammates with his emotions, but it was utter nonsense. Arsène Wenger, my manager at Arsenal, once said, 'I don't believe in leaders. I believe in good passers,' and he was on entirely solid ground with that: a team with a handful of supposed leading players will not achieve anything if the other half-dozen do not play football well enough. They may be screamed at, they may be strangled, it would be no good – apart, perhaps, from the screaming bloke getting some good press: 'Good attitude on that one, at least he's trying.' What use, though, is his big mouth if the ball bounces away from him? All authority would be gone in an instant. In the game, leadership is not characterised by senseless yelling but rather by organisation. That much-coveted marker is laid down in a different manner: through good footballing action that picks up the team and makes the rest realise that with this player on good form today, we could actually do this. By contrast, the screaming fit or the deliberate, stupid foul was a typically German fallacy leading to nothing at all.

Many players only talk towards the outside, to the press. They sit at the table with a journalist over a cup of coffee, saying 'So-and-so needs to put in some more work.' That is easily done, since the player in question is not listening and perhaps might not even read the interview. It takes a wholly different kind of courage, a different kind of self-confidence, to say something like that to that person's face in front of everyone else. The ones who know how to do that are the true leading players, the ones a team needs, because by criticising others, they put enormous pressure on themselves. Saying something of that sort makes you vulnerable; you must not permit yourself to make even a single mistake on the pitch or your colleagues are finished with you. Experience has taught me that this kind of greatness is most likely found in players of whom there is little or nothing heard in public.

# A Different World
# – The Motherland
# Of Football

A RED CARD AFTER ONLY SIXTEEN MINUTES – NORMALLY, I SHOULD be feeling as stupid as a keeper who has thrown the ball into his own net. But the sending-off during the semi-final of the DFL-Pokal left me rather cold; even the suspension I received subsequently did not bother me. It did not concern me any more, since, five days later, I would no longer be part of Borussia Dortmund but number one at one of the best clubs in one of the best leagues in the world: Arsenal FC. In 1999, I could have moved to the Premier League, but Liverpool simply did not appeal to me. Now, however, the destination was London – a metropolis, in which the family I had started by now would find optimal conditions. Until this point, I had only known London as a tourist, sightseeing in Hyde Park. This city was now going to be our home, where we would all adapt to a foreign culture and learn a foreign language. At the end of the day, these things that advance you as a person are more important than titles; those are evanescent.

Of course, it would be nice to win the league or the cup, but later in life, that was not going to leave me with much. If, however, I developed as a person, I could draw on that until the end of my days. I could not speak any more than passable school English, enriched with the footballing gobbledygook I had needed in Milan and for international games. Now, I was given the chance to learn something proper, both on and – more importantly – off the pitch, which is why I could not and would not reject such an offer. 'We're going to London, there will be no discussion,' I told my wife, making one of the best decisions of my life – not only for me but for the whole family, who developed further thanks to this departure to another world, and who were welded together even more.

There are only a few absolute top clubs in the world, that is something with which most professionals agree: Real Madrid and FC Barcelona, Juventus, Inter and AC Milan, Chelsea, Manchester United, Arsenal and Liverpool to top it off. In Germany there is Bayern Munich. Being able to move to Arsenal was akin to being knighted. I was supposed to be David Seaman's successor, the man with the ponytail who had been England's number one for a long time. I took that as a good sign right away: the fans would merely need to switch one letter in their cheering chants, and perhaps I could emulate Seaman and become my country's number one. Up to that point, I had only lived a shadowy existence as Germany's eternal number two, so receiving two or three lucrative offers from abroad made me think that I was being appreciated more by everyone else than the various national coaches. At times, players struggle for recognition in their own countries, which made the move to Arsenal all the easier for me. To top it off, money in Dortmund was slowly running low. Suddenly, it was doubtful whether the whole system with expensive stars and a massive stadium, all constructed after the Champions League win in 1997, was at all financially feasible any more. As a player, this was something not learned from the papers but rather from first-hand experience, during contract talks and premium negotiations. 'Money isn't flowing through the league any more, and building the stadium was expensive' – hearing such arguments during salary negotiations meant having to watch out. Luckily, I had always had a good relationship with president Gerd Niebaum and the DoF Michael Meier. Every now and again, the latter would let slip that things could become difficult if Dortmund one day no longer qualified for the Champions League. This was why, after I had received the first phone call from England, my decision to move there was sealed. However, sporting director Michael Zorc and manager Matthias Sammer disagreed, with Sammer putting in a veto against my sale. 'No, no, he's not going anywhere!' he said – but their financial situation left the club without a choice. I only had one year left on my contract and could have moved on a free transfer the next summer, leaving Dortmund empty-handed. This way, though, they were able to pocket four million euros. Considering the subject was a 33-year-old goalkeeper, this was like winning the lottery, as they also saved on my salary.

So, how did such a move to a top club go ahead? Well, everything began with a phone call from Otto Addo, my colleague at Dortmund. I had never been in contact with Arsenal before, but Otto knew a German scout, Thomas Kost, who worked with Arsenal head scout Steve Rowley. That may sound as if Rowley was paid poorly to stand, freezing, around the world's recs to look out for talented players, but far from it. At Arsenal, he was the second-most important man around, with his office being directly next to Arsène Wenger's. Rowley was a kind of cash-point for the club; he kept the system going that bought young talents to be sold as stars. In addition, he was a good soul: during a scouting trip to Hamburg, for instance, Moritz Volz's girlfriend phoned him to ask for a favour. Rowley had an almost fatherly relationship to Volz, who had moved from Schalke to Arsenal at sixteen. 'Steve,' she said, 'you need to go to the BOSS shop and get me a coat they don't sell over here.' 'But I'm already on my way to the match,' Rowley replied, 'I have a player to watch.' 'You can do that afterwards, can't you?' the retort came. And so, Steve yielded, simply missing the game by a little.

It was Rowley, too, who made contact between Arsène and me after receiving my number from Kost. During the first phone call, he passed the handset directly to him, and the Arsène made short work of it: 'Hello, I'm interested.' That, already, had made me something special to Arsenal – the oldest player Arsène had ever wanted to sign. 'How much do you want to earn?' he asked, 'And how much, do you think, are you worth?' After all, it was not as if the Gunners could afford to throw money out of the window. No, Arsenal had to do the maths, and that was something Arsène Wenger knew full well how to do. However, because I was hell-bent on moving, I hinted at Borussia's shaky financial standing and their need of money, no matter how much.

Nevertheless, we did not agree straight away. What followed was a three-week-long impasse during which Arsène had me watched once more; after all, I had not been playing for three months due to a strained thigh muscle. Eventually, he did make up his mind and told me to come to London. Up to that point, I had negotiated all details by myself, because I thought I was old enough for that now. I knew what I wanted, and in any case, any kind of special agreements concerning personal rights were as yet out of my league. Now, however, I needed someone who would be able to devise an English contract, and so decided to take with me Andreas Urban, a friendly business lawyer from Düsseldorf. We met at the house of David Dein, Arsenal's vice president, with whom every single detail was discussed precisely. Dein and his lawyers were hard as nails during the negotiations, a typically English demeanour: even the smallest matter was hashed and re-hashed, to the point where I found myself wondering who could possibly care any more. Besides my salary, two things were important to me: a house for the family and a good school for the kids. But that, of all things, was something with which the club was being least helpful: as they usually signed rather younger players, they lacked understanding in this particular field. Dennis Bergkamp had the same experience after signing for Arsenal in 1995.

After we had brokered the details, Steve Rowley took me for my medical. That might sound like routine, but considering I was having slight knee problems at the time, I was rather nervous that they would examine my old bones extra-thoroughly. The doctor's surgery was based in a pretty Victorian townhouse, with his office located in a hall with a 20ft-high ceiling; he himself was enthroned at his desk at the far end. Initially, we made casual conversation, until he led me into a kind of booth squashed into a corner of the hall where, on one side facing the wall, stood a cabin bed. Lovely, I thought, this way he can only examine me from one angle. And he did. Tinkering about with my leg for a while, pressing here and there, he eventually nodded contently and declared the exam over. That was it; I had become an Arsenal player.

I was standing on the street in front of the surgery with rain pouring down all around me, when Conny phoned. 'How did it go?' 'It's a dream,' I replied, 'the sun is shining as well.' Sometimes, a person should not be burdened with the truth. A few days later, however, I could no longer pretend, as she came over herself with my older son, Lasse, to look for a house. Although he did not have to, Rowley offered to drive us around. We had to search for a long time – even for someone with my handsome salary, finding a house in London's really pretty corners was no mean feat. We had to stay at Sopwell House, an aged, shabby place where each new Arsenal player was given initial accommodation, as it was close to the training ground. Ultimately, the solution to our problem came in the shape of

Steffen Freund, an old Dortmund colleague who had been playing for Tottenham until that point but was now moving to Kaiserslautern; and he offered us his house. It was great, but located in Totteridge, a suburb far out in the northwest of the city. Our decision was made, however, when Freund added, 'Listen, my kids won't be going to school here any more; maybe yours could take their places.' The way it worked, we thought, was that parents simply went to the school of their choice and signed up their children. When we did interview at Grimsdell Preparatory School, though, we were given funny looks for the matter-of-fact way in which we were behaving. In the end, our kids were accepted, but it was not until much later that we were informed by our English friends just how lucky we had been. 'Usually, you have to register your child as soon as it is born; that's how rare the places are,' they told us. Apparently, even an Arsenal bonus would not have helped me out there. Just as well, really, seeing as the club were not offering much support in these matters: when later on, we moved house once more, they inquired for us at a different school and were rejected immediately.

Nonetheless, our luck in inheriting the school places from Steffen Freund's children aside, my sons had a difficult start in London. 'You can't just move to London, what about the poor children?' our parents had scolded us before our departure. While still in Dortmund, we had invited the whole family to Sunday tea, to tell them we were going to England. The grandparents struggled to cope with the news, as did the kids. Lasse was seven at the time and, having only just made his first friends at primary school, he now had to leave them behind already – and worse, to move to a neighbourhood and a school where, initially, he did not understand a single word. He began to suffer from stress-induced hiccups that would not stop during the first few days. Luckily, the school was not large – a small, pleasant building – and one of the teachers spoke a little German, which made it easier for Lasse to settle in. Mats, my younger son, also struggled in the beginning. Granted, he had no idea just how big a step a move from Dortmund to London was; to him, even Bochum, a few miles from Dortmund, would have been completely new and strange. Nevertheless, the foreign language was too much for him, too. He felt a total outsider, an alien, whom no one understood and who had to fight for anything he wanted – quite literally. In the early days, his teacher took us aside two, three times a week, telling us that our son had hit his peers

'*Yet again*'. We were terribly sorry about that, of course, but what were we supposed to do? Luckily, children tend to learn a foreign language awfully quickly, and Mats did end up making some new friends.

I myself could not be of much help to my kids as I had to go to work, in other words, training. To me, too, many things were still new. Granted, the game they played at Arsenal – football – was still the same as at Schalke or Dortmund, but there was a difference in pace and speed. I still remember the very first goal I conceded as an Arsenal goalkeeper; we were still at a training camp in Bad Waltersdorf, Austria. Chop, chop, the ball went from man to man, until suddenly, Dennis Bergkamp stood before me, completely free. In my seasoned manner, I spread out like the Michelin Man, but Bergkamp lobbed the ball over me, cool as you like, so that it moved out of my reach. Behind me, though, the ball dropped to the ground like a stone, rolling into my goal. Executing such a shot so close to the keeper is something only very few players in the world know how to do; I knew immediately the kind of aces with whom I would be playing from now on. This lot were, by all accounts, in a league of their own. I was jolly glad to be 'only' the goalkeeper, as I was sure that, had I been an outfield player, it would have taken me half a year to get used to the speed with which the ball was being passed, and the fact that everyone had to know at all times where their teammates were standing. It was at Arsenal that I experienced the famous concept of one-touch football at its finest.

Quickly, it transpired that not only could I be content with my new club, but that the Gunners had, if I may say so myself, made a lucky find in turn. Thanks to my ability to calm a game down by swiftly intercepting crosses and speeding up the ball again by throwing it towards the half positions, we performed *gegenpressing* again and again, much more dangerous than regular counter-attacks. *Gegenpressing*, of course, has since become a popular word in football language due to Borussia Dortmund's success with it under Jürgen Klopp. In Germany before, I had never been able to exploit the possibilities offered by this way of playing, because my teammates quite literally turned their backs on me as if to say, 'Leave me alone.' For Arsenal's fast way of playing, however, my style was downright pre-destined. Everyone wanted the ball, at all costs, and swiftly understood that they would receive it from me rather promptly. Moreover, they profited from the opportunity to play up high: a back four pushed far up the field towards the halfway line, the optimal situation for every team – the higher the back four are standing, the less running effort is required from the rest of the side. Every long ball that did not need pursuing because the keeper stood out front saves a thirty-yard sprint – energy that could now be retained for the remainder of the game. We virtually only played in the opposition half, which was why we were in a position to keep up our sprinting abilities over the entire length of the match. Often, it took no more than two or three touches for us to reach the other side's goal, and once there, it was a matter of moments until we scored.

Really, everyone had written us off already for the 2003/04 season, as Arsenal had given away the previous title carelessly and were now starting with a single new signing: an aged, crazed German goalkeeper. As usual, Manchester United were favourites to win the league, joined for the first time by Chelsea, who had been reinforced by Roman Abramovich at incredible expense. In fact, they were supposed to be solid rivals for the championship, but we were having none of it, deciding many games in the first twenty minutes by taking a 2–0 lead and refusing to give it away. It went this way in my very first match against Everton on 16 August 2003, which we won 2-1, and in our second match against Middlesbrough, in which we were 3–0 up after twenty minutes. Later in the season there were 5–0 and 4–1 wins against Leeds, and Liverpool, 4-2.

Nevertheless, on occasion, I had to take a lot of flak. Sometimes, I would play thirty or forty yards in front of my goal, where I was able to intercept 95 per cent of balls coming in. It did also, however, lead to my making two mistakes in the Champions League, handing the opposition striker an assist with my head or similar. Moments like that make you look like Mr Bean, and since the English, whether down the pub or in the papers, interpreted every single situation of play as intensely as if it were a passage from the Bible, the exegetes soon delivered their verdict: that keeper was bonkers. 'The mad German is coming,' *The Times* had written, even before my arrival in London. Eventually, opponents adjusted to my way of playing, my coming out of the goal, and as a result tried to block me. During corners, two opposition players were instructed to bar my way towards the ball. I, of course, exerted pressure and thrashed about, which led to a great kerfuffle with the referees. 'I'm only trying to get to the ball, but they're blocking me,' I attempted to explain. It took a while for them to recognise my problem and to blow their whistles in my favour every once in a while. Eventually, however, everyone concerned understood my game – and the advantages that came with it. Today, anyone who wants to be a good keeper plays that way or at least tries to do so. I am not suggesting that I invented this way of goalkeeping; perhaps, someone else had been doing the same but did it in the wrong team. I was lucky enough to join a side to whom this style fitted perfectly. A few years on, Jürgen Klinsmann once listed his criteria for a good keeper: he has to play along; he has to intercept balls; he has to keep up the speed of the game; and being alert on the line goes without saying. Nowadays, German keepers in particular stand far outside, running towards the edge of the area with every ball they have intercepted, trying to speed up the game.

I did, therefore, fit quite well into Arsenal's system of play. My first season there was one of the best in all my life; I did not make a single mistake in 38 Premier League games. On English soil, Arsenal were virtually unbeatable. At the end of the campaign, we had registered a record that may never be repeated: 26 wins, 12 draws, and not a single defeat. The last time something comparable happened was 1888/89, when Preston North End remained unbeaten; although, a complete season at the time only comprised 22 games. We had accumulated 90 points, and I had conceded a mere 26 goals. Thinking about the reasons for this incredible run today, I recall a few things in particular: firstly, the squad had been put together perfectly, a fantastic mix of young and experienced players, who all had one outstanding quality and ended up playing themselves into some sort of frenzy. Secondly, our fitness: Chelsea, our fiercest competitors, ran out of steam towards the end, so that we were confirmed champions three days before the campaign had even finished. Thirdly, perfect analysis of all game parameters: that season was the first time that Wenger's coaching staff made use of *Prozone*, a computer program that allows examinations of both the opponent and your own game down to the very last detail. It delivers data on possession periods, sprinting abilities, fitness, distribution of players on the pitch, and so forth. Additionally, it produces animated recordings of every attacking move. Wenger knew how to use *Prozone* to turn both his own and the opposing side into transparent teams. Finally, the matter of tactical education: a computer system alone is of little use if managers cannot get the findings across to their players and have them be applied on the pitch. Specific training methods exist that practise this flow of the game; at times, we would play 11 vs none. Alternatively, warm-ups could consist of 11 vs 11: one team does not defend but merely gets in the way of the other, who practises forms of passing for five or ten minutes, with a change of sides after each goal. Everything revolves around continuous play, as if you were circling slalom poles. Yet a different version would see the forwards and attacking midfielders play against a back four. All the while, the manger corrects every single wrong path, every pointless pass. To me, Arsène Wenger was the unrivalled master of developing the offensive game.

After all, that is what people come to see. Arsenal's Highbury was always packed, while Chelsea's support, occasionally, left much to be desired, despite all the stars and successes. Even when we lost a home game to Inter by 0-3, our fans did not boo us but released us with a very short round of applause, as if to say, 'You had better up your game next time.' They would have only lost respect if we too, like some of our rivals, had begun to park the bus, constantly returning the ball, and trusting the football gods with long balls during attacks. People do not want aggressively defended 1-0 wins; they want a spectacle, pace combined with technique. And this was exactly what that Arsenal team offered to perfection during my first English season.

Unfortunately, we only managed that in domestic matches, not in the Champions League. We, who in that year had certainly been the best team in Europe if not the world, were eliminated in the quarter-finals, against Chelsea of all teams. It was one of the bitterest moments in my footballing life. Five times we played Chelsea that season, winning three games and losing only one, which unfortunately was decisive. At this point, in April 2004, the scheduling of fixtures worked to our disadvantage. Within a few days, we were due to play Manchester United, Liverpool, Chelsea, Newcastle and Manchester United again, this time in the FA Cup - all of them matches that would test our limits.

Eventually, it was time for the return leg against Chelsea. We were up 1-0 from the end of the first half, when Claude Makélélé simply took aim at my goal from thirty yards in the 51st minute. The ball was a newly issued Nike specimen that came fluttering towards me like a bat pissed out of its mind. I failed to grasp it as it fidgeted between my arms and my chin, only for it to fall at Frank Lampard's feet, who put it across the line to make Chelsea level. For me, of course, this was anything but ideal – however, after the 1-1 draw in the first leg, all was not yet lost. We were simply flattened, though, and in the 87th minute, Wayne Bridge made it 2-1. It was Chelsea's first victory over Arsenal in nine years, but at that moment, this fact gave us as little solace as Chelsea's defeat to AS Monaco in the Champions League semi-final some time later. I believe that, had we beaten Chelsea, we would have gone all the way to the final, which was eventually won by José Mourinho's FC Porto. But words such as 'if', 'would', and 'had' carry no significance in football; the subjunctive mood is the loser's enemy.

The new season turned into a roller-coaster ride. Initially, our winning run continued spectacularly: 4-1 at Everton, 5-3 against Middlesbrough – the latter in particular reflected the mood within the team very accurately. After 53 minutes, we were trailing by 1-3 on our own turf, with the Middlesbrough players celebrating as if they had won the game already. If they kept this up, they would become the first team to defeat us in a very long time. A minute later, Dennis Bergkamp made it 2-3. We continued to play swiftly and directly, and barely ten minutes later, Robert Pirès equalised: 3-3 and the stadium was surging. We no longer allowed Middlesbrough to come through and instead whirled around in their half. The 65th minute saw José Antonio Reyes make it 4-3, and a Thierry Henry goal made it 5-3 just before the end. What a game. The fans were raving with excitement, and Boro could not believe what had befallen them in less than twenty minutes. In the dressing room, we exchanged high-fives, but before long were merely sitting there quietly with a modest smile on our faces, as if to say, 'This is why we're alive – playing perfect football.'

Ultimately, we remained unbeaten in 49 consecutive league games – until 24 October 2004, when yet again we were due to play Manchester United. For a long while it was 0-0, until Wayne Rooney went down in my area and was immediately awarded a penalty. The referee's name was Mike Riley, and I remember him to this day. As Ruud van Nistelrooy arranged the ball on the spot, my mind went back twelve months. Almost exactly a year previously, the Dutchman had missed a penalty, virtually giving a starting signal for our incredible run. I really wanted to choose the other corner as before, when Patrick Vieira called out to me. 'You know his corner!' Such heckling is always unwelcome with keepers, as it makes you think twice. If I did not go for Ruud's corner but he chose to aim for it, Patrick would reproach me. 'I told you that was his corner!' And so I thought back and forth, with van Nistelrooy eventually simply putting it across the line. We ended up losing 0–2, our historic run broken by a dive. One win and three draws later, we played Liverpool away, and a certain Neil Mellor, who neither before nor ever after would play a great role for the Reds, popped a fluke shot into my net from twenty yards – defeated again. It was my second-ever Premier League loss, and yet the manager comes up to me and says, 'Jens, you're not as fresh any more; you seem tired; I'm taking you out now. If you start having problems with your national team because of this, you may as well leave.'

After just two defeats. I did know, of course, that I would be under particular pressure at Arsenal. As a foreigner in this league, you are never held in quite the same regard as you would be as an international in your own country. There were so many international stars playing in England that I was reduced to a mere number, and because everyone would like to move to the Premier League, I was in competition with the whole world: for all I knew, a super-keeper from Antarctica could arrive out of the blue. Travelling via Canada, he could be standing next to me all of a sudden, ordering me to give up my spot between the posts. While I had learned to live with this pressure, being taken off the team after just two defeats was not something I had been expecting. Later, Wenger explained to me how he was merely afraid of my age, having once trusted two older keepers for too long. Ever since, his rule of thumb has been to substitute too early rather than too late. Hence, he now brought on our new second goalkeeper, the Spaniard Manuel Almunia, whom Wenger apparently trusted more than me due to his immense bounce. As it turned out, however, this idea was destined to go down the drain.

Before I was banished to the bench, a team meeting was held, during which we wanted to discuss our little crisis internally. No one, however, said a word, and so I, as the eldest, eventually opened my mouth. 'okay, I haven't played all that well in the last few games either; I need to make more of an effort,' I admitted, 'But this applies to all of us: after that little breather, we need to toil again, show more commitment and a sense of togetherness.' I was expecting some of my colleagues to add something to this, but the room was utterly silent. How strange, I thought; I was relatively new here, and I seemed to be the only one with anything to say. Shortly afterwards, I had to vacate my place in goal and was unable to shake the feeling that it had something to do with my public self-criticism and my muted criticism of my colleagues. Perhaps those players who were closest to the manager had told him they were not sure about the keeper. Whatever it was, I shall probably never find out whether or not my gut feeling was right.

Naturally, I felt completely wronged and felt like going up the wall in my anger, especially when I had to read Wenger's line in the papers: 'If Jens wants to leave, he leaves.' Without the experience in Milan, which was still bothering me, I probably would have searched for a new club. This time, however, I would not be bullied. I was no longer a single man who could pack his bags from one day to the next: my kids had finally settled into the country after a year and a half; I could not force yet another move onto them. Shortly after I had been sent to the bench, my friend Andreas handed me a ground-breaking book: Dr Joseph Murphy's *Erfolgsbuch* (literally, 'Book of Success'), which described techniques to manipulate the subconscious. With hard work and an unwavering faith in God and the goals one tries to accomplish, it said, one could achieve anything. I began to combine the techniques of Philippe Boixel, our osteopath, with those from the book. The result was something that might be described as daily meditation.

Of course I want to play here, I told myself, but since that decision is made somewhere else, in a higher place, I should not try to force anything; and I did not want to do so, either. On the very evening when I was pondering this, Didi Hamann phoned me; he was playing for Liverpool. 'Listen, Jens,' he said, 'We need a new keeper.' That was certainly tempting, the perpetually terrible weather in Liverpool aside. But since I had been listening to my own thoughts so carefully earlier, I declined. 'No thanks, I want to keep trying to continue at Arsenal.' And promptly, as if it were a sign, Manuel Almunia played poorly against Bolton Wanderers the next day. After another defeat match against Manchester United two weeks later too, I found myself back in goal. I could not help but give in to a feeling of triumph. I had had the last laugh: over myself, because I had remained patient; over the German media, because they had already written me off for the World Cup and were constantly favouring Oliver Kahn; and lastly, over my manager, who had been debating my departure. When, finally, he put me back into the team, I confronted him once more. 'Boss, if you think I'm not fresh any more, I would've expected you to talk to me first and not take me off the team straight away,' I said. 'I was on such a roll, and it's not like the others were all that fresh, either.' 'Jens, you're right,' the manager replied, 'The whole team was no longer fresh, no longer hungry. It was more down to the other players rather than you.'

I sat on the bench for ten long games before I was allowed onto the pitch first to warm up in the match against Aston Villa, which was taken by both the fans and me as an unmistakable sign that I was number one again. I received very pleasant applause; after all, the fans did know that, I had always given my all for the club and done much good. Meanwhile, the wind had turned, too, in the British press, with discussions about why I had taken me off the team in the first place, when the team needed experience at the back of all places.

The Villa match was won 3–1, followed by eleven further games without defeat, in which I conceded just four goals. In the end, we came second, which sounds great initially, but really does not mean anything other than being the first loser. Following our super previous season, it went without saying that we wanted to defend our title and were accordingly disappointed about second place. The main reason I did not consider the season lost, though, was a game played six days after the end of the Premier League: the FA Cup final on 21 May 2005.

In England, the FA Cup is a myth, an absolute blockbuster. I thought it to be something similar to the DFB-Pokal: a pretty pot, but nothing compared to winning the league. In England, however, the perception differs: 'Mental!' was my friends' reaction when we reached the final. While a championship is a long process, a team effort, a final match may be decided by a single player making a certain difference, and on that grey Saturday afternoon in front of 71,876 spectators, that single player was me.

At the end of 2004, when I was not allowed to play, I had begun to focus inwardly on a possible final. Already during our 2–4 defeat in the league to Manchester United in January, I was sure that it would turn out to be my game. At the time, I said to United's assistant manager, Carlos Queiroz, 'Congratulations on the win. We will definitely meet again in the cup final.' And so we did: as the new Wembley was still under construction, we played at the Millennium Stadium in Wales. It was to be a game focused on one goal – ours. Manchester were vastly superior and had chances galore, but I was able to save them all, helped by my friend Freddie Ljungberg, who walloped the ball off the line after I had been beaten by a van Nistelrooy header from five yards. We reached extra time, and the match became even more exhausting and one-sided. The only words hammering my skull like so many little cylinders were 'Fight, fight.' I knew I was going to have to deliver that day: my manager was poised to take me off the team again at the blink of an eye, and that would mean bidding London goodbye, a new school and perhaps a new country for the kids, all that rubbish. Immense pressure.

Somehow, however, we survived that half an hour and, yet again, a penalty shoot-out loomed. Dutchman van Nistelrooy took the first and scored, but was followed by Paul Scholes, and suddenly it was time for the old classic: England vs Germany. I again was the lucky one, and saved his shot. Our next four penalties went in, leaving it down to Patrick Vieira to win us the cup. He scored, and it remained his last ever Arsenal goal, as he would move to Juventus after eight years in London. Later, in the showers, a colleague nudged me. 'What's that you've got there?' he asked, pointing at my shin, where a fist-sized lump had emerged. Normally, such a thing should be extremely painful, but I was not feeling anything. Then, I remembered: the bruise was probably the result of that one passage of play just before the finale. Philippe Senderos had miscalculated a long ball, allowing United's Ryan Giggs free rein. We cannoned into each other like two express trains, the classic one-on-one. If I came a split second too late, Giggs would be through and free to score. Alternatively, I might hit him instead of the ball and be sent off. We clattered; I reached for the ball and, apparently, Giggs hit my shin. Being up to my eyeballs with adrenalin, however, there was no pain, no nothing. Until later, that is, when I was being treated on the dressing room table: all tension fading, tears ran down my face once more; only this time, they were not indicators of pain but of relaxation, relief, and joy. For the first time, I was voted man of the match, and marvelled at the way things had taken a turn for the better. Not three months ago, I had been perched on the bench, being tortured by thoughts of moving away. Now, through positive energy and hard work, I had pulled myself up by my bootstraps and with it, had achieved my greatest goal of the season. All decisions I had made had been the right ones.

# Everyday Life Among The Stars: The Inner Workings Of A World-Class Side

HENRY, BERGKAMP, VIEIRA, CAMPBELL, KOLO TOURÉ, EDU, CESC Fàbregas, Gilberto Silva, Ljungberg, Robert Pirès, Rosický, Emmanuel Adebayor, Theo Walcott – the international Who's Who of world-class footballers. If today I were a young fan, I might own the shirt of some of these players or perhaps have their posters hanging on my wall.

For a few years, I was a colleague to these exceptional footballers and had been given a box seat at Arsenal to observe their work. Sometimes, I would simply stand between my posts and delight in how beautiful their game was. Patrick Vieira, our captain, was a kind of lighthouse on the pitch thanks to his physical presence and his fantastic technique. He could give the game rhythm by turning it and himself quickly via a successful move with his back to the opponent, playing a pass from deep towards the strikers. Such a midfielder is rare; if they find themselves with their back to the opposition goal, most of them play the ball backwards. His nature may have meant that Patrick was relaxed to the point that he had to be given a push in training at times, but when he was on fire, he was incredible.

In the defence, there was Ashley Cole, who would later move to Chelsea. He, too, was physically and technically strong, and being educated in Arsenal's academy, he was a role model for the entire nurturing system. Despite his age, Cole had already secured a permanent spot in the English national team.

Thanks to Kolo Touré and Sol Campbell, I learned about the advantages of having fast defenders on your team. Whenever possible, they would try to shift the game into the opponent's half, and even in the case of an opposition through ball going past them, they were fast enough to overtake both player and ball. Behind them was Martin Keown, an English defender who, if he was not playing, always made sure the tone in the dressing room was respectful. On the right Lauren, a warrior second to none, fantastically gifted in both technique and aggression. An absolute pro on the pitch, he was above all relevant to the team's balance and social fabric, and in this respect I learned a lot from him.

The midfield boasted two World Cup winners with Gilberto Silva and Robert Pirès, who were also the measure of all things when it came to technique, joined by the fast Freddie Ljungberg and then Ray Parlour, a true Englishman and one of the funniest players I played with. Beside the genius Thierry Henry, the attack was made up of Dennis Bergkamp, one of the most technically perfect players there has ever been. He had no weaknesses whatsoever; even his heading was flawless. Bergkamp was the only player never to travel by plane. Apparently, he had experienced a terrible flight during the 1994 World Cup in America, after which he announced he would fly home and never board a plane again. He kept his word: Vic Akers, our kit manager, would transport him by car to all away games in the north. When it came to European games, he would simply not be included in the squad, and he was chauffeured by his wife to our training camp in Austria. There was no need to worry about him getting on one's nerves during long journeys, though; Dennis was a man of few words. The only time he would let go of his usual restraint was when he made jokes at my expense; I do miss that.

Many fans may ask what daily life is like in a job where the colleagues are world stars. I vividly remember my first day at Arsenal. It did not take place in London but in Bad Waltersdorf in Austria – almost something of a home game for me, as my mother-in-law was born a mere 93 miles from there, and I knew the area from my family's annual holiday trips. Nevertheless, of course, I was still nervous when I was flying from London to Graz after the signing, where my wife picked me up and drove me to the team hotel. New people, a new manager, a new language – how would things be done? True, I did have some transfer experience, but Germany to England was something else. When I entered the dining hall at lunchtime, I shook hands with everyone first, as that was what people in our culture did. I knew some of them a little; after all, the previous year, we had played Arsenal twice with Dortmund in the Champions League. Back then, I had already caught a first glimpse of that turbo football, of which I was now a part: the attack preceding Arsenal's second goal in a 2–0 win for the home side at Highbury had taken exactly thirteen seconds from my predecessor Seaman to Ljungberg, the scorer. Thanks to my time in Dortmund, I was used to discipline being the highest virtue not only during the game, but at all times. Meals had always been taken together and, like in kindergarten, we were only excused once everyone had finished eating. I had made quite a few enemies at the table, because I am such a slow eater, but eventually I had found a merry group around Torsten Frings, Kehl, Metzelder, Reuter and Christian Wörns. We could not be all too merry, however, or our manager would intervene. Matthias Sammer was known as the party killer: 'Men, I can understand your good mood, but we've got a game on tomorrow, so you need to be already focused by now. Too much cheerfulness can only hurt that.'

Punctuality is another German fetish. If you were late for departure before a match and the game was lost, the manager would take it up with you personally: 'Well, what do we expect to happen if certain gentlemen are already late for departure on Friday?' Excuses were not accepted, not traffic jams, not accidents, not even the argument that there was little point in your risking your licence or even your life for the sake of making up a few minutes. Drilled as I had been, I was now encountering an English team who were even sitting at the table differently: mature professionals who did not forget how to play football even if they arrived for meals a quarter of an hour late and got up from the table once they had finished. All that mattered was for them to be on the training pitch at 4 pm, ready for action. Naturally, those who did not manage this were punished harshly. Graham Stack, our second keeper, was axed just before a cup game in Leeds at the beginning of the year, because at training at 3 pm on New Year's Day, he had still smelled like a half-full pint glass.

Personal responsibility instead of rigid Prussian organisation was the name of the game. And of course, I got stuck in traffic on my way to my first home match. Of course I did. We were supposed to meet at 10 am, but since I had not yet got to know properly that monster called 'London traffic', I had left my Totteridge home far too late. At five to ten, panic-stricken, I called our team organiser. 'I'm so sorry, but I'm stuck in traffic, so I'll be late. What am I supposed to do?' 'Well, just keep driving,' he replied, 'You'll arrive sooner or later.' I could not believe my ears, and when I eventually turned up five minutes late, I threw myself onto the floor, as it were, in an act of German self-deprecation. Oh, God, I thought, if we lose this time, they'll definitely put the blame on you. I apologised repeatedly – traffic, underestimated, sorry, etc. 'Relax, don't worry,' was all Johnno said. Then, he explained the rules to me: a waiting period of fifteen minutes would always be applied; if that was not enough, one would simply have to drive to the hotel independently. No stress.

Similarly uncomplicated was the interaction with my colleagues. My English was okay; it was more than enough for communication on the pitch. Since we were an international outfit, barely anyone spoke without flaw. The natives, for that matter, appeared to have something gushing from their mouths which, initially, I highly doubted to be English. Father-and son kit managers Vic and Paul Akers were speaking with a Cockney accent so strong that, to me, their early conversations were nothing but people making noises with their mouths open. Unfortunately, busy as kit managers tend to be, my standard phrase during the first few weeks was a question: 'What?' Over time, my ears acclimatised, aided by the foreign colleagues correcting each other – apart from Robert Pirès, who after three years in the country still could not be bothered to learn the language: in all matters off the pitch, he would let his wife do the talking.

Arsenal under Arsène Wenger at that time was almost more French than brie or baguettes. At mealtimes, there was a French table with Henry, Pirès, Vieira and others. And as the rule there, like in any other establishment, was 'no seating plan, but don't you dare take my seat', I dropped a clanger. In any case, they were giving me baffled looks when I simply plonked down into a seat which, as I would learn later, apparently belonged to Kolo Touré, our Ivorian defender who, of course, spoke French too. Despite having had four years of French lessons at school, I barely understood a word, let alone being able to join in the conversation. In turn, however, no one made an effort to speak English for my benefit. As a result, for the next meal I toddled off to the international table with Bergkamp, Ljungberg, the Nigerian Nwankwo Kanu, and the Brazilians Gilberto Silva and Edu. And that was where I stayed, always beside Bergkamp, with whom I developed a typical German–Dutch friendship – much to the delight of our team-mates, as we would regularly tell jokes at the expense of each other's nationality.

Manners at training took some getting used to as well. In one of my first training games, I was on a team with Henry, and when he lost the ball once, I did what I still do to this day: get players moving. 'Hey, Thierry! Go on, pursue the ball, go and get it!' Henry, whose extraordinary abilities meant he was already considered England's real king, lifted his head another few inches and abused me in French. Evidently, I had committed *lese-majesty*. We Germans ousted the nobility more than eighty years ago, I thought to myself, so now, everyone had better run the same length. Subsequently, after each loss of possession, I goaded him further, until even the others took notice and Henry could no longer simply come to a standstill, wondering what sort of idiot was standing in that goal. Eventually, he ran after lost balls – nothing special to me, but apparently a huge step for our colleagues. I had not meant to show him up; I merely considered myself a player of a certain status who was in some charge when it came to his team-mates. I was, after all, the only player besides Dennis Bergkamp who had won the UEFA Cup. I was ahead of even Thierry in that respect, although, of course, he had won the World Cup and the European Championship, just like Patrick Vieira, Robert Pirès and Sylvain Wiltord. Over time, we developed a very, very good relationship based on mutual appreciation. I was very upset when he left for Spain, and I was not the only one: really, all of English football was mourning, because he had become a kind of common property. His playing ability, his pace, his goal-scoring abilities and his effectiveness had ennobled the entire league. At the height of his fame, no one quite dared attack him properly any more – which made him even more dangerous and, it goes without saying, more royal.

Frankly, I do not think much of declaring a player the world's best in absolute terms. There are always two or three playing on that same level, and in the end, the form of the day decides who has the edge on the others. As a keeper, I have always had the greatest respect for Ronaldo, not the one from Portugal but for the Brazilian Ronaldo. He was able to switch from placid trot to high-speed train immediately, which made him unpredictable. Moreover, he was the fiddly type, who, even in seemingly hopeless situations, managed to find a way of securing a clear chance. I must have played him eight times, and I kept wishing for each match to be over soon.

When it came to assessing quality, colleagues were of one mind most of the time. You had the ruthlessly overrated, whom I nicknamed 'Ball too hard sun too bright pitch too dry', as those were their standard excuses whenever things had not gone well again. Some were even capped by their countries: Thomas Brdarić, for example – master of excuses but no shots, no dribbling, no passing. Over the years, I have been lucky to have had the pleasure of playing with a lot of very good footballers, from Olaf Thon to Andi Möller and Lothar Matthäus. In the end, however, it was Henry who impressed me most. Not only with his speed and the spectacle he would create on the pitch but with that so very different, intelligent personality of his. To me, Thierry Henry during his Arsenal years was the best player in the world.

Yet, his particular status never unsettled our team: it was composed of so many great players that every single one had to learn some humility, which was why no one went out of touch and grew too big for their boots. Yes, sure, one or two of them did own three, four cars, but when everyone is a star, no one is. For the most part, being a professional footballer is a completely staid profession: one simply cannot afford to stay out late if there is training or a match scheduled for the next day. The greatest eccentric was Freddie Ljungberg, with his soft spot for fashion and that stint as an international Calvin Klein model. When he went to a nightclub, he was the one most popular with the girls. Before my family had moved to London, he showed me around town at night, giving me an idea of what it meant to be a heart-throb. Within the team, Ljungberg had some fool's licence, although that did not amount to much more than occasionally being late for training or forgetting to put on his top. Besides, our manager liked him and readily excused such little antics.

When I later moved to Hampstead with my family, a pleasant little circle came about, with Freddie and the French lot, who would meet for lunch after training at Base. While it was really more of a location for housewives' gatherings, we were undisturbed in this Hampstead bistro, which, when most people know you from TV and the papers, is a precious asset. Sometimes I have got into the habit of not looking anyone in the eye when walking down the street, because people take eye contact personally at once and then feel the need to say something. It is a somewhat peculiar fad. Most of them are pleasant, agreeable and enthusiastic about football, but they do consider you something special, because you appear on television. If they knew what a normal and reserved person I was, they would surely lose interest. The widespread image of the obscenely rich footballer is a misbelief, too, and always needs to be considered in relation – especially in London. Already in my second year there, real-estate prices exploded in such a way that I could not afford a house like the one in Germany. Our first abode, the place we had taken over from Steffen Freund, was very nice but at the same time one of those English lightweight models: draughty in the winter, it was never quite rainproof. Later, we moved into the city – great areas, but every time I converted the pound prices to euros, my insides would go all funny. Yes, I earned handsome money, but compared to London's top salaries, it was a little sum. Looking at the excessive lifestyle of the sheiks from the Middle East or the Russians, one learns humility, realising just how small footballers can be when surrounded by such wealth.

Of course, during this time, not every one of my teammates was my best friend. In modern football, a side's composition changes so quickly that one does not have any time to establish long-term friendships. In the end, it does not matter to me with whom I am playing. What is important is my teammates bringing me success and vice versa. A team is a community of purpose; at the end of the day, it functions like a wolf pack: if one falters, he will be driven away with teeth and claws, especially if he was dominant before. It takes a great stroke of luck to have colleagues whom one finds thoroughly pleasant. We were graced with this luck during the title season when, despite the national and international seating arrangements at the lunch table, we managed to find real harmony and a stable hierarchy on the pitch. Without the latter, things cannot work, unless the side consists exclusively of tolerant, intelligent people, but that is not the case in any team anywhere. The hierarchy always obeys one simple principle: he who plays well is at the top, even if he has never been a so-called leading player before. Age barely plays a role for a position within the team, either. In my last year at Arsenal, for example, at just twenty years old, Cesc Fàbregas was suddenly a very important man. I remember his first game for us, three years previously, in the Champions League away at Celta Vigo. We were standing in the lift together, his gaze glued fearfully to the floor like that of a fifth-grader on his way to the headmaster. Later, he was supposed to put a few crosses towards my goal as a warm-up but could not find any rhythm. 'Cesc, you're with the pros here; you should be able to manage a cross,' I told him, resulting in his not hitting any ball at all any more. However, fast-forward a few years and he was suddenly at the top, with my task changing to telling him to stay grounded. Out of everyone in a team, it is the best ones who have to show respect to the others in order to be accepted as outstanding. If they do not, the team cannot have maximum success, since the figurative Indians will not fight for the Chiefs. A team made up of twenty stars will still not play good football if they do not combine well with each other, both on the pitch and in private. The soft factors – a player's wellbeing, his family's happiness – all have a decisive impact on his performance; already at scouting level, Arsenal were attaching great importance to it, as if they were shooting an expensive Hollywood film that can only captivate an audience if all roles are cast fittingly. Arsène Wenger had always had a great knack for good casting. Just how great it was only became clear when important players left the club. The first were Ashley Cole, Sylvain Wiltord, and Edu; followed by Patrick Vieira and Kanu; then Thierry Henry, Freddie Ljungberg, Robert Pirès and Sol Campbell; finally, Alex Hleb and Mathieu Flamini to name only a few. None of them played as outstandingly at their new clubs as they had at Arsenal – surely, one of the greatest compliments to the boss. Not only did he have a knack for choosing players, but he knew how to read statistics well and recognised in advance when a player had exceeded his zenith and it was time to part with him. At Arsenal, the system made the players successful, not the other way around. Conductor Wenger managed to have everyone in his perfect orchestra stand out through synergy with their colleagues. I asked a few team-mates, and they all said they had not found this kind of interplay at any other club.

It was only in my last year that Arsène went a little off the mark once. He appointed me club captain, a sort of elder statesman representing the team outwardly. Besides shaking a few hands in the VIP rooms post-match, this role requires paying attention to one thing: the dressing room. Observe the tone and see that the players show each other enough respect. I had to call the younger players to order a little on occasion, but all together, we harmonised quite well. At times, things were jolly in the dressing room, for instance when my colleague Emmanuel Eboué involuntarily showed off his white long johns, making us laugh like a band of pubescent boys on a class trip. Legendary, too, is the story of a UEFA Cup match in Bremen before I joined the club that was recounted to me time and again. During the morning walk around Bürger-Park, the players were larking about with a physio called Winky. Ray Parlour gave the latter a push, causing him to collide with a cyclist who happened to be passing by. She fell headlong off her bike onto the pasture, did a roll or two, and finally ended up covered in leaves. Winky ran up to her at once and, in trying to wipe the leaves off her, he touched her breast. 'Off, off, you bastard,' screamed the woman, who, luckily, remained unharmed. The whole team was laughing so hard that the pre-match team meeting had to be postponed by fifteen minutes. While the game was still going, Winky was summoned via the loudspeakers and, shortly after, taken away in handcuffs. The cyclist must have reported him to the police. Winky was able to clear the matter swiftly and was let go before the game was out – in which Ray Parlour, of all people, ended up scoring a hat-trick. Later, Arsène Wenger would say, 'Ray, from now on, I want you to push Winky into a female cyclist before every game.' Among all this, I myself learned one thing: as representative, one does not always get to play. My club captain colleague, World Cup winner Gilberto Silva, for example, found himself sitting on the bench most of the time.

And speaking of captains – already in my time, having William Gallas head the team was problematic. We had learned of his appointment in the papers and we all shook our heads. During the 2006/07 season, he had repeatedly turned up very late for training or had left the training ground without permission. With the promotion, Wenger apparently wanted to appeal to Gallas's sense of responsibility, trying to turn him from Saul to Paul. Initially, this went successfully, until Gallas once briefly lost his nerve.

We were due to play Birmingham away in February, and Arsène took me out of goal again. The evening before, he had not yet made his decision. I was lying on the massage bench, knowing that if the goalkeeping coach did not call me to arrange a talk with the boss, I would be playing the next day. However, even as was lying there, the phone rang. 'The boss wants to talk to you.' It was like a death sentence; I knew beforehand which way the decision would go.

Downstairs in the conference room, the boss informed me about my renewed banishment. 'Jens, I know you've been playing well and are looking fresh and sharp on the pitch again. But I need to give Manuel a chance; it's what you, too, would expect me to do after an injury.' He was making a mistake, I retorted, as now, during the final sprint for the title, he would need experience on the team, and Manuel was playing his first proper season at this level. He had been playing very well, but when a player starts playing at top level this late, he struggles to lead others in big games. The player focuses on himself and his performance, but is unable to support the others in a difficult situation. Wenger ended the dispute with the words, 'If he plays poorly, you're back in,' followed by a chat about private things and my future. This was how we interacted: we would argue, but only on a professional level. As soon as the conversation swerved towards things aside from football, it became harmonious and relaxed.

The game the next day was fateful: after only three minutes, Birmingham centre-back Martin Taylor shattered Eduardo da Silva's ankle with a tackle. We were all shocked, but were leading 2–1 shortly before the end, when Gaël Clichy was late for a ball while in his own area. His opponent fiddled the ball around him and then went down – time for a penalty and time for captain Gallas to spring into action. Instead of standing at the edge of the area and clearing a possibly parried penalty like any other defender in the world, he abandoned the team, ran towards the halfway line and, in his anger, kicked an advertising hoarding. After the match, which eventually ended 2–2 thanks to the converted penalty, he refused to leave the pitch but sat down in the centre circle like a sulky child, until the manager himself came to collect him. In the dressing room, Gallas came to blows with Gilberto, who accused him of seeking attention in a daft manner – the row dragged on for the remainder of the season. Finally, it contributed to us finishing only third, four points behind Manchester United, despite having been six points ahead in March. My prediction, unfortunately, had proven correct: experience cannot be substituted.

The Gallas case was yet another chapter of my little private mentality study around the footballing nations, because – especially in critical situations – certain fundamental types become apparent. If things do not go well for a German player, he thinks, 'I need to pull myself up by my bootstraps – at the end of the day, I want to win, no matter how.' The Frenchman says, 'I'm not at fault; the others are.' He never addresses a problem directly, as that could make it bigger. Every now and again, though, they grow too big. The Englishman, like the German, always wants to rev it up. While the attitude is the right one, sometimes, the self-esteem is only borrowed: he will do what the manager tells him, without giving it much thought. If that approach does not go well occasionally, he will expect the manager to help him, support him – but the manager is sitting way out on the bench and cannot intervene. Perhaps that is why the English national team keeps failing so early in big tournaments. The Spanish and the Italians build on similarly shaky terrain: if everything goes well, they are the world's best players, but if the ball or the game does not do as they wish, they quickly lose courage.

I also experienced this Janus-faced character with my colleague, Manuel Almunia, with whom I had fought a bitter struggle for Arsenal's goal in my final year, the 2007/08 season. He is a very good keeper with great anticipation and explosiveness. From the beginning, our relationship had of course been shaped by rivalry: both of us wanted to play. Perhaps he thought that, at 27, he would be able to drive out the 35-year-old crock. But since things were not as simple as that, we went into battle headfirst. We were constantly training together – the third keeper put in the crosses, Almunia played the forward, and I was what I am: number one. While Almunia kept complaining that I was challenging him too hard, he would also moan when the roles where switched – something about me using my body too much during duels. For revenge, he would hit the ball towards me with such force as if he hoped I would break my fingers.

As a pro, I did not really want to get myself into these little psychological games. Child's play. Once, though, we did clash properly, ultimately due to a triviality in a training game. I moved towards a cross, Nicklas Bendtner went up using his elbow, and headed the ball into my goal. The assistant manager, however, indicated a free kick, prompting my friend Almunia to shout all the way across the pitch, 'Hey! That was no free kick; that was a regular goal!' When the match was over, I went up to him. 'Listen, when something's happening at my end, you're not to yell at the back.' That was when all his rage broke out of him. 'What do you want, *bastardo*?' 'What are you saying? Why are you insulting me?' I shot back. 'Shut the fuck up, *bastardo*!' came the reply. 'Ah, at least now you're openly saying what you really think of me,' I said. 'This is your true character – insulting colleagues!' By now, the other players and the boss had noticed our argument and tried to calm us down, having to positively restrain Almunia so that he would not smack me. I, of course, would have welcomed him losing control, since that would have meant getting rid of a rival. Unfortunately, he cooled down again.

However, despite this confrontation, my relationship with him had never been all bad. In private, Manuel is a rather nice bloke, and we would always have chats off the pitch. A few days after the incident, during a meal shortly before the end of the season, I approached him once more. 'Manuel, I know you hate me, but it will do you good during your development as goalkeeper,' I said. 'I, too, have often had to struggle with rivals. It will help you to come into training every day, knowing that there's that damned German who wants to play and who attacks me whenever he can. And that leads to you attacking me, just like the other day.' 'Well, yes, that's right,' he replied, 'But that thing a few days ago, that simply wasn't okay.' 'Neither was your reaction, but what was I supposed to do? I have to and want to play,' I retorted. 'So, I have to give everything, every day. I cannot rest, not during the game, but not in training, either. That does bother me quite a bit, but if I'm no good, you or someone else will play in my stead. That's why have to make sure I'm always, every day, better than whoever is next to me – and at the moment, that's you,' I explained. 'One day, you'll be doing the same thing. But I can tell you that I don't have a problem with you in private; you're a really good bloke.' Afterwards, we and our wives sat together for quite a while, and it transpired that, before my move to Arsenal, Almunia had been one of my admirers – only to realise now that I knew neither friend nor relative when it came to rivalries and would do anything in order to play. In Spain, he had been used to an entirely different situation: there, an undisputed number one was always playing, while the substitute keeper provided support and even jollied him in a crisis – come on, you'll be fine, etc. After all that, he ended up with the German, who had a completely different mentality, who wanted to play, who was ready to exploit the other's mistakes ruthlessly.

Of course, to me, this type of dispute is no fun, but it is educational and performance-enhancing, especially for someone of my type. At the height of my duel with Almunia, I would wake up every morning thinking, I have to be good in training again today; I need to bump the other bloke somehow. Especially a perfectionist like Arsène Wenger would give no quarter, and neither would I. At times, I regretted my own attitude as well as that of others, but if you wants to play at top level, this stance is essential.

I do, of course, take care to support and advance every comrade – it is what others expect from me, and what I demand of myself. But when it is clear that all effort is futile, it is no longer worthwhile to waste any more energy.

That is why, on the pitch at least, proper friendships between goalkeepers cannot exist. While outfield players may also compete with each other for certain positions, it is never such an unconditional conflict as it is for the keepers. Even considering that players are becoming more and more specialised in certain tasks, at the end of the day, the defender can still grind in defensive midfield if there is someone better out there in his permanent position. The fight for the goalposts, in contrast, is like *Highlander*: there can only be one.

# My Managers –
# Of Tough Dogs, Keen
# Thinkers, And Men
# Of Few Words

I CANNOT QUITE SAY HOW MANY COACHES I HAVE WORKED WITH in more than twenty professional years, even though the manager is the most important man in a footballer's life. All power lies with him: he decides who plays; he decides what is being practised and how; he chooses who is to assist him in coaching and fitness matters. Thus, he lays down the framework inside which a great part of my job takes place; he determines my everyday experiences, for better or for worse.

To me, the first formative character in this regard was Klaus Fichtel, 'Tanne Fichtel', the Schalke legend, who played until the age of 43. I even played alongside him; at the same time, he was my first goalkeeping coach. A *libero* by nature, he nevertheless taught me a few interesting things. But he was not setting spectacular exercises or revealing secrets about penalties – it was his entire way of life that would become exemplary to me. Fichtel looked after himself and his body in such a way that still allowed him to keep pace with the Bundesliga at 41. He was one of Schalke's biggest stars and yet remained humble: for ten years, he would drive the same car, wearing normal clothes – no swanky watches or similar bling that makes some modern players glitter like a Christmas tree.

Fichtel's highest command to me, the youngster in goal, was to do everything necessary for my manager and my teammates to trust me, for that was the only way they would allow me to play. So, I initially appeared polite, modest, pleasant, just as my parents had taught me. The fact that this does not make one a good goalkeeper was pointed out to me, in turn, by a team-mate, Andi Müller, who would be Schalke manager for a long time. After I had played a few good games, Müller was asked what he thought of me. 'He has talent and delivers good performances,' he replied, 'but he needs to yell at us properly, or I won't know he's there.' As a result, I positively flipped a switch on the inside. Of course I had directed teammates at the under-19s, but here in the pros, there were seasoned men before me, in some cases fifteen years my senior. And I was supposed to order them around like a sergeant did his recruits? Very well – I tried, and it turned out good enough for me. Not that I was always yelling the same orders, but over time, I developed an infallible feel for the right thing to say on the pitch.

At the time, tactical intricacies did not yet play such a great role in football. All teams employed a *libero* who had to clean up everything, while the rest more or less did whatever they wanted. The decisive factor was having the better players, who could lend enough trust for them to play at the upper limit of their possibilities. One of my former managers, Peter Neururer, always supported me a lot, which I considered very important. Until, that is, he overdid it a little. To him, I had always been 'the titch' and one day he said in an interview, 'The titch is the next national keeper.' That, of course, pleased me greatly, and when *Kicker*, the German football magazine, asked me sometime later, I said, in my naivety, 'Of course I want to play in the national team one day.' However, since I had not revised the text properly before publication, the paper suddenly read, 'Jens Lehmann – I'll be playing on the national team before long.' That sounded like delusions of grandeur and set me back accordingly in my Germany career, as I would hence be considered overly ambitious, one who at once will make a fuss if he is not playing. As a result, I was not even invited any more as stand-by. But at the end of the day, I had learned something from Neururer, and that was how not to behave in this situation. Neururer is a very intelligent man; he is a highly gifted rhetorician, and at the time, he led very good training sessions. His insatiable urge to communicate, however, did not go down well with everyone. He even picked a quarrel with president Günter Eichberg, which resulted in his dismissal at Schalke despite the fact we were occupying second place in the table. In all my years of professional experience, it was the only managerial sacking I thought to be completely idiotic. Neururer was followed hard on the heels by the manager under whom I suffered most: Aleksandar Ristić. Already during training, he would give his players such a bollocking that they might have known what to do on the pitch, but every single one was so intimidated that he could only deliver 50 per cent of his actual performance. Out of sheer fear, no one took a risk any more, and a bunch of scaredy-cats will never make a good team. During the team meeting before a game, he threatened us in such a way that we would go all small, hoping we might evade him. Once, he asked a colleague, 'Boy, why do you think you're playing here? Only because you know how to do a throw-in. You don't have to do anything else. When we've been awarded a throw-in, you move up and throw the ball as hard as you can. That's all you do.' There is nothing that could demotivate a footballer more.

We did, however, get promoted to the Bundesliga under Ristić – by the looks of it, there was something about the fear-and-terror method after all. Of course, we did have a good team that year, and perhaps Ristić thought he would pile on the pressure no end and see who withstood it, since he would have to get rid of the rest anyway. I agree with the belief that the true whizzes are only ever identified under pressure, but is it necessary to degrade players the way some managers do? Even without little psychological games, we players are automatically under pressure: due to the rivalries at the club, due to poor results impairing our market value and income opportunities, due to the circumstance that we can practise our profession at a high level for only a dozen years and then need to be home and dry. When this constant pressure is raised systematically, eventually the entire system, that is to say the team, will blow up in one's face.

Back to Ristić, then. Before a match against Stuttgarter Kickers, he said to me, 'Boy, if you play as poorly again as last time, you're gone, I promise you.' Promptly at the first goal kick, I practically served Dimitri Moutas the ball – Bam!, 0–1. Bugger, I thought, I'm gone now. In the end, we lost 1–2, though it was not Ristić who came to see me the next day but president Eichberg, asking what I thought of the manager. 'He's impossible,' I replied, 'He's only demotivating us.' Since a few other team members had apparently expressed similar views regarding

Ristić, it was not I who was gone a little later, but him.

I shed as few tears over him as I did over most other managers whom I saw coming and going. Almost every departure I had witnessed had been justified in the end. After all, there is only one thing a manager needs to know how to do: teaching the boys the kind of football they need to be playing, and not only in terms of good technique – if someone cannot stop the ball, he is not going to learn it as a pro, either. No, what is essential in a manager's existence is showing the players solutions on the pitch. He has to tell the right-back what to do when we attack via the left; he has to explain to the centre-forward where to go when his attacking partner moves to the right. This may sound incredibly simple, but the fewest managers know how to do it. With some of them, it does not become as apparent, because they always have great players, but when there is a balance of means, the manager's quality and know-how are decisive – and those are measured by his ability to sign the right players in consultation with the club, putting them in their proper positions, and showing them how to operate there. If one is no ogre, one will be in a position to lead a team well. That is all.

I'd like to think I'd be a calm manager. I have truly yelled enough in my footballing life; I could not be bothered to keep that up. I also think poorly of the method of challenging the players' morality and casting doubt over their characters, something that happens quite a bit in Germany. I know a Bundesliga case in which the manager first greeted his side as follows: 'What are you doing here with your flashy cars? Looking at your performances over the last years, you haven't earned them at all.' He was merely displaying social envy without understanding the players' motivation in the slightest. If they are good enough, they need and want to make as much money in as relatively little time as possible – enough, in any case, to be able to live off it later, since nowadays, hardly any player is properly qualified for anything but the game. Ultimately, every employee wishes to earn as much as possible, according to their output. I, for one, was lucky to be playing a sport in which everyone takes an interest. In Germany, compared to other countries, this debate unfortunately tends to be held with much envy. When a player is not allowed to take on the lifestyle he is able to and wants to afford, he will swiftly denounce his loyalty to the club. This can be problematic, as a player's identification with his employer is an important asset – he can only be successful if he takes joy in his profession. A content player who receives his salary on time, whom the club protects from unjustified external criticism, will pay all that back in good performances. Fines, in my experience, do not work in most cases; they merely enhance the club's funds but not the relationship between player and manager.

Udo Lattek, under whom I played both at Schalke and Dortmund, is a great psychologist, one of my favourite managers in Germany, a fatherly type, who makes his players strong through unconditional trust. 'Boy,' he said to me, 'I don't know that much about goalkeeping, but you have your coaches, they'll sort things out. You're talented, you work hard; I have complete faith in you.' Perhaps he had not always been as liberal but quite the conservative discipline fanatic, as one would already expect him to be based on his age alone. A few weeks after I had been late to that Easter match against Bayern due to the infamous egg hunt, he told me how his stubborn insistence upon discipline had once led to him being taught a terrible lesson. At the time, Lattek had been manager at Köln, who were on a visit to Schalke. I remember the match well: we were 1–0 up shortly before full time, when Maurice Banach had a huge chance after an extended corner. Having moved from Wattenscheid recently, Banach was one of the great forward hopes for Germany. Now, he was standing before me, unrestricted. I threw myself into the path of his shot and with it foiled the last scoring chance of his life. Lattek had always insisted players drive together from the match venue back to Cologne, no matter where they lived. That was why Maurice Banach was not allowed to drive back to his Westphalian home in Münster, but had to go to the Rhine first before rushing back to his wife and child. When I turned on the TV the next day, the first news item was a fatal accident on the A1 near Remscheid. Banach had been killed. To this day, I think of it whenever I pass that bridge. Lattek told me that he was still blaming himself for his narrow-mindedness, out of which he had insisted that Banach make that long detour via Cologne. Had he not done so, the accident might never have happened.

Henceforth, Lattek was much more responsive towards people and trusted them more readily. As a result, his players had the feeling that there was a manager for whom they had to give their all in return – as he was treating them well, they considered it their duty to give back something, particularly in difficult situations.

How well this could work became apparent later in Dortmund where, together with Matthias Sammer, Lattek saved us from relegation in a precarious position. However, to avoid any misconceptions – Lattek still remained a tough dog despite the mellowness of old age. In all my life, I had never had a properly soft manager, but perhaps I was only being handled especially roughly because everyone had noticed that this boy was only ever any good under pressure. Very early, I had found myself in a position of egging on the entire team and pushing them to a better performance. The mere fact that I had done my *abitur* (at Schalke, Andreas Müller was the only other one with matriculation standards) seemed to have led my managers to believe that I could cope well with pressure and responsibility, even at a young age. In any case, no manager ever treated me with particular empathy, but it was not as if I had ever missed it. I wanted to play, and if I was not allowed, I would get angry – and I would make them feel it, long enough for me to be back in the game. This stubbornness ran through my career like a common thread. Never did I go up to a manager and praise him out of pure self-interest, on the contrary. Currying favour is not embedded in my nature, unfortunately – with the use of a little more diplomacy, I would have saved myself a fair amount of trouble.

Once, as captain at Schalke, I was in the awkward situation of having to bring about a managerial change when Jörg Berger was in charge. It had nothing to do with the fact that he had sent me to the bench immediately after his arrival, on the contrary. He was a funny man, with whom I was getting along well; a keen player of backgammon and chess, whom I would duel time and again on those endless drives to away games. He had certainly earned his reputation as the ideal firefighter; a manager, who, with simple methods, could put insecure teams back on the right track. His *Wendelauf* exercise [the bleep test as it is known in England], normally part of the acceptance test for German police, was particularly infamous. He would bring a large watch that counted down the seconds on the edge of the pitch, while we hurried back and forth. It did help, though. We were fit and, as a result, organisation within the game came more easily to us. In addition, Berger preached patience: the way out of the relegation zone is long, but we will manage; the next game is going to be better – a kind of faith healing which he executed to perfection. 'He would have saved the Titanic, too,' they would say of him later in admiration. However, once he had spruced up a tottering side, he would at times let himself and the team go a little, and in the end he was no longer able to flip the switch. Eventually, it got to a point at which we players became aware of the fact that we were simply not training often enough. We were a troop of young, hungry, ambitious players: Olaf Thon, Youri Mulder, and Ingo Anderbrügge were on the players' council, while I was the elected captain. We wanted more than to merely avoid relegation. Among us, we agreed to meet for training alone on Monday morning. Come if you like, stay home if you like. In the end, by their own choice, 20 out of 24 players stood on the pitch, sealing Berger's departure from Schalke. He was stuck with a team who were full of impatience, and who wanted to get to the top faster than he trusted them to. Yet, at least in Germany, our uprising had been an absolutely unique process. Eventually, the whole team even ended up going on a football show to justify themselves in public. That was followed by quite some drama, as especially the fans did not understand this step.

In such a case, the media always resort to condemning a side for playing against their manager, but that is a common misconception. No team, no player, can be bothered to play poorly on purpose, only to end up in a relegation spot – especially because everyone knows how long it takes to get out from down there. Sometimes, there is no getting out at all, and with every relegation, the chances and market value of every single player decreases. For that reason alone, no one plays consciously against their manager, but at some point, there rises a feeling of simply accepting his departure. It is not an active vote against him but a passive bearing. And that, then, is how the team will finally play: without passion, without the final devotion. Eventually, the final thought is an optimistic one: better have it happen now than four weeks later.

Jörg Berger was succeeded by Huub Stevens, who, to us, was quite literally worth his weight in gold – or, rather, silver: thanks to his school of technique and organisation, we improved enormously as a team and ended up winning the UEFA Cup. The public only ever sees General Huub Stevens, because his credo is discipline, organisation, efficiency. Privately, however, the Dutchman is a cheerful soul, who likes to make a sarcastic remark or two in training: 'Ah, are we on time today again?' Mind you, I was also a little afraid of him, because he pursued his goals relentlessly. When, for instance, I wanted to change clubs, he positively blackmailed me. 'You're not going anywhere; you have a contract to fulfil – and if you plan to leave, I will send you into the stand for all of next season.' Eventually, he did allow me to leave, but I only ever felt entirely safe from his threat when all contracts had been signed.

The most astonishing training I ever had was when Erich Ribbeck –Sir Erich; he carries that title with entirely good reason, gentleman that he is – was managing the national team. A pleasant man, a master of ceremonies, who presents himself perfectly in public. His was the time when the rest of the footballing world still elected to play with a traditional back four, but Sir Erich's secret weapon was called Lothar Matthäus. Ribbeck had activated him in a state of need and specifically invented a system for him, the *Loddar* system. Since Ribbeck did not dare still play properly with the antiquated *libero*, he would call Matthäus his 'freelance worker'. The latter was allowed to play before or behind those four players who had been condemned by the manager to form a back four without anyone knowing how that actually worked. How to divide space, how to calculate the distance in which players had to stand to each other, how they should move – not many managers at the time had any notion about these things. During the preparation for Euro 2000 in Belgium and the Netherlands, this heap of chickens was supposed to be put into some sort of order. However, the first training match in the camp in Majorca was stopped after five minutes, because Sir Erich and his assistant managers Uli Stielike and Horst Hrubesch were debating the execution with a number of players. They were standing in the centre circle, racking their brains as if attending an advanced seminar in political science, while the rest of us did not quite know what to do. A few had some shooting practice into my goal while others played five against two in a corner of the pitch. In the end, the first few began to leave like discontented spectators. By the time the three coaches had finished their guideline debate, most of the players were already on the bus. That was how the German national team prepared for the Euros.

Later, there was a funny team meeting during which Ribbeck tried to explain his tactics with the use of some oranges on a table. His line-up could only be guessed once he had told us which players were supposed to be in the wall during a free kick against us. At that point, at least, five people knew that, apparently, they were in for the match. Perhaps this was his belief in the 'thinking player': we were supposed to read the fruit bowl the way a seer reads the crystal ball. As a person, though, Sir Erich was great, and on occasion, that indeed resulted in success.

A team sees misery coming, but without unity, there is not much to be done about it. And this national team was anything but united. To the tabloids, the resurrected Matthäus was top dog, while Oliver Bierhoff as official captain was fighting a losing battle, since there was also a strong Bayern faction within the side. What, really, would have been the benefit of complaining to the DFB president? Incumbent Egidius Braun had been sidelined after a bypass operation; business was already conducted by Gerhard Mayer-Vorfelder. Presidents, whether at clubs or associations, usually do not know at all what to demand of a manager. After all, what boss trundles across pitches themselves to see how potential candidates for a coaching job actually work? German officials have no way of judging whether or not he actually does good work and fits the team; to them, it is important that the manager sells well in the media. In most cases, the signing of a coach goes by the concept of Pandora's box: buying the shiniest thing around, without anyone really knowing what lies inside. One lifts the lid in first training, hoping to find sweets rather than pickled cucumbers.

Occasionally, though, there are surprises in store, such as in the case of Rudi Völler – born under a lucky star, especially considering how he secured his first job. Following the cocaine scandal around designated national coach Christoph Daum, the search for a replacement had begun, and Rudi was in the right place at the right time. Since he was not actually a qualified manager, he might not have been able to offer the latest thing in training methods, but nonetheless he had a good way of dealing with the team. Back then, football was not as developed as it is today; the pace was nowhere near as high, nor was the players' physical and tactical training as sophisticated. Not until 2002, when all foreigner restrictions in the clubs ceased to apply and, suddenly, footballers from all over the world courted the few places at European top clubs, did the entire sport have a boost in development. All at once, boys from the Ivory Coast or Ukraine played in the Champions League with their clubs, superbly trained and fit as a fiddle. It was the point at which we Germans started to trail internationally.

With Rudi at the helm, we finished as runners-up in the 2002 World Cup, a great success. The name of our first opponent after the group phase, however, was Paraguay. During the phone calls home, my friends would say, 'Last sixteen, mental! How do you think that'll go?' 'A German team does not lose to Paraguay at a World Cup,' I replied. Indeed, we did not, and before long, we were set to play the US in the quarter-finals. A German team does not lose to the United States at a World Cup, either. A simple law of nature, just like the one according to which a German team does not lose a World Cup semi-final to South Korea. Since our opponent seemed to agree with said laws, we suddenly found ourselves in the final, and I answered the reoccurring question of 'Where's it going against Brazil?' with a pensive 'It'll get tricky now.' Ironically, the final was our best match, and we still lost it.

Finally, the necessary revolution came in the form of Jürgen Klinsmann. Jürgen has two prominent strengths: firstly, he can set a team's psychology optimally before a big game, because he himself has played many of those matches on a knife's edge. Secondly, he has the greatness and the talent to delegate important tasks. Add to this his steadfastness towards the media, and players will notice that here is a man who will not be bent, nor will he compromise. Together with Jogi Löw, he brought the national team to the next level in terms of fitness and tactical order. At the 2006 World Cup, this was our major plus. At Euro 2008 in Austria and Switzerland, it showed how quickly teams like Croatia, Spain and even Turkey caught up with us and even overtook us. Towards the 2006 World Cup, we had suddenly processed upwards very quickly from a low base: we were extremely fit, absolutely keen, and boasted defensive organisation, topped with opponents who had not yet reached the peak of their possibilities. The next step would be to develop the national team's offensive play. The players' potential was good, but they suffered from simply learning too little from their German clubs about the organisation of attacks. At that point, in spring of 2010, hardly any German top player was part of the Spanish or English leagues, where one could pick up on those things – apart from Michael Ballack and Christoph Metzelder.

When I returned to Germany from the Premier League, my first manager was Armin Veh, an affable fellow, relaxed in a pleasant way. In my opinion, he had picked out his assistant manager well, too; work on the pitch with Alfons Higl went very nicely. Eventually, the one thing missing were the points, and in that situation, even a top coach is no longer safe – a shame, I thought. In exchange, I witnessed the flash promotion of an old national team colleague, Markus Babbel. Overnight, he was hauled from third place in the coaching hierarchy into the top spot. I used to paint the town red with him; now, he was the first manager younger than me. This did not bother me, and whether he struggled with it, I may never know. Addressing our largely unsettled group, he was dead on. 'I believe in you because you're strong,' he said. 'In play, you're one of the best teams in the league, and there is great individual class here.' Everyone enjoyed listening to this; it was constructive and motivational. However, when, after a sensational march from eleventh place to third, the team was later plunged into turmoil, he simply did not manage to find another tone of voice. The papers wrote of the manager's double burden being the reason for 'the Stuttgart crisis', as Babbel constantly had to go to Cologne for manager training courses. However, the situation was not as simple: Markus often led the session in person and only ever drove to Cologne during longer international breaks. No, after all the euphoria of the previous year, he merely did not manage to offer justified criticism. In Seville, he tried to still our trepidation by pointing out that he was the only one who had to fear for their job, a big mistake. As manager, one should never give players the feeling that one's future depends on them or the outcome of a match. Nevertheless, I took to the open way in which Babbel coped with his situation. With a certain sense of fatalism, he walked an extremely fine line – after all, his time at Stuttgart could be over any day. Players, though, do not want to hear dirges when it comes to problems on the pitch. They want solutions, and well-founded criticism is a vital part of that; it is the only way one improves. In all my years as a pro, this has always been the standard I set myself: in every training session, I want to be a little better than the day before. At the beginning of his time at Bayern, Jürgen Klinsmann said something similar and was brutally mocked for it. Yet, he was proved right.

Babbel's successor, the Swiss Christian Gross, was a man of clear messages. He had probably learned this in the Ruhr region, at VfL Bochum, where he had played for two years in the early 80s. Since I, too, had been socialised with exactly this directness, I could live well with his manner. With Gross, everyone knew where they stood. Before a friendly, for example, he would tell us clearly that, in this match, two centre-backs were fighting for the one free position in the next competitive fixture. In addition, he ordered players into the weights room a lot, which might have made some of the young colleagues groan, but I do like hard training. That, ultimately, the slog is good for something shows in the successes of Felix 'Quälix' Magath with such diverse teams as Bayern, Wolfsburg and Schalke. I used to have my difficulties with Magath, because as Bayern manager he would understandably always sponsor his own keeper, and his name was Oliver Kahn. Apart from that, though, I would have liked to be tormented by him in my old age.

Admittedly, all toiling aside, some successes are very difficult to explain in a rational manner. Why, for instance, did my team, that Stuttgart side who had been staggering around disorientated for months, score those three beautiful goals in the first fifteen minutes of that Champions League leg against Unirea Urziceni, and why did we do it in that end of the ground which in the past had been like a curse to us with its constant construction site? The manager's weight training could not have been effective yet at that stage, and his pre-game statement had been quite plain, too: 'If you want to score goals, you need to try to penetrate the penalty area.' No sooner said than done. Sometimes, football is a very simple game indeed.

The manager from whom I learned the most is Arsène Wenger. He is a perfectionist, who does not only know how to defend but who has an exact idea of the game's movement when going forwards. The possibility of training moves and automatisms forwards as well as backwards appears not to exist in some managers' awareness. That concept has found its master in Wenger, who, over a longer period, has always been successful with his analytical and perceptive way of working. Not for nothing has he won big titles in all his jobs in France, Japan and England – only the Champions League trophy has eluded him so far, unfortunately.

After we had won the FA Cup with Arsenal on penalties, he once said that he never actually enjoyed the win, because our success had not been based on his way of playing but rather on 'winning ugly', as they say in England. Dirty victories were not his cup of tea. On the return flight from the Champions League final in which I had been sent off and we ended up losing 1–2 to Barcelona, he sat next to me and said, 'I knew that if they scored one, we could no longer win.' I was confused: we had gained a 1–0 lead after my red card; surely, conceding did not mean all was lost. It merely meant parking the bus and pulling the handbrake, followed by winning on penalties.

Notwithstanding all tactical brilliance, needless to say that I have suffered under him on occasion: after all, he removed me from goal twice. However respectful his treatment of seasoned players at the club was – of Vieira, Ljungberg, Pirès, Bergkamp or Henry – if he thought it was time for a change, he did not make allowances for big names. Time and again, the boss viewed the statistics, and as soon as he noticed a player's running time or playing time decrease, he would rather sell him at once and at a handsome profit, than let him enjoy pleasant footballing twilight years in London. The club's politics dictated a maximum of year-long contracts for over-thirties; Wenger believed it to be the only way of meeting the Premier League's enormous physical standards. To my luck, being keeper made me an exception, and in any case, at 33 I was already the oldest player Wenger had ever signed. When, eventually, my age and the successes of the previous years meant I was becoming too dominant, I had to leave, so as not to stand in the way of a new team hierarchy – a tough decision but a reasonable one at that.

Aside from his eloquence, Wenger is someone who does not speak a word in excess. He does not argue loudly but rather builds incredible pressure through his silence and perfectionism. Occasionally, during shooting practice, he would stand motionless behind my goal, his arms crossed. When I failed to save a shot, I knew that he was raising an eyebrow in utter disdain. As a result, I always tried to build myself up beforehand: there are twelve players coming up, each of whom is going to aim at your goal two or three times. Don't let a single one pass, or the boss is going to wonder immediately whether you're too old now. Situations like this required some getting to grips, as did sentences like this: 'Jens, the next half a year needs to be perfect; only then can we still achieve something.' When the reporters kept asking me in the build-up to the 2006 World Cup whether the fight for number one was putting me under too much pressure, I always said, 'The real pressure is at Arsenal. This here, this is incidental.'

# How I Became Germany's Number One

'JENS.' ANDY KÖPKE'S VOICE ON THE PHONE SOUNDED AS IF HE HAD just learned of his best friend's death. 'Jens, we have had to make a decision today.' It is Friday, 7 April 2006. For almost a year now, the so-called *T-Frage* has been rumbling on, the question of who should be in goal for the national team at the World Cup in Germany – Oliver Kahn or I. In the meantime, football had become almost an affair of the state; delegates even wanted to summon national coach Jürgen Klinsmann to a commission at the Bundestag, because we had lost 1–4 to Italy. He was jeopardising the success of the World Cup, they said. The tournament was not his, they said, but that of the members of parliament and, therefore, that of the entire German people. That was why the *T-Frage* was being discussed for months as if it was the country's presidential election.

Back then, whenever I went to meet with the national team, the hullabaloo was quite embarrassing to me, especially in front of the other players, for whom, apparently, there were simply no other topics to discuss. Luckily, living and working in London, I was usually far away from the German fuss. One morning, I was preparing for Arsenal's match against Manchester United. A strict mobile ban applied during training, which normally meant I was not available. Around 2 pm, however, one of our press officers, handing me a phone number and telling me to call Jürgen Klinsmann. I went to my car and turned on my mobile to discover eleven missed calls, including one from Jürgen. I dialled his number, only to hear Andy Köpke's funereal voice – apparently, I had confused the numbers in my excitement. 'We have asked Oliver to come to Munich,' Köpke was saying now. Well, there you have it, I thought; he sounded so downtrodden that they must have decided against me. 'It really wasn't easy for us,' he went on. 'We've been sitting together since last night, but we've opted for you.'

Almost 24 years after sitting on my parents' sofa in Essen and deciding to become a professional footballer in order to one day be better than Toni Schumacher in that World Cup semi-final, I had made it. I was number one in the German goal. Finally, it had come as I had always hoped it would. But what to do now? Give a cry of joy? Take a lap of honour around my car? Do the Mexican wave by myself? In the end, all that left me was a small, contented smile.

It had taken me 35 years of my life to arrive at this point; by now, my first cap for Germany lay sixteen years in the past. Back then, in May 1990, I was allowed to play a half against Switzerland with the under-21s, in front of 1,500 people in Muri. We had won 2–1. My career with this team had been a complete roller-coaster ride, as if the football gods had wished to prepare me for those exhausting years ahead. After my move to Schalke, I had initially joined the German under-19s, which was quite gratifying, since before, I had not even been considered. Shortly afterwards, I had become the under-21s' first choice – after all, I was the only very young keeper playing regularly for his club. Mehmet Scholl told me to count myself lucky that Kahn was not half a year younger, or he would be in goal for the under-21s. I went to see how much truth there was in this, but Kahn's performance was not such that I really needed to be afraid. Back then, however, I had no way of guessing just how our fortunes would be linked.

The great aim among the under-21s was qualification for the 1992 Olympic Games in Barcelona. Granted, to a footballer, the Olympics is not as important as a World Cup or the Euros, but for us young players, it was the absolute top event. Suddenly, though, manager Hannes Löhr opted for Dortmund's Stefan Klos in goal. I was disappointed, of course, but at least I was left with Pierre de Coubertin's famous utterance as solace: 'it's not the winning but the taking part that counts'. In order to take part, however, we still had to come away with two points from the last two qualifiers against Scotland, something that should have been manageable with a team that boasted Christian Wörns, Christian Ziege, Horst Heldt, Heiko Herrlich, Karlheinz Pflipsen, and Mehmet Scholl. The first leg in Bochum saw Klos in goal again; Löhr reckoned it was like a home game for the Dortmund man. He expected high crosses from the Scots in the return leg, though, and wanted to play me, since he thought I would offer some advantage. The home game ended 1–1, not good but still promising: a draw in the second leg would suffice. Contrary to the manager's promises, I was once again not included in the line-up, Löhr's argument being Klos's good run at Dortmund. We had been 3–1 up after seventy minutes when the inevitable happened: high crosses into the area and, before we knew it, Scotland had got one back. In the 85th minute, there came another high cross – 3–3. During injury time, a final high cross came sailing in, followed by a header – 3–4, game over. Master Löhr, whose wrong decision regarding the keeper's position meant he had to answer for the defeat, merely commented curtly. 'Well, the show goes on.' But for us, it did not. We did not go to Barcelona, and after that, I was finally too old for the under-21s.

It was nearly another six years until I was allowed on the pitch for an international again. By the time the 1996 European Championship came around, I had almost made it. Being voted the league's best goalkeeper meant that national manager Berti Vogts could hardly avoid me. Ultimately, though, I was only on standby for the tournament in England – a substitute, in case one of the first three keepers should suffer an injury. As improbable as that might seem, it actually occurred. I was already getting excited, but Vogts had other plans. He preferred to take Oliver Reck, because he believed me too ambitious – according to him, I was dying to play, compromising the side's harmony. That was utter nonsense; I would have been glad simply to be part of the squad, and as it transpired I would have been allowed to call myself European champion. Eighteen months and a UEFA Cup win later, it was finally time: I was standing in goal for the German national team. On 18 February 1998, I was brought on in the second half for Andreas Köpke, the man who would later tell me – in his role as goalkeeping coach – that I had been selected for the 2006 World Cup. All I remember, though, is a nice hotel, pleasant temperatures and palm trees: we were on a visit to that great footballing nation, Oman. We won 2–0 in front of 10,000 people in the capital city of Muscat. Ours was no bad team, really, with Thon, Kohler, Wörns,

THE MADNESS IS ON THE PITCH

Häßler, Bierhoff and Kirsten. But Berti Vogts once said a clever thing: one is only a proper international player after twenty caps. Now, I might have got an entry in the DFB's statistics books, but to be a proper international, I needed at least another nineteen games . . . and a half. And accumulating those would take me some time. Out of all international players, I am probably the one who took the longest period of time to reach 61 caps: ten whole years. Had I prevailed after my debut, chances are I could have rivalled Sepp Maier as Germany's record appearance-maker as a keeper, but I remained stuck with a few games here and there.

At least when the team went to France 1998, I was allowed to join as third man. Being third meant training, keeping your mouth shut, and being on call in case one of the players wanted some last-minute shooting practice. We were staying in St Paul de Vence, half an hour from Monaco. Since I was not playing anyway, I drove to a Monte Carlo nightclub one evening with Andi Möller and Lothar Matthäus. As there was training scheduled for the next morning, we eventually wanted to make a move around 3 am, but Lothar had met people from Munich, delaying our departure until four o'clock. In the car, with me at the wheel, Matthäus tilted back his seat roughly. 'Are you bonkers, watch for my knee!' screamed Andi Möller, and it took a while for Lothar to free him. Afterwards, Lothar fell asleep at once, his mouth open, his arms flopping left and right from his seat. At 5 am, we arrived back at the hotel knowing that, in two hours, Berti Vogts was going to go for his morning jog. We wanted to serve him his favourite player for breakfast in all his hungover glory by simply leaving Matthäus in the car by the hotel entrance, but then we came to dread the awful trouble that surely would have pulled us into the abyss, too. So, with great effort, we manoeuvred Lothar to his room. Considering the rest of our performances in France, we probably should have left him in the car: Vogts put Matthäus in the team instead of Olaf Thon, who was being sacrificed in spite of good efforts. Every remaining evening from then on, Olaf enjoyed himself with a bottle of wine, which, admittedly, fitted the ambience perfectly. In the quarter-final against Croatia, Lothar made a mistake that had to be smoothed out by Christian Wörns, who was sent off subsequently. We lost 0–3.

After the World Cup, Andy Köpke retired as national team keeper, and for a short while I thought my time had come. But I had not reckoned with the Bayern lobby. Franz Beckenbauer, Uli Hoeneß, Karl-Heinz Rummenigge and Sepp Maier campaigned vehemently for their keeper – and his name was Oliver Kahn. Considering my Italian adventure's abrupt end and me being new at Borussia Dortmund, I, by contrast, had no one who would make their presence felt for me. After the World Cup, due to Oliver being injured, I had played the first few matches, and done so outstandingly. And although Oliver, once he was fit again, had kicked off our rivalry with a decisive mistake during the 0–1 loss against Turkey, I would not have one fair chance against him over the years that followed: Erich Ribbeck, the new national coach, had formerly managed Bayern Munich; a little too often he agreed with *Bild* when it came to personnel decisions. Since man tends to tread the path of least resistance, this distribution of power would remain in place for the next few years. At the Confederations Cup in Mexico, 1999, I was allowed to get a good hiding, conceding eight goals in three games, but at the big tournaments that followed, it was always Oliver Kahn standing between the posts. Of course, it was not easy for me to be number two for so long. My way of playing had been the same over the years but, unfortunately, football was not quite ready for it yet – managers did not yet appreciate the advantages of perceived risks. Apparently, life also punishes those who rush.

After Euro 2000, for the first time, I got up my hopes about playing. Following a disastrous first round exit without a single win and a concluding 0–3 defeat to Portugal, I set out to attack again. The entire team had played poorly, but solely Ribbeck had come under media fire and was made to retire shortly after the tournament. On the final evening, we players gathered to conclude the events with laughter and some ranting, and after a few beers and glasses of wine, the world was not such a bad place any more.

But back to my personal rivalry. Prior to the next big tournament, I had got my hopes up again. I had played a very good season during which we had won the league with Borussia Dortmund and reached the UEFA Cup final. The new manager, Rudi Völler, however, only chose merely to acknowledge the fact that he had a very good substitute keeper: Oliver was allowed to keep playing. He did genuinely deliver a fantastic performance at the 2002 World Cup in Japan and South Korea – apart from the final. During the dinner after winning second place, he and I had a pint together. I congratulated him on his performance during the tournament and asked what his plans looked like. 'I don't know,' he replied, 'Had we won the title, I would have stopped.' 'Well,' I said, 'Seems we're keeping this thing going until 2006.' And that was what happened.

Until then, our relationship had been good, actually. Up to that point, I had respected his performances without envy, but I moved to Arsenal the following season, and immediately, we won the league undefeated. I played the best season of my career, and Kahn had one of his worst. As a result, I figured my chances of playing the Euros in Portugal were good, and with that, began to make demands. And in football in Germany, the way to do that was by giving interviews. Really, I had only wanted to say that I had kept well that season and he had not. But I was, of course, also asked about our relationship and our topics of conversation. At the time, Kahn's private life had been a big subject; he had separated from his wife and was with a new girlfriend. So, entirely truthfully and without any ulterior motives, I said, 'At the moment, there isn't much we talk about. I have a family and my kids; he has a new girlfriend and a completely different life.' Consequently, a storm of indignation erupted in the media, as if I had accused the Pope of having a lover. 'Lehmann thinks he's something special, just because his family's still intact', etc. Yet my answer had in no way meant to be moralistic, but entirely practical: what was I, a boring father and husband, supposed to talk about with a man newly in love? But the scandal wind machine was working so hard that it even blew Rudi Völler all the way to London. We met at Scalini in Chelsea, where he, in all seriousness, said to me, 'Jens, we can't have you attacking Oliver in this way.' I simply could not believe that he, too, was taking the issue so seriously. 'With all due respect, Rudi,' I replied, 'I meant no harm at all; I just don't know what to talk to him about at the moment.' Making the most out of his London trip, I added, 'Rudi, I want to make one thing very clear: I am having a great season, Oliver is not. And I want to play.' As soon as I had finished speaking, I realised that Völler either could not or would not make such a weighty decision. Would I have to count myself lucky to be going to the Euros at all? Eventually, though, Franz Beckenbauer granted me absolution in one of his columns, claiming my supposed attack on Kahn had not been that bad after all.

So, with the matter clarified, I travelled to the Euros as second man. The pleasure was to be short-lived. During the group phase, we conceded goals that would never have been scored two years previously, and after a 1–2 defeat against the Czech Republic's reserves, it was game over. The next morning, before departure, Völler announced his resignation to the team. In his likeable way, he asked us not to wash any dirty laundry in public, and we adhered. As we were getting off the plane after the return flight, Rudi wished me luck – and then said, 'Sorry, Jens, I should've let you play.' I could not believe my ears and was angry as never before. Surely, one of the basic characteRistics of any manager who wants to be successful should be resistance to the public's machinations and opinions, otherwise, he will lose his team's respect immediately. On the other hand, Rudi is characterised as being perceptive, rather than a stubborn old devil who believed until the very last minute that he had done everything correctly. His official reason for resigning was that he was sick and tired of the constant pressure from the media, and that the national team did not deserve to be denigrated until his head rolled. Later, I learned from Bernd Pfaff, then the team's general manager, that apparently Rudi had had to make some very painful decisions – against some of his 2002 World Cup players – and by the looks of things, he no longer wanted to do that.

Despite Völler's resignation, I did not get my hopes up for better conditions – on the contrary: Ottmar Hitzfeld was being tipped as potential successor. Lovely, I thought, I was going out of the frying pan and into the fire, yet another ex-Bayern manager who would prefer his man. While I did have a kind of verbal assurance from Völler that it was my turn now, to a new manager, such a promise was worth nothing. Briefly, I had hoped for Guus Hiddink, the globe-trotting Dutchman who had brought South Korea all the way to the World Cup semi-final in 2002; I knew that he liked goalkeepers who could play good football. But then, surprisingly, the announcement said that the new national team coach was to be Jürgen Klinsmann. Well, I thought initially, that is not too bad for me, at least. The immediate public reaction, however, was that Klinsmann was a friend of Lehmann's, which was not true at all. He might have captained the national team with whom I made my debut years previously; he might have looked after the younger players, explained to us about factions within the team and warned against group formations; and he might have created my connection with lawyer

Andy Groß who had sorted my move to Italy. But the latter had not advised me in a long time, and I had not had much contact with Klinsmann either, who was now living in America. Hence, there could be no talk of any advantage over Kahn. Nevertheless, Jürgen's first official act made me prick up my ears: he took the captain's armband away from Kahn and gave it to Michael Ballack.

The first international of the Klinsmann era took place in Vienna against Austria on 18 August 2004; Oliver and I played one half each. In the end, we won 3–1; the goal against us was not scored while I was on the pitch. In a private talk a few days before the match, Jürgen had told me that from now on, there were no longer a number one and a number two keeper. Instead, Kahn and I were to be equals; there was to be a fair fight for the spot in goal over the next two years, and each of us was to be given the same number of games. On one hand, of course, I was delighted about the new motto, 'rivalry on all positions'; on the other, I was at odds with the fact that Germany, as host, would not have to go through qualification but would merely play friendlies. Otherwise, the decision would have probably immediately been made in my favour. But the following day, shortly before his press conference, Jürgen unexpectedly pulled me to one side once more. 'Listen, Uli Hoeneß has just called to say it wasn't too bad that I had taken the captaincy away from Kahn, but if I told him on top that he wasn't number one anyway, he would be completely finished and end up falling apart. We cannot afford that with Bayern.' Puzzled, I looked at Jürgen. Was he going to bin me yet again? 'So,' he continued, 'I'll phrase it differently in the press conference from the way we've discussed. I'll them Kahn is number one and you're the contender. But in our internal evaluation, you both have the same status.' Oh dear, I thought, he looks downcast already, but before I could say another word, he was already on his way.

The battle, then, was on, and the lobbyists were already getting to work. Even my old friend Toni Schumacher suddenly emerged from the shadows, but in quite a different manner than I would have expected. When I went to Arsenal, he asked me at once whether I could not arrange a training visit for him with Arsène Wenger. As I had worked well with him during our time at Schalke, I took care of it right away and, when he was granted the place, let him stay at my London home. In the mornings, he would go to training with me; in the afternoon, he would sit around the house, not even going for a look around town. It was all the same to us; Conny enjoyed making him coffee. Eventually, as soon as Klinsmann took office, he approached him and said, 'I would keep Kahn as number one.' Toni, I thought; are you demented? He had lived with us not two years ago. Even if he believed in Kahn, respect and decency demanded that he keep his mouth shut for once. But to Schumacher, decency will probably forever be an alien concept.

Klinsmann remained steadfast. Kahn and I took turns in goal, I kept a clean sheet most of the time, he conceded a few. Looking at the statistics of saved shots and conceded goals, I was in the lead, but then came the match against Italy in Florence that almost killed off 'Project Klinsmann'. It was supposed to be Oliver's game; I was supposed to play against the US three weeks later at my old Dortmund ground. Oliver, though, was clever and called in sick for Italy; it was as if he had sensed something. The journey alone was an utter catastrophe: with the airport blocked, we were unable to land in Florence and instead had to drive two hours through Tuscany, starting from Bologna, across an old, curvy motorway, without anything to drink. In order to get to the training ground, we stumbled through Florentine traffic for another 45 minutes before returning by bus in drenched clothes, taking more than half an hour to arrive back at the hotel. The next morning, several players reported to the doctor with a cold. I had lost my voice, and before such an important game, too. The match itself was practically finished after only seven minutes: the Italians were 2–0 up and we still had not arrived on the pitch properly. In the end, we drove home with a disastrous 1–4 on our backs, a mere few months before the beginning of the World Cup.

I knew what was now to befall the side and, of course, the manager. The national team, the Germans' dearest child, was suddenly considered to have behavioural problems. As usual, though, there was no constructive criticism this time either. Instead we, and especially Klinsmann, faced a smear campaign because he had flown to his family in California after the game instead of participating in the FIFA workshop in Düsseldorf. For this he received the ultimate punishment: a public shaming in *Bild*, carried out by football's emperor, Franz Beckenbauer. The debate even went as far as Klinsmann's sacking being demanded in order to avoid humiliation at the World Cup. No one really cared what had actually gone wrong in that Italy game. Again, I was vindicated in my old feeling that none of the self-styled experts really conducted any investigation of causes. During his 1990 World Cup triumph, Beckenbauer himself was able to draw from a reservoir of almost 200 East and West German players. By now, there were barely sixty left in the Bundesliga who were worth considering for the national team. They were joined by Didi Hamann at Liverpool, Robert Huth at Chelsea, and me – the only Germans at renowned foreign clubs. Especially where Hamann was concerned, I had always marvelled at how readily the public overlooked his success and experiences. In 2005, following a poor game against Holland, he asked the coaches not to pick him for the time being. From conversations with him, however, I knew that secretly he was still hoping to be going to the World Cup. We had met in mid-February during a reception for the English Prime Minister, Tony Blair, where Franz Beckenbauer was also present as part of his never-ending world tour, visiting all World Cup participants. For us German players, of course, it was an honour to meet the British head of government. A few minutes after his arrival in the drawing room of 10 Downing Street, Blair approached Didi and me, and began a conversation. He was a Newcastle United fan (one of Didi's former clubs), and one of his sons supported Liverpool. The impression he gave was one of likeability without any airs and graces. Later on, I was standing together with Beckenbauer. What was I to talk about with this man who always took a stand for Kahn as 'best German goalkeeper'? We did not waste any words on the national team but rather talked about the English he had managed to pick up during his time at New York Cosmos. Despite him not making life easy for me with his lobbying for Kahn, Franz Beckenbauer is a very polite and pleasant man, who exudes modesty in spite of his popularity – including this evening, during which he also chatted animatedly to my wife about the children.

Later on, Wolfgang Niersbach, the former DFB press officer, took me to one side. Now vice president of the World Cup's organisational committee, he wanted to know what I would do if I only ended up as second choice. 'I don't concern myself with that at all,' I replied. 'I'm quite certain about becoming number one.' Slightly bemused, he asked whether I was prepared for the worst-case scenario. Again, I retorted that I could not imagine not being number one. Now, in a kind of implicit threat, he made it clear that I, in case of degradation, should under no circumstances make a scene, as that would only cause a problem. I took that to mean that I was not to delude myself about the answer to the *T-Frage* while at all times grinning and bearing the stitch-up. After this conversation, I got the impression for the first time that, politically speaking, I did not have a chance of playing. Nonetheless, I still believed I would – the differences in the performance level between Oliver and me were simply too great for me to be pessimistic. The only uncertainty was the issue of me being unable to assess whether, in the end, Jürgen Klinsmann's decisions would be based on a gut feeling or on objective criteria.

The international against the Americans in Dortmund had suddenly become a key match for Klinsmann; another defeat, and the pressure would become unbearable. As a result, everyone was poking around the *T-Frage* debate all the more thoroughly. Apparently, at the DFB, all involved were grateful for this sideshow, as it was distracting from the bigger, more pressing questions. Kahn opened the international week with a kind of government statement in *Bild*: 'I'm number one.' Klinsmann had assured him, he said, prompting me, of course, to ask whether that was true. He, in turn, assured me never to have said such a thing. During the press conference the next day, however, Kahn repeated his claim; I denied it whenever I was asked – this way, utter chaos à la Chinese whispers came to reign, at the end of which, no one knew just what was true any more.

But I was not going to be bothered. I had lost my great athletic respect for Kahn some time ago because, since 2002, his performances had not justified his self-regard. A journalist once showed me a statistic: since the 2002 World Cup, Oliver Kahn had not played a great game against a good opponent, neither with his club nor with the national team. In addition, I had radically shifted my training towards quality and intensity; I was now simply working faster and more explosively through every exercise. Every day, I subjected myself to a tight rhythm: I was the first to arrive in the morning to be treated, either with a massage or by Philippe Boixel, our French osteopath at Arsenal. He became very important to me, because he taught me how to cope with stressful situations using his techniques. After a few minutes of breathing, I would notice exactly what might not be quite right with my body.

I focused intently on every single training session and every single match as if they were finals. Constant dripping wears the Klinsmann stone, I thought, and I indeed managed to play better games. Even after the 2005 Confederations Cup, when Klinsmann said that if the World Cup was around the corner, Kahn would be playing, I could not care less. I was a little frustrated, of course, but I am not prone to strong self-doubts; they are not something a goalkeeper can afford. I know that, over the course of my life, I have trained so much and worked so hard on my weaknesses that I was close to being perfect where my technique was concerned. If, in addition, my fitness and focus on the next aim was right, nothing would stand in the way of a convincing performance. I swore to myself I would do it just like I had in London with Arsène Wenger, who eventually could not help but bring me in. Every day, I meditated for a quarter of an hour using Philippe's breathing techniques, and together with Dr Murphy's advice and my faith in God, I became imperturbable. To top it all off, I worked on manipulating my subconscious: whenever I was asked in an interview about my situation, I would always reply, 'I am firmly convinced that I will be playing at the World Cup.' This way of commenting must have sounded very persuasive and self-assured: eventually, not only the press but Bayern, too, thought that Jürgen was bound to have given me a positive answer already. But I had not received anything. Perhaps I had made people think just like me purely through my choice of words and the power of my thoughts.

The key match against the US began with a goalless first half, with the fans booing the players back into the dressing room. Klinsmann paced from one end to the other, imploring the team to give it their all one more time. Never mind tactical instructions – everyone knew that if we messed this up too, Jürgen could fly back home again, but this time on a one-way ticket. Immediately after the second half had kicked off, Bastian Schweinsteiger scored, and when Kahn saved a dangerous header with a great parry, I feared a turn in our rivalry. Everything was going according to his plan again; all of his weaker games of the past had been forgotten; the crowd were behind him once more. In the game's dying minutes, though, just as I was beginning to doubt whether I still stood a chance at all, Oliver Kahn shot himself in the foot. He came out rashly when a ball was played towards his box, allowing it to bounce over him and into the goal. After the final whistle, I phoned my cousin Jochen, who, with my brother Jörg and my friend Niklas, formed my trio of agents. Over the past two years, they had been keeping me up to date about the mood of the German public and the media. According to Jochen, the commentator had screamed 'Foul' when the goal against us was scored. Even Kahn had been of that opinion, he said. Unbelievable, I thought, now he was turning mistakes into fouls and bad luck. But then, help came from an unlikely ally. Immediately at the start of the match analysis, Franz Beckenbauer made it clear that Oliver had to shoulder the blame, because coming out of his goal meant he should have saved it. Thank you, Kaiser.

In private, I thought that Oliver had to hate Beckenbauer, since the latter was the only one openly calling it a mistake. Before, Beckenbauer had already outlined the differences between the two of us: 'Lehmann comes out for every ball; Oliver, well, he prefers to stay on the line.' For that, I was very grateful, because among experts, this difference is considered the most important criterion. Everyone had to play well on the line if they wanted to feature in a top league. The difference between good keepers and top keepers, however, lies in domination of the penalty area and actively playing the game. I could only hope that the coaching team was of the same opinion.

Imagine those final, decisive internationals before a World Cup like a hustings, a grotesque drama. Oliver Kahn and I were standing not ten yards apart in the mixed zone at the Westfalenstadion, advertising our own agendas. 'Vote for me,' each of us seemed to be shouting as we pretended to analyse the game. I had known beforehand that I would have to give a statement even if I had not played. My message was, 'I cannot imagine a reason why I shouldn't be playing.' My manifesto read as follows: 'I play for Arsenal, a team who are young and whose way of playing is similar to that of the national team – the defence stand far out in front, and that calls for a good goalkeeper who can play along'. In Oliver's manifesto, one word in particular was underlined: 'tournament experience'. The campaign location in Dortmund was where candidate Kahn repeated once more how Klinsmann had told him that he was number one. He had played a good season, he said, 'Just like Jens'; hence, there was no reason to change anything. Now, apparently, he wanted to get me on board, but I would only be allowed to play supporting role. Over time, he had developed a clever strategy to distract the public from performances delivered on the pitch.

The climax of the hustings, however, was yet to come. Back in London, I

THE MADNESS IS ON THE PITCH

watched *Das Aktuelle Sportstudio* via satellite alongside my family. The peak of the show was a telephone poll: who should be in goal at the World Cup? I merely remarked that there had to be a million Bayern fans watching now and that I did not stand a chance anyway, before ceasing to watch. After a while, I received a load of text messages, all with the same content: 'You've won!' The sensation was complete; I had won, with 52 per cent of the votes. On a whim, I texted back, saying that, time permitting, I would come by their market square sometime with my campaign van. Suddenly, the early indications had given me confidence once more. I used every following opportunity to continue my campaign – for example, whenever channel *Sat.1* were broadcasting our Champions League matches. Before and after the quarter-final against Juventus, I dutifully recited my regular message: 'I believe in myself and can't think why I shouldn't be playing.' In London, we positively took Juve apart with our young team, winning 2–0. Germany was delighted with Arsenal's refreshing, fast game. For my candidacy, not conceding was just as important as the fact that we were about to break the Champions League's all-time clean-sheet record. Surely, that could be transferred to the boys in the national team's defence.

Not three days later, a sort of preliminary decision was made. We won 5–0 against Aston Villa; Bayern only drew 2–2 against FC Köln, who were likely to be relegated. On the way home, I received a text from a friend in Munster, who prepared me for two interesting Köln goals. I was home at 6 pm BST; Germany was one hour ahead – *Sportschau* time. The summary of the Bayern match was starting just as I walked through the door. The first goal saw Oliver Kahn obstruct an opposition player during a cross; on the second one, he let past a swirling shot by Albert Streit from around twenty yards. At half-time, he asked to be taken off and disappeared from the stadium. It reminded me a little of that Leverkusen game thirteen years ago, when I had been substituted after a hair-raising mistake and ended up taking the train home. On the one hand, I felt sorry for Oliver, because he had to sell these goals as bad luck while the public were lusting after a confession of guilt. On the other, some of the bullying and the unbearable moments of the last eight years were still in the back of my mind, all the attacks and accusations from Oliver's entourage, not to mention the bias and blind loyalty of Sepp Maier, who had never given me a real chance. Or, for that matter, me being forced to run the gauntlet during the opening match at the Allianz Arena. 'Lehmann, you arsehole,' the entire stadium had shouted at my very first touch. Later on, when I had clattered into Bastian Schweinsteiger during a perfectly regular tackle, causing him to crash into the hoardings, the crowd had gone ballistic. As a result, I had been whistled and booed over ninety minutes, and the stadium announcer had not said one word to alter the mood at least a little bit. Some grand opening that was, with the atmosphere being solely generated by the spectators' hatred towards a single player. Since those had been bitter moments for me, I briefly considered resigning from the national team and putting an end to the whole *T-Frage* nonsense. Luckily, Conny would not let pass this little moment of weakness. 'This can't be it,' she said, 'You can't put up with this.' And so, disappointment became fury. At this time, I had been reading Oriana Fallaci's book, *Fury and Pride*, which might deal with something completely different, but the title had stuck in my mind like a motto. As a result, my fury eventually turned into positive energy, making me even stronger.

More opportunities would follow, during which Kahn's friends charged my fury battery. Before the decisive game against the US in Dortmund, even our captain, Michael Ballack, had come out in favour of his old Munich team-mate. 'I can't picture someone else playing other than him,' he had said in an interview. I had immediately taken him to task about it, but he had denied everything. Years later, during the argument over Torsten Frings' future on the national team, Ballack did it again: without need, he pointedly got behind the veteran, undermining the ambitions of other, younger players. In order to gain more authority and sympathy within the team, Ballack needed to learn that this was simply not something captains did.

After the Köln defeat, Oliver tried on more explanations for size: he had been too ambitious; he had been bent on playing despite the back injury sustained during the US match. Uli Hoeneß came to his aid, claiming Klinsmann was to blame for Kahn's excessive ambition in that he was piling inhuman pressure onto his goalkeeper. Then the Bayern party, amid their pro-Kahn campaign, made a tactical mistake. They publicly demanded an immediate decision by Klinsmann regarding the *T-Frage*, claiming the situation was harming their keeper. According to them, Kahn was absent-minded in the league; the pressure was too high, and a shaky goalkeeper could potentially jeopardise their title aspirations. I was sitting on my sofa, smirking. Had it not been Oliver who had kept talking of the insane pressure he had withstood brilliantly in all his performances? What had happened to all that, I wondered. After all, it was I on whom the uncertainty weighed most: unlike him, I could not even be certain of playing at my own club.

For the time being, the return leg against Juventus was more important to me than the ongoing hustings spectacle in Germany. Following a goalless draw, we made it to the semi-finals. After the game, I said goodbye to Oliver Bierhoff, who was present in his role as a *Sat.1* pundit. He told me that, considering the pressure coming from Bayern, it was possible Jürgen and the other coaches would make a decision this week. We were barely into April – one month, then, before the day I was anticipating a decision to be made. Inwardly, I was quite confident. I had simply kept too well and too steadily to imagine a decision against me, especially after the two previous weeks. Experience, however, had taught me to be careful and vigilant. Two days later, then, I heard Andy Köpke's voice over the phone, delivering the good news: I was number one.

Afterwards, I spoke briefly to Jürgen Klinsmann. 'Phew,' he said, 'over two years, this has been the most difficult decision to make so far. I haven't been managing for that long yet, but it has by no means come easily to me. We want to go through this with you; we believe in you.' I could not say much more than 'thank you'. I merely promised to give it my all, because not only I but Klinsmann too had had to fight much resistance. And as a player, one will go through fire and water for someone like that. I did not want to bother myself about it much more, though, because I had to be on the pitch two days later. I wanted to talk to my wife at once, of course, but initially, due to my friends constantly phoning me, I could not make a call myself. It took me almost half an hour to finally get hold of her. 'Where are you?' she screamed down the phone. 'You're number one, isn't that insane? You've always said it; you've always believed it.' 'I know, I know,' I replied calmly, but I was welling up. 'It was about time.' 'I keep getting calls and texts,' she continued to scream, 'Everyone's congratulating you.' How did she find out, I asked. 'My mum heard about it on the radio and called me. At first, she thought it was a joke,' Conny explained, 'But even one of those financial news channels interrupted their programme. Klinsmann is talking at the moment, and they keep showing Oliver Kahn. By the way, he's wearing that same jumper you have, how funny.' 'Poor bloke,' I said, 'He must be quite sad. At least I would be if I were in his place.' 'How are you feeling?' she said. 'I don't know,' I replied honestly, 'I'm happy, of course, but somehow, I can't process it properly yet. It's a great gift, but it's not palpable. And it doesn't change anything at the moment, either – after all, the World Cup is still some time away.' In the evening, the question to the *T-Frage* was even featured up front on *Tagesthemen*, as if it were a terror attack or an increase in VAT. It was absurd where this electoral campaign had led us.

When I look back on this time, asking myself why I ended up being election winner, one thing comes to mind above all else: the fact that, apparently, I was able to cope even better with stress than Oliver Kahn. It was a comparison at eye-level; we were both driven by ambition. I, however, had developed crucially through my move to England, while Kahn was unable to improve after the 2002 World Cup. Perhaps not having competition at his own club had not been ideal, either. I was the more complete goalkeeper, and that simply had to come into play one day. My wife might have always told me I did not stand a chance anyway, but my credo had been Rudi Assauer's old saying, 'Class always prevails.' Of course, the constant duelling had been bloody exhausting and anything but fun, but all the negative experiences throughout the years had taught me to fight my way out of bad phases and to come out stronger than before. In the end, this had given me the composure simply to deliver, as they say. Occasionally, I am asked whether I had felt sorry for Oliver Kahn; after all, he was to experience the capstone of his career – a World Cup in his own country – mostly from the bench. But sympathy would not have been appropriate; this had been an athletic competition. I had respected the fact that he had tried hard, but at the end of the day, I believe I had invested considerably more into my great goal. I had been so convinced of my victory that the question of what I would have done in case of a defeat had never arisen in my mind. I probably would have sat down on the bench, too; after all, in all my years with the national team, I had become familiar with this spot, even if I had never learned to love it. In the end, professional players are still fans who support their side, and while I was playing for several different clubs, the national team had always been the only constant.

As consolation, Oliver Kahn was allowed to start in the match for third place, with which I agreed very much. This way, he actually received two testimonials – one at the World Cup and one at the end of his time at Bayern. By the time my career with the national team came to an end, testimonials had already been abolished. Hence, the new DFB era had duped me twice: there was no farewell game for me, and I would have to work hard for the coaching badges, which ex-internationals used to receive automatically. But all this fits the rest of my career: I had always had to graft for everything.

# A Record For The Ages: 852 Champions League Minutes Without Conceding

AS RONALDINHO WAS CLOSING IN, I HAD A MERE FRACTION OF A second left to decide. Should I stay in goal or go out? There was no use bickering about how, really, Alexander Hleb was at fault, even though it had been he who had lost the ball on the right-hand side. My defenders, Campbell, Touré and Eboué might have been standing in position, but Eboué had failed to warn us of Samuel Eto'o coming down the right. Barcelona's playmaker had used this moment of uncertainty – or perhaps it was mere fear of an ingenious opponent – to pass the ball between me and my defenders with the outside of his boot. This was the moment I had to make my decision, and it was made while Ronaldinho was still closing in.

I could see Samuel Eto'o sprinting towards me. 'I can manage this,' I thought, setting out for a long sliding tackle. Suddenly, I realised that the Cameroon forward was even faster than I had anticipated. My path-time calculations, applied intuitively like so often before, got mixed up for the first time in ages. No matter how much I stretched my leg, Eto'o would touch the ball before my foot did, and put it past me. 'No goal,' my mind yelled. It served as a warning but also a reminder that I had not yet conceded in this Champions League season – an unprecedented record, a mark for eternity. The streak would have to end at some point, of course, but not now of all times, not during the first twenty minutes of a the final. Was this the reason my hand suddenly grasped at Eto'o's leg?

To this day, I do not quite know why I had not been able to simply keep my fingers to myself in the nineteenth minute on that May night at the Stade de France in Paris, 2006. Yes, Barcelona would have taken the lead, but we would have had seventy minutes left to turn the page, to win possibly the most valuable title in world football. After all, from an athletic point of view, the Champions League final is classified higher than a Euro or World Cup final, both of which are reached after a mere six games with some luck of the draw and some exotic teams in the first round. In the Champions League, by contrast, one plays exclusively against strong teams all year round. By no later than the quarter-finals, the opponents are so well attuned that they will not make any mistakes, at least not those that will happen to less well-organised teams. Had all this been crossing my mind just before my hand touched Eto'o? Not deliberately, surely, and even if so, it was the facts that counted in the end: I had touched him, and he had fallen.

For a short moment, there even seemed to be hope for me. Barcelona's Ludovic Giuly had come sprinting towards me from the left, thrusting the ball into the empty goal. I heard the referee's whistle and thought I might be lucky; perhaps he had seen something that was going to save me. Barcelona's players crowded the ref, asking him why on earth he had not played the advantage. Realising that Terje Hauge could not reverse his decision, they changed strategy at top speed. Carlos Puyol and Mark van Bommel brandished imaginary red cards under the referee's nose, a picture which burned itself into my mind. That simply is not done. Players do, of course, run up to the referee to tell him what to do every now and again, but openly demanding he send someone off simply is not on. In the end, the only solace I get is the hope that people always meet twice. There are always opportunities to settle old scores.

As the referee showed me the red card, I felt like the loneliest person on the planet; I could not even muster the strength to complain. This could not be true, I thought, burying my face in my hands. It could not be true that I was being sent off twenty minutes into this crucial match, not after the season we had been having. For the sense of self-protection, I fumed at my defenders for bringing me into this situation in the first place with their failure to act. I sulked off the pitch as Almunia was brought on, with Robert Pirès having to make way for him. Pirès was the pawn sacrifice, and I offered him an apology later in the dressing room.

To this day, no one has asked pardon for that recklessly lost ball marking the beginning of the error chain at the end of which I had to put my neck on the line. Only the referee, whom I would meet again during an international a little later, he alone was blaming himself. He should have kept the game going, he told me. His honesty was to his credit, but perhaps he had gone into that final somewhat insecure – a mere day before the match, one of his linesmen had been replaced because he had let himself be photographed in a Barça kit. What an impartial man. But I was not going to cook up some conspiracy theory saying there had been something shady about Hauge and his match officials, including the sending-off. His early whistle had simply sealed my fate, that was all.

And to think that I had made such ambitious plans – 2006 was supposed to be my year. On New Year's Eve, I was once again on my own: as the English in their football mania never take a break, we were scheduled to play a lunchtime game against Aston Villa. Conny and the kids had already gone on a skiing holiday to Austria. The match ended 0–0 and, relatively content, we drove home from Birmingham. I asked Freddie Ljungberg what he was doing in the evening and, friendly as he was, he invited me round to his house. He lived on the same street as us, so I welcomed the New Year during a comfortable dinner alongside his godchild and their family. My resolutions were clear: first of all, I wished for the birth of a healthy daughter. Secondly, I wanted to win a trophy with Arsenal – preferably the Champions League. Thirdly, I was still playing for a new contract in London. The World Cup was to be the icing on the cake.

I went home shortly after midnight. Watching the fireworks over London, I noticed that this was another one of those moments I could not enjoy properly thanks to my discipline and my ambitious goals. Over the years, I have stopped counting the number of family gatherings, birthdays, weddings, christenings and parties I have missed because I had to play, or was on the way to a game, or barracked in a training camp. This New Year's night, however, I consoled myself with the thought of the big moments waiting for me on the pitch over the coming months, moments that would nearly make me despair with stress and strain.

On 3 January, we played Manchester United. For the first time in Arsène Wenger's ten-year-long era, Arsenal were not among the top three, so we could not afford to lose this game. For me, it was the prelude to a whole series of so-called big games. This time the previous year, I had still been on the bench, and even now, I was not immune to being banished to this worst of all pieces of football furniture. Hence, I treated every match like a small final – the prizes being my position on the team, fourth place in the table (our minimum aim), and number one on the national team. Although I only had to make a single save, the United game was a battle of nerves. Against players like Ryan Giggs, Ruud van Nistelrooy, Wayne Rooney or Cristiano Ronaldo, one moment of carelessness was enough to lose a match. We managed a goalless draw; the start of the New Year had been successful.

The following matches were numbered among the most eventful of my entire career. Usually, I did not have to make too many saves, as our defence took most of the work off my hands. However, due to the injuries of Cole, Clichy, Lauren and Pascal Cygan, I had suddenly become grandfather to a bunch of teenagers and had my work cut out. In order to keep the side on track towards Champions League qualification, I had to parry a number of penalties and make some spectacular saves. A few days after Manchester, we nearly weakened ourselves further: during the match against West Ham, Sol Campbell made two mistakes in the first half. 'I am not going back on again,' he told the manager during half-time, and simply disappeared. Although I knew him quite well off the pitch, which did not mean much considering his reserved nature, I would have never expected him to let down the team at this hour. We lost the match 2–3. Later on, I called him to leave an urgent voicemail on his mobile; we had planned, after all, to drive together to Tony Blair's reception the next day. But he remained unavailable for five whole days, not only to me but to everyone. As a result, wild speculations arose: was the incident going to finish his career? Or did he merely wish to move club? Eventually, he simply decided to reappear, something he did in some style. In front of the whole team, he gave a speech of apology for which he had specifically made handwritten notes. The boss and the others accepted his apology; apparently, he was not going to be punished. Henceforth, I kept this in mind, just in case I wanted to go on a mid-season skiing holiday one day without telling anyone. Unfortunately, Sol sustained a foot injury during the first training session after his return. With this, our defence slipped further into trouble.

Today, I can say that this pressure benefited me. Despite an eventual, last-minute 1–0 loss, I delivered one of my most spectacular performances ever against Liverpool. For the first time since moving to the UK, I was voted man of the match in a Premier League fixture; the prize was a Sky TV bottle of champagne. The broadcasters looked at me in astonishment when I vehemently refused to accept it. Boarding the team bus with a bottle of fizz after a defeat simply would have sent a poor signal, even if receiving the award was really a sensation. Playing with people like Bergkamp, Henry, Pirès, Ljungberg or Vieira, goalkeepers would not usually be man of the match, and yet, here I was. The situation offered good conditions to talk to the boss about a new contract, so we sat down in the training-ground office, where the little group of five chairs had by now been extended to ten. 'You know,' Wenger explained, 'lately, during contract negotiations, new players have begun to bring not only their parents with them but a whole bunch of lawyers and agents.' We, however, remained between ourselves. At my age, I would have considered it embarrassing to still bring along an agent, who, in any case, would only have been paid to sit around anyway. Apart from the contract length and my salary, there was not much to be negotiated; everything had been organised perfectly by the club, and my family were entirely happy and content. Eventually, my contract was extended by a year.

In late February, the last-sixteen game against Real Madrid was looming, to be played at the Bernabéu, one of football's most holy temples. If you want to learn about the significance of football in individual countries, all you need to do is to look at the locations of the great grounds. The Bernabéu, for instance, is situated right in the middle of town. Our young team was considered the blatant underdog compared to the galácticos of Ronaldo, Zinedine Zidane, David Beckham, Robinho, Roberto Carlos and so forth. To the surprise of fans and pundits, however, we delivered a perfect match. Thierry Henry secured a historic 1–0 victory, upholding once again his reputation as Europe's outstanding forward – but it would have been unfair to highlight a single player. We had been the first English team ever to win at the Bernabéu; moreover, we inflicted the first home defeat in three years on Real's superstars. The first-leg win, however, was only the initial step. Three years previously, almost to the day, on the same pitch and in a Dortmund kit, I had already felt like the winner too and still ended up losing 1–2 after a 1–0 lead. Back then, I had promised myself to return to this legendary site and to do it better. I had been unwilling to depart empty-handed again – and in the end, I did not.

There is no need to consult a pharmacist to know that such historic games do, of course, have their side effects. A match like that demands 120 per cent of a player, both mentally and physically, so that after the final whistle, one is quite literally less of a person than before. Even I, as a goalkeeper, would easily lose two kilos; it would take a corresponding length of time to come down from this exceptional state. If, then, we met a typically English team like Blackburn the following match day, who did more kicking and hitting than playing football, losing 1–0 was a possibility. Arsène Wenger, however, had always had a very good, at times even aggressive, manner of addressing a young team like us after such a defeat. He would simply challenge us to reflect on our game and to have all the trust in the world in our skill. After poor results, he would stand before us like a protective shield, but internally, everyone knew what that really meant: those who did not deliver reliable performances would be replaced by someone else no later than the following season.

The return leg against Real was memorable. After a mere two minutes, Ronaldo executed a header which I could only just block. It was immediately clear to everyone that Real, one of the three best teams on this planet, would not underestimate us again and wanted to turn the page at any cost. Suddenly, we were forced to experience the precision and speed with which those boys were able to play, but we were putting up bold resistance. The match surged back and forth with chances on either side, Raúl having the clearest one after 65 minutes: flying to the ground, I had steered his shot onto the inside of the post, but the ball bounced back to him, and even with his weaker right foot, he could have easily made it 1–0 from eight yards. But with the ball bouncing once again in front of him, Raúl was forced to volley it, which gave me a tenth of a second to get back up on my feet. Against my running direction, he curled a shot into the long corner, but luck seemed to be on my side – as I was falling, I managed to turn the ball around the post with my right hand. Highbury had not lived through this much drama in a long time. When the final whistle sealed the goalless draw, and with it our progress, I knew that this was one of those moments for which one lived as a footballer, and for which one happily did without many other things. Nowhere else can one experience such a concentrated range of chemical processes in one's own body, processes leading to adrenalin release, stress, goose bumps, and feelings of elation.

I was sitting in the dressing room after the game, completely exhausted, when my parents called. They had watched the match live on TV and were still beside themselves. As usual, before congratulating me, they asked whether I had been hurt – I suppose one never grows up in the eyes of one's parents. My German and English friends, as ever, texted me short, personal match reports, a kind of digital umbilical cord connecting me to the outside world beyond the stadium. I had been given a new nickname, courtesy of London newspapers: Jenius – I knew that from this moment on, I would have to be even more focused and vigilant. There is a game that the English media, though not exclusively, likes to play: praising players lavishly, only to run them into the ground ruthlessly at the slightest mistake. Hence, I simply could not afford to make any mistakes.

Our next opponent was to be Juventus, but I was miles away. Sometime towards the end of March, my daughter was supposed to be born; in private, I hoped that Conny would not go into labour shortly before an away game. On 9 March, we went to the clinic for another check-up, where the doctor told us that it would happen in the next 24 hours. My God, I thought, we could have a baby by tomorrow. On the inside, I rejoiced; the timing was perfect. It was a Thursday, three days before the home game against Liverpool, and the doctor was proven right. Indeed, Conny went into labour only a few hours later. The hospital bag had been packed already and everything had been organised for the night. A friend looked after Mats and Lasse, since I, of course, wanted to be there for the birth. By 10 pm the contractions were coming regularly. The Real match had only been a day before so, naturally, I was awfully tired and fell asleep, hoping someone would wake me in time for the birth. And someone did: my sons, at seven in the morning. I saw my wife lying next to me and asked, perplexed, 'What's going on? I thought it was supposed to come today.' 'I don't know,' Conny shrugged, 'The contractions have stopped.' So, the day began as usual: I dropped off the kids at school and drove to London Colney for training.

A week passed in this manner, when my wife called me during training: 'Come home, I'm driving to the hospital in a minute!' We arrived there at 5 pm, where

I, to Conny's annoyance, asked the staff for a portion of fish. The contractions worsened more and more, but for a third child, the birth did take quite a while. Finally, shortly before midnight on 16 March, our daughter, Liselotta Marie, came into the world. I took her into my arms, hoping she would start screaming immediately, and she did indeed, only to go quiet again at once. Perfect, everyone was happy and healthy. Later that night, I was finally free to go home and sleep.

Twelve days later, we played Juventus, who, unlike Real in the previous round, were surely not going to underestimate us. They did, however, make a mistake with their method of forcing a slow pace on their opponent. In this first leg, they had nothing to offer in reply; our domineering 2-0 success frustrated the Italians to such an extent that they got carried away with provocations, resulting in Mauro Camoranesi and Jonathan Zebina being sent off late in the game. We then prepared routinely for the return leg until, three hours before kick-off, a typically Italian slip-up occurred. After the final team meeting, eight or nine of us took the lift up to our rooms, but before we had reached our floor, there was a mighty jolt; the lift ground to a halt and got stuck. While the younger players began to make jokes, I was a little afraid and asked them to stop talking. Theo Walcott, Mathieu Flamini, Ljungberg, Reyes and the others might have ridiculed me, but I did not consider it a laughing matter. Once before, I had experienced such a situation when, during my time at Dortmund, I had got stuck in a lift with Jan Koller. We had been stuck for half an hour, with almost no oxygen left in the small space by the end – apparently, a giant such as Koller needs more air than normal people. This time, too, the mirrors in the lift quickly completely fogged, making my colleagues go quiet abruptly. Luckily, we managed to wrench open the doors a little to let in some fresh air, but it still took twenty minutes for us to be finally freed, and even if none of us could prove our suspicions, we all thought that this had been a little piece of Italian sabotage.

The match, in any case, turned out typically Italian. Juve tried for control, although we, through repeated quick forays, posed a threat in their half. We did not, however, make use of our opportunities, and suddenly Juve created two chances which, luckily, I was able to save. When eventually, Pavel Nedved was sent off after a terrible foul on Eboué, we managed to hold on to a goalless draw, registering in the history books a new record for games played in the Champions

League without conceding. For the first time in the club's history, Arsenal had reached the semi-finals of this competition – an immense success for the club, who had been playing the finest domestic football for years, but who had never enjoyed the same level of success on the continent. The fact that, now, we had unexpectedly reached the semi-finals was a particular gratification for all of us, especially Arsène Wenger.

Our opponent in said semi-final was to be Villarreal, a compact team who were known to be hard to beat, both at home and away. Straight after the league game the weekend before, I began my preparations. In my mind, I went through every possible occurrence, followed by the trusty pre-match ritual. Check-in at the hotel on Monday evening, dinner, massage, bed at 10 pm; the next morning, rise at seven, a game of chess on my phone (to wake up), followed by a croissant and some cocoa at the bar. In the afternoon, I would meditate for a clean sheet; at 6 pm, it would be time to leave for the stadium, with music on the bus and full focus on the game. Five past seven, time to go out onto the pitch for the warm-up, surrounded by empty stands. Then at 7.45 pm it was kick-off in a packed ground. Nothing much happened, though – an effort here and there, a feeble cross; that was all Villarreal had to offer. In the end, we won 1–0 thanks to a goal by Kolo Touré – not the lead we wanted, but at least a head start. The match being quiet at least gave me enough time to study the strengths and preferences of individual Villarreal players. Their most important man was Juan Román Riquelme: the Argentinian dictated rhythm and pace; every attack went through him and, especially during set-pieces, his right foot was a downright weapon.

The return leg followed a week later. As I went to bed the night before the match, I pictured set-pieces against us, wondering how Riquelme would take each one. Based on his movement pattern, I was sure that, in case of a penalty shoot-out, he would aim for his right, that is my left corner. On the way to the match, many of the fans we passed were holding up hands showing all five digits – apparently, that was how many we were about to concede. But I had seen such hands already before the 1997 UEFA Cup final against Inter; I preferred to take them as a good omen. During the pre-match warm-up, however, I was surprised to discover that the spectators behind each goal would be positively hanging over me. What a pleasant atmosphere this would turn out to be. To top it all off, shortly before kick-off, I learned that the referee was Russian. My mind began to work – just before the first leg, I had talked to Arsène Wenger about corruption in football and the fact that property developers had good contacts to Russia. And Villarreal's president was exactly such a Spanish developer.

The match itself saw the Spaniards piling on the pressure: Guillermo Franco from a short distance, Riquelme with a fluttering free kick, joined by long-distant efforts, crosses, deep forward passes – with hard work, we managed to retain a 0–0 at half-time. There were ten minutes of silence in the dressing room, before the boss told the midfielders to position themselves further towards the front. Up to this point, Thierry Henry had been completely isolated as our only striker. In the first stages of the second half, too, Villarreal had fantastic chances, but one of us kept throwing himself into the shots, until the Spanish appeared to lose their confidence. Evidently, we had more strength left and could finally take the initiative. Like a mantra, I kept telling myself to 'concentrate, concentrate', until, in the 88th minute, a technically harmless cross sailed towards our penalty spot. Gaël Clichy jumped up alongside the crucially taller José Mari; both missed the ball, but the Spaniard dropped to the floor, followed by a sudden whistle. I could not believe it – Ivanov, the Russian referee, had given Villarreal and their developer president a gift in form of a penalty. While my teammates abused him vilely, I kept out of it – the decision was not going to be reversed, anyway, so I might as well focus on the penalty.

Riquelme approached me, demanding the ball. Days before, I had pictured this exact situation. Not letting him out of my sight, I noticed Riquelme glancing briefly towards my right corner. Should I, contrary to my first decision made days previously, jump to the right after all? As Riquelme looked at the referee, the whistle sounded. Slowly, he took his run-up. I waited, long enough for his foot to be just short of the ball and for him to be unable to change direction any more. A matter of milliseconds. Do not wait too long, I thought, as Riquelme made his way towards the ball. Otherwise, I would be too late in any case, even if I were going in the right direction. Right or left corner, then? First thought, I told myself, jumping to the left. Plop – the ball bumped onto my hands, bouncing back into the outfield. At once, I was back on my feet, in time to see Juan Pablo Sorín coming in for the rebound shot. But there, there was Kolo, my Kolo; the fastest defender I had ever known, the only one with whom I had played every single game in our legendary invincible series. He reached the ball before Sorín and managed to get rid of it. When I had finally picked it up, my teammates came storming towards me. With everyone trying to hug me, I could do nothing but yell, 'Get back in! Keep going, this isn't the end yet!'

Eventually, of course, it did come to an end. All the world's footballers have the habit of looking for a fixed point on the pitch after big wins. Most of the time, they choose to run to the goalkeeper – perhaps because his clothing attracts them magically; perhaps because, for defenders, he is simply the nearest team-mate to cuddle. Whatever the reason this time, there was a cluster of people gathering around me in the huddle and, exuberantly, we celebrated Arsenal reaching the Champions League final for the first time in their history. The party on the pitch was followed by touching scenes in the dressing room. Feeling guilty about his part in the penalty drama, Gaël Clichy thanked me over and over again; Thierry Henry was shouting, 'Jean, Jean, Jean' – his nickname for me; others kept stammering, 'German, I can't believe this!', and someone emptied a bucket of water over my head. Even Arsène Wenger embraced me, but even in this situation, he was unable to hold back one of his typical remarks: 'I should probably take you off the team more often if it makes you play like this ...'

When, an hour and my indispensable stretching exercises later, I emerged from the dressing room, the journalists were still waiting for me. Even the tabloid guys, as they were also known, were celebrating our success. Again and again, they asked how I had managed to save a penalty in the last second. I replied that they certainly would not be as pleased if I had to save a penalty against England in the World Cup. The following day, the scoundrels would turn my answer into an English-language headline: 'I will make you suffer at the World Cup.' Safely out of reach and on the team bus, I switched on my mobile to discover 43 texts from friends, followed by calls with Conny as well as Niklas and Nick, friends from Germany and England – they had been completely beside themselves. To me, such feelings of happiness are one of the great motivators behind playing football: knowing that games like this will not only intoxicate oneself but many other people, making them happy for a few hours. Money, fame and popularity may be pleasant side effects, but at the same time, they are relative – happiness, though, is beyond comparison.

In the league, we now had to try to secure fourth place to guarantee our participation in the Champions League the following year, too. Standing in our way were archrivals Tottenham Hotspur, three points ahead in the table. Ten days before the Champions League final and we had closed the gap to a single point; our last league game of the season was on the agenda, Wigan at home – but if we won, we would have to hope for Spurs not to beat West Ham. On the day, we quickly took the lead before then trailing 1–2; a goal from Henry made it 2–2 going into the break. In the second half, though, we managed to pull away, winning 4–2, with Tottenham losing 1–2. Apparently, our north London rivals had not been able to get together eleven fit players and lodged an official complaint with the league management, claiming the side had been poisoned with spoiled lasagne – a cheap excuse for a lost game and a lost season. Later, it transpired that one player had spread a virus among the team. We did not let the drama dampen our spirits, though: the Wigan match was a historic one, the last to be played at Highbury. The club was abandoning the ground after 93 years, and for a final time, things had turned to good account on its pitch.

Since it would take until 17 May for us to top off the season with a Champions League win, we were having to keep up the pressure for ten more days. Training went as usual, really, with only a few tactical exercises thrown in here and there, designed to teach us how to corner Barcelona. Following afternoon training on Tuesday, a day before the final, we flew to Paris. As always, we passed on the training session at the stadium to which we were entitled, as the boss thought trudging through traffic to the ground and back would be too much hassle, resulting in dinner being late again. So I took an evening walk to the Louvre, which was directly across the road from our hotel. Since the French police feared criminal activity, a bodyguard stuck to my heels. In step, we marched along the Louvre among all the tourists for half an hour. What was the guard thinking, I wondered. My thoughts, for one, were already circling the game; I was trying to prepare myself for any situation I might face. It was as if a computer-simulated scene was playing inside me. Like a spectator, I was seeing my team-mates, the opposition, the path of the ball. In some cases, I knew the way a player moved and the route he normally took across the pitch, so that I could anticipate how they would run, pass and aim for target. Simultaneously, I considered the actions required of me during various scenarios. These mental images were not clear enough to make me dive for an imaginary ball in front of the Louvre Pyramid. No, it remained a game of make-believe, but a thrilling one, true to life. Contrary to my routine and the fact that kick-off was still almost 24 hours away, I was agitated: the final was going to be one of the peaks of my entire footballing life, but I was unable to savour the moment, as that would compromise my focus on the match. Following the last team meeting the next day, I phoned Conny once more around noon. My whole family had come to Paris; even our eight-week-old daughter was there, watched in the hotel by my mother-in-law. My wife, however, was distraught on the phone, telling me how our son Mats would have been run over by a car if her mother had not pulled him off the road at the last second. Normally, news like that would have got me worried like any other father, but when I heard that everything had ended well, I did not let it get to me any further; my focus on the game was simply too strong.

At the end of the day, preparation for such a big game does not differ from the norm: you flee into rituals and routines, everything not to become flustered. After all, with some goodwill, you can talk yourself into believing that the ground cannot be any more packed than usual and that the main concern is winning – just as is the case with any other match, too. My colleagues' faces were tense, but I did not talk to anyone in the tunnel anyway; I never do. Today, I cannot even remember who the mascot was out beside me. Just after half-eight French time, we entered the pitch, followed by music and the obligatory shaking of hands with the opposition players. As usual, I looked each one in the eye. Many stare at the floor or straight ahead – I have no respect whatsoever for this; as an athlete, you should at least have the guts to look at your opponent during the handshake.

Finally, at quarter to nine, it was on. Again, we played a 4–5–1 with Thierry Henry as the only striker. Contrary to his normally offensively orientated notion, Arsène Wenger had made us play this way during the entire Champions League season – successfully, too: up to this point, we had not conceded a single goal. After a few minutes, Thierry Henry had the first great chance, followed by two Spanish attempts on target which I could parry safely.

Four minutes past nine, the infamous moment had come: Ronaldinho played his pass, Eto'o began to run, Lehmann grasped, Hauge blew his whistle. Following the dismissal, I slunk into the dressing room to put on a clean shirt. What was I to do now? For a few minutes, I sat around, irresolute, before climbing up the steps to the stands. I bumped into Sir Alex Ferguson, who stared at me wide-eyed, as if he had seen Lucifer himself. 'Bad luck,' I said with a shrug, continuing on my way. When I had eventually found a seat, I was joined by Lasse and Mats, who had been sitting with my wife and brother. I pulled them onto my lap and finally began to tear up. There is no apt description nor any solace for this moment, in which all aims, hopes and ambition of the previous months disappear in a black hole of disappointment. I suspected I would never again be part of a Champions League final but did not let the thought get to me at all. Nonetheless, all was not lost. I spurred on my team, and indeed, we took the lead with a beautiful Sol Campbell header – with ten men to boot. Barcelona attacked in vain, and we carried the lead into the break.

Entering the dressing room, I saw everyone sitting quietly on their seats as usual. No one reproached me; I simply had been playing too well during the previous rounds. In order not to feel completely useless, I went up to every single player, asking him to win the match, before Arsène Wenger gave some instructions in his calm way. Shortly after, the referee's whistle sounded across the tunnel, summoning the boys back onto the pitch. None of this played out in a particularly emotional manner – had our fate been sealed already? At least we were still in the lead, but as I was running back up to my kids, I realised that the game was now going in one direction and one direction only: towards our goal. Campbell, however, was in fantastic form, and so we formed a stronghold around him. Henry covered such distances, it was as if he was hoping to receive a mileage allowance – as a result, he was granted another scoring opportunity. Following a superb pass, he sprinted towards the goal at inside-right, but his effort from fifteen yards was not strong and well-aimed enough; the endurance runner's battery was running low. Barcelona, however, still had energy left, and again it was Eto'o who reached the ball at the crucial moment. This time, he penetrated the penalty area, looked up briefly and saw that Almunia, my substitute, had moved too soon, going to the left even before the shot was fired. The ball was swooshing past his foot at the near post – 1–1. Disappointed, I fell back into my seat before clapping my hands upon realising that we had every chance to reach extra time and penalties.

Almunia, however, dimmed my hopes. His body language had changed after the equaliser; it was no longer positive. I knew him well and hoped he would pull himself together again, but to no avail. Somehow, however slowly, the keeper's attitude spread to the players in front of him, and so, the winning goal was only a matter of time. Only four minutes later, Henrik Larsson set up Juliano Belletti, who put the ball through Manuel's legs from a sharp angle.

The rest is told quickly. Straight after the match, we returned to London, with Arsène Wenger telling me that after the equaliser, he had known that we could no longer win. Why did he think we could not have done it? Why would parking the bus and getting through the shoot-out have been impossible?

Eventually, our arrival in England marked the end of the matter. It was a simple mark, too – no team dinner, no grief work, nothing. Arsenal were not one for socialising at all; in my five years there, only one Christmas do had been held. By no means did I want to party after our defeat, but a nightcap would perhaps have helped us cope. Despite all the frustration, however, I would not have been able to drink myself into stupor anyway: two days later, I had to leave for Geneva to join the national team for our World Cup preparations. I was rather glad about it, too, since it allowed me to look forward to something else, maybe something even bigger, instead of brooding over my sending-off.

What, then, was left after the first half of 2006? Well, there was my being made definite German number one. Then, there was establishing a historic record, one that might never be broken: 852 minutes without conceding in European football's fiercest competition – a record set the following season when the Champions League started back up again. Of course, such an accomplishment needs a little luck and a great team, but at the same time, it remains my personal best, and having achieved this at the end of my career is wonderful. A record is something objective; here, facts alone matter. True, I had been voted goalkeeper of the season before, but such an award always depends on the grace of a jury made up of other players and journalists with various opinions. Our 852 minutes, in contrast, are a fact over which one cannot quibble. I am likely to remain the only goalkeeper ever not to concede throughout an entire Champions League season and still lose the final.

# The 2006 World Cup

NEVER WILL I FORGET THE SOUND WITH WHICH THE WORLD CUP began properly for me: a cracking. It came from my left ankle, and it did not sound good. Crack. I had just been singing the national anthem ardently, overwhelmed by the feeling of playing at the World Cup. The icing on the cake had been the fact that this match was played in Munich, where, only a year previously, I had been booed and hissed mercilessly during the opening of the new Allianz arena.

Now, in contrast, the fans had been chanting my name during the warm-up, and again, I had been affirmed in my belief that every nadir is followed by a peak if you are willing to work on your own game. In an act of defiance, I had taken the 90-minute-long chorus of whistles as an incentive to work even harder. Here I was then, singing my national anthem at the World Cup, only to be interrupted harshly by a cracking noise.

After the anthems had finished, I went into my goal to wait for kick-off, jumping sideways on the line to loosen up. Mid-skip, my left foot turned – crack. It hurt immediately, to the extent that I was barely able to tread. My mind was racing; this could not be, it could not be. Was a ligament ruptured? Oh God, I thought, the opening match of the World Cup kicks off in less than a minute, and I cannot put my foot on the ground. Did this mean that everything had been in vain, the two years of grafting in the training camps and the whole *T-Frage* nonsense? I had even got a grip on my swollen knee in time; that had to count for something. The day before, on the way to final training, my knee had suddenly bulged,

**153**

perhaps due to the Adidas boots which I was obliged to wear for sponsorship reasons when with the national team. They always tended to be a little too small, jumbling my movement pattern. For two years I had been complaining about it, only to be told there was nothing that could be done about it, as the lasts used to make the boots had simply been designed this way. The previous evening, however, a cobbler from Herzogenaurach had suddenly turned up, saying he would get to work quickly. Apparently, the fear of my being sidelined for the opening match had made the impossible quite possible. The swelling had not subsided entirely, but it did not hurt or hinder me in my movement any more. My ankle, on the other hand, was now stinging fiendishly. This could not be happening. I am going to stay put no matter what, I thought, just let the referee blow his whistle so I can say I have taken part in the opening match.

Frantically, I waved at Klaus Eder, our physiotherapist, who came running with his case just as the referee looked at me with his hand in the air, asking whether I was okay. Of course not, but I raised my hand nonetheless. During the first time-out, Klaus emptied half a bottle of freeze spray onto my ankle; that would have to last me until half-time. Luckily, Philipp Lahm planted the ball into the corner of the goal, causing the whole stadium, if not the whole country, to go wild. At the moment, there were more important things to worry about than my ankle. With my right foot, I was without difficulty able to reverse the few back passes I was receiving, and there had not been much I could do where Costa Rica's equaliser was concerned – Paulo Wanchope had been left completely free before taking his shot. Fortunately, Klose restored our lead soon afterwards. Then, finally, it was time for the break.

Today, I cannot remember whether I told Jürgen Klinsmann in the dressing room about my mishap at all, or whether Oliver Kahn had noticed anything and suddenly got up his hopes about replacing me. He probably had done, but then again, he had not left the pitch either in Brazil four years previously, even though one of his fingers had been broken. As goalkeeper, if you think you can manage somehow, you simply do not make a fuss. I merely asked our team doctor, Dr Müller-Wohlfahrt, to take a look at the issue. 'Oh dear,' he said, 'I don't know if there's something torn here.' 'Tape it,' I replied at once, knowing that a properly fitted bandage would have enabled me to continue even with a complete

Early beginnings at Schalke. I was 19-years-old when this photograph was taken. There would be many setbacks before establishing myself in the first team. [*Getty*]

The start of something special. After beating Tenerife 2-0 at the Parkstadion in the semi-finals of the UEFA Cup in 1997, we really started to believe the competition could be ours. [*Getty*]

The first leg of the final against Internazionale was a tight affair, decided by a late Marc Wilmots goal. [*Getty*]

Embracing at the final whistle with Thomas Linke, a powerful defender who would continue his career at Bayern Munich. [*Getty*]

To Milan and the San Siro. The Schalke team did not include any star players. Ninety-minutes away from creating history. [*Getty*]

The first of my professional victories in a penalty shoot-out. Never believe it when someone claims the goalkeepers have nothing to lose. Teammates always expect you to save at least one kick. I stopped one and Inter missed another. Schalke were champions. [*Getty*]

Maybe I was too hasty in deciding to leave AC Milan in 1999. Oliver Bierhoff, my international teammate, stayed and won Serie A five months later. [*Offside*]

Back in Germany. Doing it my way; trying to score goals if necessary and taking on outfield players if necessary. It is fair to say I did not gain friends by signing for Schalke's big rivals, Borussia Dortmund. [*Getty*]

In Dortmund, I reached the final of the UEFA Cup for a second time in 2002. Having been crowned as Bundesliga champion the week before, this defeat against Feyenoord did not hurt as much as it might have done otherwise. [*Getty*]

Rivals at club level and rivals to become the national team's number 1. Bayern Munich's Oliver Kahn and I. [*Getty*]

My devoted wife, Conny. [*Getty*]

The Invincibles! Winning the Premier League in my first season as an Arsenal player. The title was secured at White Hart Lane, the home of Tottenham Hotspur – Arsenal's north London rivals. [*Getty*]

The best of enemies. Games against Manchester United were always intense. They'd decide the course of a whole season. [*Getty*]

The most important in-game penalty save of my career, repelling Juan Román Riquelme's shot in the dying seconds of the Champions League semi-final second leg in 2006. [*Getty*]

The last match at Highbury, such a special football ground. [*Getty*]

The Champions League final of 2006. A dark start to a beautiful summer. A red card after eighteen minutes against Barcelona. [*Offside & Getty*]

Germany waited…another decisive save in a penalty shoot-out, this time against Argentina in the quarter final of the World Cup in Berlin. [*Getty & Offside*]

Dejection after an extra-time defeat to Italy in the semi-final. [*Getty*]

Though my frosty relationship with Oliver Kahn thawed during the World Cup to some extent, it would return later. This photograph was taken after a third-place play-off win over Portugal. [*Offside*]

Two more seasons in the Premier League would test my limits. [*Getty*]

Preparations for the 2008 European Championships in Austria and Switzerland. I would retire from the national team as the country's number 1 goalkeeper. [*Getty*]

A return to the Bundesliga with Stuttgart. It would be an eventful couple of seasons. [*Getty*]

I had retired when Arsenal asked me to return after a goalkeeping crisis. I would play one game, a 3-1 victory in Blackpool. [*Getty*]

The media game with Jürgen Klopp. [*Getty*]

On the grass, where I like to be. With Arsène Wenger at Arsenal's training centre in Colney. [*Getty*]

rupture. And so we went out for the second half, eventually winning the match 4–2. 'Brilliant, boys,' Klinsmann was shouting in the dressing room afterwards, 'The first win at our World Cup. Well done, men!' I decided to ignore my ankle.

To this day, I cannot explain properly how it all happened. Perhaps, after all those difficult months and years, I had been a little too sure that nothing could go wrong any longer, and my subconscious had wanted to teach me a lesson. Perhaps it had simply been bad luck. For the further process of the tournament, however, the opening match had been positively ideal. Not only had we won but we had scored four times, which had turned anticipation into pure euphoria. When we had arrived in Munich from our Berlin headquarters the day before the match, an immense wave of expectation had formed. Suddenly, summer had arrived; countless people had been lining the streets on our way to the hotel. We had tried not to be infected by it too much and had adhered strictly to our routines. In the evening, opponent analysis was on the agenda, and the conclusion was positive: no easy start, but if we gave 100 per-cent, they would not stand a chance. That night, we had all faced the challenge of sleeping despite the haunting thought of having to represent our country in front of more than one billion people the next day. In the end, though, the TV numbers were never going to matter; the crowd in the stadium were going to make all the difference. Luckily, I have never had an issue with this sort of tension and pressure. I, like everyone else, wanted to be world champion. I had my doubts, of course; I did not have any illusions with regard to our side's performance level: Arsenal, my club, were certainly stronger than this German team. But the other nations' selections, too, had to form a team out of their superstars to begin with, and so I did not let it trouble me, sleeping all through the night.

One who struggled with the concept of nonchalance was our captain, Michael Ballack. He was once again having problems with his calf, which would resurface two years later before the Euros final. Evidently, there are two types of people: those like me, whose minds affect their mood, and others, whose minds apparently affect their lower legs. In any case, Michael was axed from the squad for the opening match. By the looks of things, the *capitano* had thought that to be playing on Friday, it would be enough to take part in training on Thursday. He had not, however, reckoned without Jürgen, who remained true to his principle which, over his entire time in office, had been '*fitness* first'. 'You're not fit; this isn't on,' he said, earning the respect of the whole team, for whom nothing would have been worse than double standards being employed. In the end, Michael would start in all other games apart from that for third place, but his calf problems never really left him during the tournament.

We would not, however, be deterred by our captain's absence before the opening match, strictly adhering to schedule on the day. Already during the customary pasta meal four hours before kick-off, a sense of something special hung in the air. We ate in silence, our thoughts circling the game. The fuss in the stadium was greater than usual, as the corridors were still packed with the artists who were performing at the opening ceremony. Yet, I did not let it get to me; after all, at 36, I had seen it all, really. If only that cracking noise had not been. At the end of the day, even that could not throw me off course, but I was worrying about our defensive performance against Costa Rica. By no means were they a top side, and still they had managed to score against us twice, because our defence had been porous. All things considered, though, these two goals had been the best thing about the opening match, as they led to a fierce and fruitful system discussion which we would have avoided after a 4–1 or even 4–0.

Back in Berlin, Jürgen and Jogi Löw showed the defenders their mistakes with the use of video. During the first goal, the entire midfield around Schweini, Tim Borowski, Torsten Frings and Bernd Schneider had been standing much too far apart from each other and tiered in depth, making the pass towards the front easy even for the boys from Costa Rica. To top it off, the defence had been trying to employ an offside trap, only for Arne Friedrich to make his move too late. Following the tormenting screening, I said the defenders had to learn to pay more attention to their teammates in front of the penalty area rather than the opposition players. If we stood properly on our defensive line, all that would be left for the opponent would be a barely outlined space in which to move around. This would give the defenders the advantage of knowing just where the forwards might be going next. During the ensuing discussion, none of the defenders bar Robert Huth said a word – their clubs had simply not taught them how to play this system properly. Torsten Frings even insisted on the defenders pursuing the forwards all the way into midfield, the cardinal error when playing the 4–4–2: as soon as just one defender ran after a forward into midfield, the defensive chain would be ripped apart. For this reason, defenders like Christian Wörns were no longer relevant to the national team. He might have been 'the best German man-marker', but among national defenders, Wörns was certainly the worst zonal marker with the poorest understanding of the system. It was his bad luck that Jürgen Klinsmann did not like players who could only act for themselves but not for the team. In order for his system to work, Klinsmann was looking for other players, such as Christoph Metzelder, who was intelligent enough not only to realise that he needed to orientate himself on the pitch but also how to go about doing so. In addition, he added the necessary speed to the system. The other centre-back, Per Mertesacker, experienced his very own eureka moment in November 2005 during a game against France: we had been playing consequently far away from our own goal, with the defenders merely leaving the back line for safeguarding, which resulted in the quick forwards Henry and David Trezeguet barely ever making it into our final third. 'I never thought that would work,' Per had told me after full time.

The tactical debate continued in a perfectly factual manner, despite the occasional 'Oh, rubbish!' and my ranting about how to play a back four. The only one who really knew the system was Robert Huth. He played for Chelsea, where, unfortunately, he was not starting much, as some very good players were blocking his path. In our internal discussion, however, he played an important role and I was lucky to have his support. Eventually, even the midfielders had been convinced that we needed to play a little differently, with them being responsible for the opposition forwards if they pulled back behind. Philipp Lahm, too, kept asking for details and was intelligent enough to put them into practice during the games that followed. The same could be said for Arne Friedrich, who had often been presented as a problematic case in public, although he was extremely important to us as a right-back with pace and keen perception. Jürgen Klinsmann and Jogi Löw in particular supported our notion of a proper system; after all, we defenders above all had to be comfortable with it. As a manager, you cannot employ a system which your team neither understands nor wants to play. The discussion was a milestone in our side's development: now, everyone knew what they had to do and, as a result, we emerged as a union, in which even sceptical players like Torsten Frings ended up delivering fantastic performances.

The improvement was much needed, since Poland, our next opponents, were of a different calibre to Costa Rica. On the flanks, for instance, they had extreme pace at their disposal, and these players knew how to put in some dangerous crosses. But we were now standing more steadily, and when David Odonkor ignited his turbo just before full time, setting up Oliver Neuville for a 1-0 lead, the lid finally flew off this cauldron named Germany, in which a temper had been bubbling away already. Our venue was Dortmund, where we had been greeted by thousands of people on the observation decks at the airports, and there was a vast car park at our hotel in Castrop-Rauxel, filled with people cheering our arrival. The reports covering the opening game had been dominated by sceptical undertones; after all, who were Costa Rica? But the fans had long since abandoned all concerns and gave us a reception we would never have thought possible. Since we deliberately did not read any papers in our Berlin hotel and purposefully only watched the other games on TV, we did not know what was going on in the rest of the country. The liberating 1-0 was the initial spark for that relaxed patriotism that became characeRistić for the republic, outlasting the World Cup. More German flags than ever before were flown in the stadiums; the fans were singing the national anthem, and yet the atmosphere never became so martial that you might see marching German troops in your mind again. The director of the Bonn Haus der Geschichte museum later told me that this had been a completely new experience which was only possible three generations or sixty years after World War Two.

There is a famous scene in Sönke Wortmann's World Cup film, showing Jürgen's dressing-room address before the Poland game: 'Lads, we've achieved so much; we're not letting anyone take it all away, least of all the Poles!' Considering the difficult German–Polish history, this might sound unpleasant to some, but such a situation makes you forget all political nuances, and I am sure that in Jürgen's statement, Poland could be substituted with any other country – he would not have said anything different about politically innocuous opponents such as Ecuador and Sweden. Most of the younger players probably did not even have a clue about the fact that the German invasion of Poland started World War Two and that our neighbours were still glancing westwards with some unease.

Even if they had known, though, this was no history lesson but the hot phase before a football match we absolutely wanted to win, because that would already ensure qualification for the last sixteen.

The Ecuador match, the last one in the first round, was to be played in Berlin. In any event, we wanted to finish top of our group, in order to be matched with a supposedly weaker runner-up in the next round, which potentially could have involved England. I had some acquaintances in the team's entourage, who told me that the Three Lions would do everything in their power to avoid meeting us in the second phase. Hence, if we were to finish second after all, they wanted to do so too, so as not to get involved with us. Typical English, I thought – such a thing would have never crossed our German minds. If you want to be world champion, you have to beat everyone, no matter where and how. But we acknowledged this insular avoidance strategy with satisfaction – evidently, we were to be reckoned with once again.

Before the match against Ecuador, Sönke premiered one of his motivational videos, including highlights from the first fixtures, thrillingly edited with great music. Even without such an accelerant, I would have been fully motivated, but I still enjoyed watching it all: our willingness, the crowd's excitement, the cathartic goal against Poland. The mere existence of these videos displayed some of that new spirit which had reigned since Jürgen Klinsmann had taken over. In the years before him, the sign of utmost concentration in the dressing room had always been an atmosphere fitting for a funeral. No mobiles had been allowed on the bus coming to the stadium; even playing cards had been out of bounds. Arriving in England, I suffered a culture shock when I had witnessed phone calls and card games on the bus until the last minute, and when resounding music greeted me from the dressing room before my first game, I had been flummoxed. The music does indeed hype you up and perhaps prevents one or two people from tensing too much before a match. Jürgen Klinsmann with his American experience was certainly familiar with this concept. In any case, he never gave us any grief whenever resident DJ Gerald Asamoah set up his iPod and speakers to play what later became infamous hits among the team – Xavier Naidoo's 'Dieser Weg' and Nelly Furtado's 'Maneater'. To this day, these songs give me goose bumps; they will forever be the theme tune of this World Cup.

Fuelled up, we beat Ecuador easily, 3–0, with the zero being more important to me than the three, since it showed that the Berlin system debate was bearing fruit. I had not been able to contribute much to this win; I might have been on the pitch, but had practically nothing to do. But far be it from me to complain about that; after all, I had not been keen on trying to look good during shooting practice on my goal. A World Cup is about being organised and granting your opponent as few chances as possible, and if the goalkeeper does not get to shine in the process, fine by me. Besides, I was certain that the game was still to come in which I would be needed more urgently.

Of course, we were still not working as well together as a Champions League winner, but neither had we seen much in the other groups to fear, on the contrary. Moreover, there was one thing about which we definitely did not have to worry: our fitness. Here, Klinsmann and his American coaches had done outstanding work. Initially, their approach had been mocked as 'Chinese jump rope' by the press, but after the tournament preparation was finished, we players had gained a basic trust in our physical abilities. No one was going to outrun us any time soon, we thought, not even in the ninetieth minute – and we would be proven right, up until minute 119 of the Italy match.

In addition, the excitement was a further incentive to us. The last sixteen saw us positively run down the Swedes: we were 2–0 up after a mere twelve minutes and soon after, the Scandinavians were down to ten men after a sending-off. In the second half, however, there came, out of the blue, that moment when I, the keeper, was suddenly in demand: penalty to Sweden. Had that been converted, a young team such as ours might have just lost our nerve after all. I simply stood still on the line, because I knew that Henrik Larsson liked to aim for the middle. He did so this time too, although I did not need to take action, as his ball flew over the bar. Nonetheless, the scene itself had a much more far-reaching symbolic meaning: all potential opponents had now seen what I would do during a penalty – nothing, initially. In case of a shoot-out, all participants would know that they had to opt for a corner no matter what. Out of three potential possibilities during a penalty, then – right corner, middle, left corner – only two remained. My chances were no longer 30:70 but 50:50, and the pressure on the shooters was rising. Here it was, if anyone had been wondering, the connection between football and probability theory.

Eventually, the game finished 2–0. Again, thirty or forty text messages were piling up on my phone; my brother and my friends proclaimed the incredible mood all over the country, of which we only ever got to see snippets. They told me how, on match days, people were not working properly but merely killing time until kick-off; how strangers were lying in each other's arms during public viewings; and how hundreds of thousands were celebrating completely peacefully in fan zones across Hamburg, Frankfurt and Berlin. At first, we had not wanted to believe the figures; Sönke Wortmann might have read of 500,000 supporters in Berlin alone but at the same time he assured us that it must have been a typo. Now, we were discovering that reports of half a million were indeed quite true, but the numbers still appeared strangely abstract to us – who, really, could imagine so many people gathered in one place?

Prior to the World Cup, I had hoped that my homeland would present itself relaxed and open-minded to our guests; after all, I had friends from England coming to visit, who were not supposed to take home a bourgeois and uptight impression of us. But just how merry we Germans could be was probably something no one had been expecting. My parents told me that after every game, convoys of cars were driving past our house, their horns blaring and people shouting my name. Wherever we drove by team bus, traffic more or less came to a standstill. Normally, in this nation of drivers, that would have been a near catastrophe, but these jams appeared to be joyfully endured; at any rate, everyone was waving to us from their vehicles. Even the notoriously fussy German police turned two blind eyes, something which I experienced first-hand: after the Sweden game, we had a few days off, during which my wife wanted to stay in Berlin. I was to pick her up at the airport but got Schönefeld confused with Tegel and ended up running late. So, I hurtled through town at top speed with no seatbelt on and my mobile by my ear to announce my delay. Before I knew it, a patrol car had blocked my path, and I was being flagged down. To top it all off, I looked like a typical roadhog in my cap and sunglasses. 'You're not wearing a seatbelt; you're speeding; and you're using your phone behind the wheel,' the officer began. 'That'll be three or four points on the register and a driving ban. Let me see your papers,' he snapped. 'I'm sorry, I don't have any on me,' I replied, 'And the car is just a rental, too.' 'Where do you live?' he inquired. 'London.' 'Street?' he pressed on, as if that would have been of any use to him. Whatever, I thought, just tell him. 'Wait here,' he ordered, returning to his car. Bugger, I thought, they'll take away my licence. Finally, the cop reappeared. 'Apologies, Mr Lehmann, I don't know much about football and did not recognise you at all,' he said. 'I'm very sorry.' 'That's okay,' I replied, still tense, 'But what am I supposed to do now?' 'Just go. Go.'

It was like this all through the World Cup: a state of exception of some sort, during which you got the feeling you could demand anything from people, along with the note, 'Just do it, it's for Germany.' Even in our Grunewald hotel enclave, we let ourselves get carried away with it and, perhaps as a result, we played better than anyone would have expected. By no later than our marching through of the last sixteen, even the media had to slowly acknowledge that we were not a mayfly who would buzz forcefully once and then crash. No, with this crowd and this euphoria behind us, we were a force to be reckoned with.

It was almost a week until the quarter-final against Argentina. The Albiceleste were at the top of FIFA's world rankings, which, really, made them the best team in the world at this point, and beside Brazil, they were one of the favourites for the title. Just two days after the Sweden game, Jürgen Klinsmann ordered strength training at the tennis centre. Normally, the second day after such a match is always set aside for regeneration; we, however, had to graft under the guidance of Mark Verstegen's coaching team. Once again, it was made clear what such a World Cup really was: no four-week-long celebration but brutal, uncompromising work. Our reward: those emotional minutes singing the national anthem before the games, and the moments celebrating together afterwards.

I began to focus on the Argentina match; during break times between training and lunch, I went up to my room and had a lie-down. For ten minutes, I did my focus and relaxation exercises, imagining how successful I and we all would be in this game. In my mind, I saw specific situations; saving shots and returning them into the field, for example. Afterwards, I took a nap for an hour before the usual daily schedule continued. Prior to bedtime, I programmed my subconscious to success mode and a deep sleep. This genuinely works – if you are thoroughly determined to stay in bed until a certain time the next morning without allowing any distractions, it will only take a few days for you to sleep according to this programming. Just like on a few occasions before, I dreamed of the upcoming match this time too. In my dream, a penalty shoot-out was happening, and I ended up saving the decisive shot. I was surprised; this was the dream of a small boy, not that of a mature professional. During my relaxation exercises the next day, I dissected the dream images in more detail. In case I really saved a penalty, I wanted to leave the pitch immediately; after all, I had to act differently than during that Champions League match a few weeks previously. Back then, against Villarreal, I might have saved the decisive penalty in the last minute, but I had stayed and celebrated on the pitch. What had followed had been my dismissal in the final. Hence, by no means was I to revel after the Argentina match; I would have to focus on the next game.

After the match against Sweden, we were surrounded by optimism and a summery mood; everything seemed easy and natural. Jürgen Klinsmann, however, had a knack of knocking us out of the skies with his lectures. Before one training session at the tennis club, he summoned us to hear an inflammatory speech. For the first time, he was properly angry, mistrusting this lightness that was giving us the deceptive feeling of easily storming into the semi-final by beating the world's number one. Klinsmann positively threatened us: if he noticed even a single one of us to be slacking, he would be on their tail immediately, breathing down their necks. We were all somewhat bewildered by his anger, but that was exactly what he had wanted to achieve. The following day, he again forced down our throats the fact that it was finally time to beat a 'big one', as he put it. For years, we had had to live with the prejudice that we were unable to win against the, well, real footballing nations. After those speeches, Jürgen would occasionally come up to me, asking how I was feeling. What was I supposed to reply? 'Fine,' I countered. 'We'll beat them,' he said again and again. Having nothing to say in return, I merely nodded.

Two days before the match, a surprise team meeting was scheduled for after dinner, where our analyst Urs Siegenthaler introduced the opponent, his organisation, and his tactical manoeuvres, leaving us quite impressed. Thanks to my games with Arsenal, I was already very familiar with Riquelme; to my mind, he was the decisive player in Argentina's offence. Urs, however, had merely shown us a picture of Sorín, the left-back, so I asked why Riquelme had not been included. Slightly annoyed, Urs pulled an eyebrow – apparently, opinions varied where the opponent's true strengths were concerned. Tension was in the air, but that was how it should be ahead of such a fixture.

The final training was scheduled for Thursday and, contrary to our usual practice, it took place not in the stadium but on a reserves' ground of Hertha BSC. There had been trouble with FIFA before, because we had only been allowed to train in the stadium for an hour and were forbidden from setting foot in the penalty area. The pitch was the officials' Blessed Sacrament and was supposed to leave a good impression during worldwide broadcasts. The fact that we were unable to prepare properly because of this dubious image and grass cultivation was irking Jürgen terribly.

All other pre-match rituals were observed as usual. Dinner was served at 8 pm; soup, salads, meat and fish, vegetables, pasta and potatoes; curd and fruit for dessert. By this point, however, we were sick of the sight of it. Our cook, Saverio Pugliese, was a wonderful person and a fantastic chef, but even he could not escape the fate that awaited all DFB cooks: after a few years, a team will get fed up with one chef's personal style; however good the quality of their cooking, you simply do not enjoy the food any more. This evening, of course, there were other things at the forefront of people's minds. As, to everyone's surprise, no further team meeting had been scheduled, I was free to dedicate my time to the treatment of knee, ankle and muscles. Klaus Eder, Wolfgang Bunz and Christian Müller took care of me, in addition to Craig and Shad, who helped with stretching and mobilisation. The session was topped off by Oliver Schmidtlein and Adi Katzenmeier with their hard and soft massages. The national team was famous for its outstanding medical treatment; after such total care, nothing could go wrong. I knew I would be fit the next day, and there was no worry about potential pain, either – the adrenalin levels during a game like the one ahead would be simply too high.

As much as I struggled on this mild summer's evening to pass over the pretty hotel garden with its beautiful tents, I still went up to my room at 10 pm After all, if we wanted to beat one of the big ones, we had to be able to renounce pleasures. Upstairs, I phoned my wife, but whenever she cut into a topic with which I could not be bothered – the children's upbringing, for example – I told her now was not the time and that the match the next day was more important. When she still would not let up, I played my best argument: 'You'll have to shelve this; I need to go to sleep now – for Germany.' That, finally, made an impact. Again I tried to prepare my subconscious for a penalty shoot-out. I knew I had to win it; it is the fate of the German goalkeeper. But I also knew that I was especially good under pressure. In any case, tomorrow on the pitch, it was going to be I who would have concerned himself the longest with wanting to become world champion. At this point, I had been doing so on a daily basis for a year and a half. It was going to work; I knew it would. Shortly before midnight, I fell asleep and only woke up nine hours later; I had not managed such time in ages. It would be a pleasant day, a successful day, I told myself, getting out of bed. As always, the daily schedule was lying on the floor in front of my door. Under the cue 'Kick-off 5 pm', it said in bold letters: 'In case of win → semi-finals!' The usual warm-up began at eleven, with Jürgen giving a short address during which he beseeched us once more that today was the day and that Argentina's number was up. The rest was common routine – stabilising exercises, eating, sleeping. Considering my age and level of experience, I was surely the last one allowed to be nervous compared to my team-mates. I slept splendidly for an hour, only waking up at half-two; thirty minutes later, we were on our way. As always, I took my washbag and my keeper's bag myself, containing Nike gloves and the Adidas pair I had been wearing during every match of the tournament. Shortly before departure, Sönke showed one of his hyping films with highlights from the previous games. He was emotional as always but in a merry mood at the same time, loosening us up. In the end, we boarded the bus clapping and cheering. I kept my eyes shut for the first ten minutes of the drive and focused once more on the match, iPod headphones in my ears. Opening my eyes a little later, I saw a plethora of people standing to attention by the side of the road. 'Don't you disappoint us,' one placard read – I turned my gaze and repeated my mantra. It was going to work.

The dressing room and the pitch at the Olympic Stadium were an awfully long way away; we had to go down several stairs. As ever, the first thing I did was check the grass and adjust my studs accordingly. Returning to the dressing room, I walked very slowly, so as not to strain my muscles too much on the steep steps. Once back in the dressing room, I asked kit manager Manni Drexler for the appropriate studs and, looking up for a second, I saw Sönke. He would always simply be there with his black camera, no matter where we were. Chances are that he was the most envied man in the film industry at the time; he had access to the host team's dressing room and team meetings, the Holy of Holies at the most important tournament in the world. Never before had anyone been granted such admission. Over time, Sönke had become something of a team member; he had, after all, played professional football himself for some time, at Westfalia Herne.

I wrapped my ankle and fingers in tape and looked for a spot in the dressing room to do my stretching exercises. An hour before kick-off, Jürgen commenced the team meeting. The closing remarks were left to Jens Nowotny this time, but I could not tell you what he said even if I wanted to – I had been too preoccupied with the match. At ten past four, Andy Köpke and I were the first to enter the pitch, where ear-splitting noise greeted us. The ground was nearly full already; it was boiling, and we could tell that the crowd were expecting something special today.

FIFA had set up a minute-by-minute schedule for the final pre-match moments. After warming up, for instance, we were to assemble in the dressing room. Normally, before a team properly leaves for the pitch, a few players and managers would shout something at random, thinking it important. To this day, I am unsure as to whether this actually amounts to anything, but most of the time, I was one of those who in their tension needed to shed a few words. Again, the exact words never stuck; I could never for the life of me remember them after a game.

In the tunnel, the Argentinians were waiting already. Now, they appeared quite calm; when we had seen them arrive on the team bus, they had all been singing – probably for courage and intimidation. It was a tactic that never worked. Of course, you do loosen up a little after the initial yelling, but you will need to recover from it all, and it certainly will not make you any braver.

As ever, the playing of the national anthem a short while later was an emotional moment. Putting our hands on each other's shoulders, we glanced at the stand until, suddenly, I froze. What on earth was that, I thought, frowning. Our wives had unfolded a giant banner that said, 'You can do it; we're right behind you!' They must have lost their minds. I frowned, hoping my wife had not played a part in this. Not until later did I learn that I had by no means been the only one with that thought. By the looks of things, some WAGs had had the urgent need to present themselves in public too and not just yield the floor to the men on the pitch. Apparently, the ladies had even arranged a special meeting at our hotel. Originally, each of them was supposed to hold up a heart with a shirt number before the game. Luckily, Conny had said she could not imagine I would consider the idea a good one. In the end, she had not been alone in thinking this, and so they had opted for the smaller solution.

Finally, the match, the classic, began. By now, our team had grown and established itself to such an extent that we were able to shape a match against even the best team in the world in a balanced manner. We went into half-time with Jürgen Klinsmann hyping us up once more: 'We can do this; they're done for.' Back onto the pitch we marched, knowing we were the physically dominant side and that we simply had to wait patiently for our chance. We followed this guideline until the 55th minute, when a failed clearance by Philipp Lahm led to a corner for Argentina. Terrible timing, I thought, as I had not had to save a single shot so far. Trying to organise my defenders, I was still wondering why Per was standing so far back, when the ball already came across Ballack's head towards the near post. I was expecting one of our giants to jump up and clear the shot, but the only player near it was Roberto Ayala, who headed the ball in at the near post. This could not be, I thought, the match had gone so uneventfully for me, only for the first effort to make it past the line. It took us a few minutes to get back into the game – the Argentinians got a few opportunities to break. Eventually, I finally had a chance to save a ball and even start an argument with someone, which raised my adrenalin levels again and egged on the crowd, too. In addition, David Odonkor came on later, and his dashing up and down the line in that inimitable Speedy Gonzalez manner finally woke everyone up properly. So much, indeed, that Argentinian manager José Pékerman got nervous and, to our surprise, took off the attacking Riquelme and Hernán Crespo. Apparently, he wanted to run down the clock.

But then something happened that was specific to Germany and that made this team the envy of the world: a goal born out of a harmless situation. Almost with a hint of desperation, Ballack crossed the ball towards the six-foot-three

Tim Borowski, who directed his header into the box and into the path of Miro Klose. Klose, who was looking shattered after all his running around, closed in and slammed the ball in the near post. He was always there when you needed him, that Miro.

The stadium exploded. As a player, you do not sense your body any more, no matter how much you were running before or what sort of pain was plaguing you – the adrenalin has filled you up to the brim. The great trick is continuing to play immediately after such a surge of emotion, as there are millions of examples in which teams have conceded straight after such a lift. Besides, Michael Ballack's calves were cramping up so badly he could barely walk; unfortunately, Jürgen had already made three substitutions, but at least the Argentinians were struggling too. Eventually, extra time began, where we switched to zonal marking during corners and Borowski moved into the middle, with the tired Ballack playing front left. This way, we gained more stability and, above all, more power in the centre, as Tim was still relatively fresh. By the end, we had wound down the clock all the way to penalties. A year previously, almost to the day, I had won the FA Cup final with Arsenal against Manchester United on penalties – now, I did everything just as I had done back then: a gulp of water followed by a short review with the goalkeeping coach, who was now Andy Köpke.

It was he who gave me the note. That same morning, we had been sitting together, analysing the statistics of Maikel Stevens, the son of former Schalke manager Huub. Like his father, Maikel had built up an immense database full of penalty-takers, four or five of whom he had available to us. Andy had written the most important bits of information on that small piece of paper which would later come to such fame.

Now, its moment had finally arrived. Suddenly, and to my surprise, Oliver Kahn came up to me, wishing me good luck. 'This is your thing now,' he said. 'You'll manage.' A great gesture; unfortunately, as I had to concentrate, there was not enough time to acknowledge it appropriately. I lay on my back, searching the skies for some intuition; it would be of good use in a minute. Of all the players on the pitch, I was certainly the one who had been preparing for this moment the longest; now, I had to deliver.

I stuffed the note back into my sock and approached the referee. We must have been talking about something, surely, but whatever Ľuboš Micheľ was saying evaporated immediately amid the immense tension. As we were first to shoot, I had to wait another while. I was quite sure that Oliver Neuville would score, what with his splendid technique, and despite Argentina's Leo Franco going into the correct corner, we took the lead. Then, Julio Ricardo Cruz grabbed the ball. His name was written on my note; hence, I knew he would probably aim for my right corner, just as he had during his last converted penalty. When he had taken his run-up, I jumped into my right corner, but his shot towards the right had been aimed too well and with too much power: 1–1.

Our turn again. Even though Ballack was unable to run, we could always rely on him delivering a well-placed penalty. He was followed by Roberto Ayala, a calm and very good defender whom I knew a little from my time in Milan. 'Shallow, right,' the suffix to his name said on the note. I simply had to save this one, but how? Should I really just trust that piece of paper? Just before Ayala hit the ball, I jumped to the left. Why, I do not know. Intuition, I suppose. Whatever the reason, the Argentinian shot the ball directly into my hands.

I did not notice the stadium raving; I merely went back to my place to the left of the area. My counterpart, Franco, came towards me, barging into me. What was that about? I did not, though, have any intention to let myself get distracted. It was Lukas Podolski's turn now. Kudos to the kid, I thought, he was taking such an important spot kick at just 21. Even before he scored, I had already taken out the note from my sock. The next shooter was to be Maxi Rodríguez, his favourite corner was the left. Suddenly, I found myself struggling to put the note back into my sock. What was I supposed to do now, just leave it lying on the ground and pick it up later? No, an Argentinian might get his hands on it, steal it or rip it apart. So I stuffed it back somehow and went to take up my positon. Run-up, jump, shot – 3–2, bugger. I had gone to the correct corner, but this one too had been placed simply too well. Tim Borowski was next; having come on late, he was still quite fit. As I consulted the note once more, he scored cold as ice at half-height. 'Fantastic, men,' I thought, 'We Germans can be relied on.' Clutching the note, I went to stand in goal.

When I looked up, I saw Esteban Cambiasso taking the ball. He had been brought on late; I had not seen much of him during the game. What now?

I glanced at my now rather strained piece of paper, cursing Andy for using a pencil – how was I supposed to read this? Desperately, I searched for Cambiasso's name, but to no avail: he had not been included. 'Cambiasso, Cambiasso, Cambiasso,' I murmured as if in trance, even as I was already hopping up and down the goal-line, until suddenly, within a split second, it came to me: Champions League quarter-finals, Inter vs Villarreal, Cambiasso had shot a dangerous free kick across the wall into the left corner. Now, he was taking his run-up and had almost reached the ball. I jumped back into the middle to spring into action from there. 'Cambiasso,' I said one last time, before jumping towards my left.

Smack.

I stood up. I had delivered; we had passed the round.

I do not know what went through my mind at that point; the pressure and the impression were simply too great. I saw David Odonkor running towards me, our fastest man; the others close behind him amid much yelling and roaring. I was merely surprised that my exact imagination had come to life, exactly what I had seen in my dreams and my subconscious. Remembering that I had been sent off in the Champions League final after revelling exuberantly in the previous round, I stayed true to my principles and refrained from celebrating too much. I ran to the dugout, where I high-fived Oliver Kahn, thanked the fans, and disappeared down the tunnel. Climbing the steep stairs up to the dressing room, I uttered random noises to disperse the tension I was still feeling. Beaming, entirely unfamiliar stewards and FIFA officials were talking to me animatedly, but I did not understand a word. For a few minutes, I sat alone in the dressing room until Oliver Kahn entered eventually. We look at each other. 'That's where you were four years ago, too,' I said. He nodded silently and disappeared in the rear of the room; I was alone once again. Gradually, the others turned up: Maxi Drexler first, followed by the physios. We high-fived and hugged in quiet indulgence. Of all people, the team behind the team, with whom I had been working for almost a decade, appeared to know exactly just how much stress and struggle I had invested in those past two years. There were Klaus Eder, Wolfgang Bunz and Georg Behlau, the young executive from the DFB's Frankfurt office. To the latter, the world within the team still seemed to be like life on another planet. At this moment, we probably all shared the same thought: our perseverance and patience had paid off eventually.

The rest of the team had arrived. The hugging did not seem to want to end; the spirits rose; finally, Poldi climbed the bench and played 'Viva Colonia' on his iPod, and we lost control. Rampaging, we screamed along with that peculiar song which we had never heard before. All those things you normally had to fight during such a game – the pain, the weariness, the exhaustion – disappeared abruptly. At one point, someone gave me a peck on the cheek, and even the managers were screaming the 'Viva Colonia' lyrics. Eventually, Oliver Bierhoff entered the dressing room at long last, looking so dishevelled and worn out as if he had been playing too. Only sometime later did I hear that our Guardian of Public Morals had got into a brawl on the pitch after the whistle. It was lucky that I had disappeared into the dressing room as quickly as I had, or I surely would have got involved – as goalkeeper, you are filled with such aggression after a game like this that a hearty wrangling would have been very welcome.

Only gradually did peace set in again. I got undressed and, as usual, threw my things onto the pile in the middle of the room. As I went to pack away my gloves, my eyes fell onto something crumpled together in the farthest corner of my locker: the note. I smoothed it out a little and read it one more time. Well, I thought, you were not much use to me after all, were you? I balled it up again and glanced around for a bin. Not finding one straight away, I looked at the piece of paper again. Perhaps the kids will enjoy a souvenir, I thought, putting it into my goalkeeper's bag.

I was supposed to give some TV interviews next, and my subconscious came knocking. You want to be top fit for the semi-final, so do not let yourself be lauded too highly. Hence, Monica Lierhaus's *ARD* was given a single sentence, and Boris Becker at *Premiere* was left flat. He was not used to such treatment, but my grand plan did not leave me any choice. The same scenario was repeated in the mixed zone among journalists from all over the world. At least ten times, I said that I wanted to prepare for the next match and that a German goalkeeper was always expected to save at least one effort during a penalty shoot-out.

When, finally, we left the stadium by bus, the side of the road was crowded with a company of soldiers, who performed the Mexican wave for us, while the police applauded us at the end of the stadium premises, and some fans were standing on the roofs of their cars, cheering us on. In the meantime, I was receiving calls from friends and fifty to sixty texts; everyone was expressing their gratitude for the emotions we as a team had released in people. We heard that this time, the fan zone at the Brandenburg Gate was filled with a crowd of one million. I tried to imagine such a number, but it was simply impossible. Approaching our Grunewald hotel, we saw the long road leading up to it lined with people forming a guard of honour – such excitement everywhere. I was looking out of the bus window, when I fully realised that what lay ahead was probably going to be the most wonderful time of my life. First, there had been the birth of our daughter, to which we had all been looking forward, followed by the decision that I would be playing at the World Cup, and now, this euphoria was in the air, turning an entire country into a nation of revellers.

When, finally, we disembarked from the bus, little girls were standing at the fence, screaming as if we were the most happening boyband of the day – which, in a way, we were after the recent rejuvenating wave: Poldi, Schweini, Marcell Jansen, David Odonkor, Philipp Lahm – they all could make young hearts leap with joy. With typically Prussian discipline, however, we went straight to the meeting room to listen to boss Klinsmann. He congratulated us but, in the same breath, pointed out that things were only just kicking off properly. Yet he allowed our families to stay at the hotel until Sunday. For dinner later that evening, I met Conny and the kids on the patio. By now, it was half-ten, so we did not sit together for longer than an hour. A pleasant atmosphere surrounded us all, but we were now slap-bang in the middle of the World Cup; there was no time for pondering or hanging about, since the next match against Italy was coming up. The Azzurri being our next opponent was a clear matter, since they were leading Ukraine 3–0 at this point.

After regeneration training, we had the day off; I spared myself any media appointments too, as they would only distract me. The family and I would have liked to spend our precious family time at one of the nearby lakes, but they were crawling with people. In any case, the kids preferred to play at the hotel, which appeared to them like an entertainment paradise that took care of every possible fancy: table tennis, table football, PlayStation, a swimming pool and ice cream. On Sunday morning, though, they had to leave the hotel, because the World

Cup routine was about to return: training, treatment, food, care. A day later, we departed for Castrop-Rauxel, where we would spend the night in the same hotel as before the Poland game. The whole route from Dortmund airport to the quarter was lined with people, and slowly, we realised that we had not been told fairy tales: our football really had changed the whole country. 'Public viewing' was the English phrase of the hour, a term that had now been integrated into the German language just as 'foul', 'party', or 'Internet'.

Again, I tried to manipulate my subconscious into bestowing me a dream with a good ending, but this time, it did not work as well. Would I still win another shoot-out and secure us the final? According to some English friends, London radio had joked after the Argentina game that, 'with Lehmann, the Germans would have even won the Second World War'. It had been one of those typically British witticisms.

I knew that I was able to rely on my team-mates, but it would have been presumptuous to claim that I would definitely keep a clean sheet, even after penalties. To clear my mind, I went to see our team psychologist, Hans-Dieter Hermann. I was to program myself to 'I will save everything,' he said. It was a much more constructive and positive approach – and one that would have worked had the match ended two minutes earlier.

For all intents and purposes, the match against Italy did not go too badly for us. After the Azzurri's strong first half, we had understood that we could leverage their concept of 'outnumbering when in possession' with quick changeovers. Above all, Bernd Schneider, whom we called the Brazilian due to his great technique, executed those changes very well, tiring the Italians and allowing us to create chances like that header that Poldi really should have put past the line. Eventually, Jürgen took off Schneider – just as in the previous games, he wanted to create pressure on the right-hand side by bringing on David Odonkor and his remarkable speed, but the Italians knew what was coming. They simply blocked our right, and since Odo, unlike Schneider, did not know how to play the surprising pass towards the other side, we lost our good rhythm and no longer reached the Italian goal. As a reaction, Marcello Lippi, the Azzurri's clever manager, brought on new, faster forwards. Twice at the beginning of extra time, they hit post and bar. We, too, had another chance and a half; one saved by Gianluigi Buffon, the other evaporating past the goal.

Then came minute 119. We had probably already braced ourselves for a penalty shoot-out; in any case, we lost focus for an instant. When Fabio Grosso's left-footed shot curled around me, I was still hoping for Odonkor to be standing by the post, but he had run out already – 0–1, finished, done. My grand dream of becoming world champion, fostered over years – decades, really – had burst. At the 2010 World Cup I would be forty years old, and even if I were to play there, who knew if we would have managed to assemble such a committed squad again. There will never be words appropriate to describe the feelings in this situation. It did not matter that Italy scored a second time just two minutes after their first goal. We were left with nothing but that incredible void you feel after a defeat. Jürgen entered the pitch to console his players – at the end of the day, it was a means of hiding his own grief. We trotted around on a lap of honour and glanced into the faces in the stands, but there, too, we saw nothing but tears. One thing, however, remained palpable even in this saddest of moments: the fact that this World Cup had created a closeness between players and fans like never before.

There was deadly silence in the dressing room. Torsten Frings, who had been banned from playing after the Argentina brawl, was sitting somewhere in desperation. Everyone else had fallen into lethargy, railing against their fate. Frantically, I reflected on what I could have done better in order to save Grosso's shot. After a while, our country's dignitaries came into the dressing room, President Köhler and Chancellor Merkel. What had been planned as a triumphant visit was ending as an expression of sympathies. Instead of hugging sweating men, all the Chancellor could do now was seal our disappointment with a brisk handshake.

What had been the critical reason for our defeat? I had the feeling the Italians had simply been ahead of us both in terms of experience and being well practised. Their game, their running paths, their pressing had simply been that little more automated. To achieve similar levels of perfection, we would have probably needed no more than another two or three weeks of preparation. Apart from Robert Huth and me, everyone else was employed by the Bundesliga, who still had to catch up where tactical demeanour was concerned. When they had joined the national team, none of those players had had any profound schooling or an understanding of the 4–4–2 and 4–5–1 systems, or at least not everyone had the same. This had become apparent at the Berlin system debate following the opening match. The managers simply had had to make do with the fact that each Bundesliga player considered different things to be correct, and catching up with such a challenge in the space of three or four weeks had been very, very difficult. At the end of the day, we had come quite far indeed.

I agreed to let Oliver Kahn play in the match for third place. Normally, these games were dead rubbers, but as hosts, we had a particular responsibility. At our arrival in Stuttgart, we were greeted by a mob of excited fans. 'Stuttgart is much nicer than Berlin,' they chanted in their thousands, trying to cheer us up. In line with this, Jürgen prepared us accordingly for the Portugal game, which went fantastically. Schweini had an especially good day with his two goals and a half in a 3–1 match. Specific credit had to go to sponsors Adidas, who had developed a ball called Teamgeist, a sphere that had turned out to be football's very own Pandora's box: no matter who hit this ball, no one knew how it would move. Philipp Lahm had benefited from this peculiarity in the opening game, as had the Argentinian Maxi Rodríguez in scoring his winning goal against Mexico during the last sixteen.

The game for third place saw Oliver Kahn perform brilliantly. Later, during the farewell lap around the pitch, he told me that this had been his last international match. In the end, we were all glad that the season was over. As wonderful as a World Cup was, after an already exhausting season it had stuck in our bones as a six-week-long mental and physical state of exception. The psychological pressure had been particularly high for us; after all, no one had wanted to disappoint the fatherland during this biggest of all home games over the last fifty years. In order to make the leap into this team at all, I myself had not been able to afford a single mistake throughout the previous 24 months. In short, we were finally allowed to indulge in a beer or two in the dressing room. The mood was great; after all, it was better to win a small final than to lose a big one. Besides, it did not take much to stir our blood: after such a long time without alcohol, a single beer was enough to get me drunk. The others did not fare any better, apparently, since there was no other reason why we yet again found ourselves singing 'Viva Colonia' on the drive home.

At the hotel, incredible scenes were taking place. 'We want to see the team,' screamed thousands, and whenever one of us showed their faces in the bus window, a cry would go through the masses as if we had won the big final after all. I threw some of my tops into the crowd and would later take my wife to the farewell dinner, which was known as the Blue Hour among the DFB – probably a reference to the face colour of some of their officials by the end of the night.

In the hotel courtyard we met Sönke Wortmann, with whom we chatted about the possible title of his film. Should it be *Germany: A Summer's Dream* or rather *Germany: A Summer's Tale*? At dinner, I asked DFB president Theo Zwanziger what he planned to do if Jürgen Klinsmann were to resign. He was hoping to be spared that situation, Zwanziger said, insistently. I told him what I considered to be a good solution – looking at whom he ended up choosing, my advice might not have been all that poor.

The evening faded as happily as the whole World Cup had been. One of the jolliest guests was Michael Schumacher, who had visited the dressing room after the awful 1–4 defeat against Italy in March. 'Will you be fielding your under-19s next time too?' he had asked with concern. Within a mere three months, this team of derision-riddled whipping boys had transformed into glorious winners – and they had taken an entire country along with them. Still, we had not won.

# Loved And Hated In Equal Measure: My Relationship With The Fans

I HAD NEVER THOUGHT I WOULD BECOME A KIND OF NATIONAL hero alongside other international players towards the end of my career. Of course, the fans had always been incredibly important to me. 'What a shame,' was always the first thing going through my mind every time I walked into a stadium that was not completely filled. Apparently, I tended to take empty seats personally; in any case, a full house would always give me that final boost to turn 99 per cent of performance into 100. I did not care, either, whether or not the supporters were on my side – the noise level, the drama in the stands, those were the things that motivated me, no matter whether my name was being chanted or I was receiving abuse. Because I, as goalkeeper, was always nearest to the fans – both my own and the visiting ones – my relationship with them was always particularly intense, for better or for worse. As long as I did not have to fear for my safety, I would not want to go without these strong emotions. That said, I only ever felt properly uneasy once or twice. One time, when we were occupying the relegation zone during my last season at Stuttgart, riots had broken out among the fans. Stuttgart's ultras were besieging our bus and the stadium exit – I had experienced similar at Schalke, but this was different. 'If you get relegated, we will kill you,' the cries had sounded through the air. It was a new quality of hostility that had indeed made me queasy.

Most sets of fans do have a sense of which player gives it their all, so you should really take their opinions seriously – but by no means does this mean that you should allow the fans to decide on club policies, much less if such central subjects are at stake like a managerial change. When, for instance, Markus Babbel was sacked, I had got the feeling that this exact situation had arisen. A week before, president Erwin Staudt had attested his loyalty to his manager. Then, however, following a superb last-minute Bochum goal, the fans had started a terrible riot. The pressure from the outside had appeared to have outgrown the officials; they simply were unable to keep Babbel in office any longer.

The second rather precarious case also played out while I was at Stuttgart. We were playing Cottbus, and during the second half I had innumerable objects hurled at me: lighters, crown corks, you name it. I was, of course, worried that some lunatic would throw something at my skull – my colleague, Georg Koch had had to end his career after a firecracker had exploded just short of his head. His ear had been shattered, his sense of balance impaired, and his goalkeeping life was over. To my luck, I have been spared anything of the sort over all those years, although I had always played in front of a massive, fanatical crowd from day one. I had been barely eighteen when I started for Schalke in the second division, after all. At home, we had had an occasional 40,000 if not 50,000 people watching, and the grounds had been filled on away days too; after all, our big name made us the centre of attention. And since I had been perhaps not straight from Gelsenkirchen but from the immediate area, I had become an instant crowd favourite. The people took a liking to me, a young lad who gave it his all.

At the beginning of my career, then, it seemed that you could not fit a sheet of paper between the fans and me. Unfortunately, this period of harmony was not to last, and I have certainly contributed to the henceforth erratic relationship. Initially, I had simply not been as familiar with the mechanisms of the footballing business, in which a few words could define a player's image for years to come. From day one, I have uttered casual quips and made jokes – which would always look very different in print. Suddenly, I was no longer the easy-going bloke I saw myself as but rather the overachiever, who framed his ambitions forcefully. When, on top of it all, Peter Neururer said that I, the titch, was going to be next national keeper and I, as mentioned before, did not object directly, my public image became a dead cert: an arrogant player on the edge of megalomania. The person who was most shocked by this was myself, as I am really an inherently modest individual, but I learned quickly that in professional football you could barely afford to be modest. Especially in my position in goal, you always had to show strength, no matter how weak you might feel inside. Display weakness and you would be driven out – not only by your rivals but by the fans, too. The Schalke fans' initial excitement about me peaked with the chant of, 'Apart from Lehmann, you can all leave.' A mere three years later, however, before my memorable half-time exit in Leverkusen, I received ruthless abuse from our own fans, resulting in me leaving the stadium – the worst thing that could happen to a footballer. Often, it is enough for one or two hundred people to be hissing and booing – you hear them as if they are in their thousands. In any case, it was a defining moment for the whole of my following career, because I realised that you could be as little sure of the fans' affection as of every other thing in football. In this profession, just as is the case with every little detail on the pitch, every encouraging shout has to be earned. At the end of the day, the fans' love is easily explained: if you are playing well, they will like you. Eventually, all fanaticism aside, they weigh up how much any player will contribute to their club. They might not like him but will look past that if a performance is delivered.

As I never again wanted to experience this crushing feeling of being booed by my own fans, I threw myself into it more than ever. This way, I managed to turn the corner even after hitting rock bottom in Leverkusen, found a way back into the team and, finally, into the hearts of the Schalke supporters – which was not as simple as it may sound. Just consider how unforgiving the Schalke fans can still be today, in a time when loyalty to your club does not and cannot matter to players any more the way it used to in the 1990s.

Certainly, during this comeback, I benefited from the fact that a goalkeeper only ever needs to react. You stand there, waiting for the ball – you do have to get your hands on it when it comes, mind. As an outfield player, you cannot wait around; you have to act and take the initiative – and at times, this does not work, especially when you are giving it your most desperate attempt. The crowd, however, will only honour your efforts for a while; in the end, what is important is what has worked and not what was attempted. A goalkeeper is easily judged in this regard: he has either saved the ball or not, whereas an outfield player's success is not defined as clearly. Anyway, when Schalke had qualified for the UEFA Cup for the first time in a generation and I had been voted UEFA Goalkeeper of the Year, everyone was fond of me again. When we even won the cup and I headed that last-minute equaliser against Dortmund half a year later, I had become a definite Schalke hero. After the UEFA Cup win, our families had entered the pitch, and we had done the lap of honour together. The public got to see us as those perfectly normal boys we all were and perhaps liked us all the more for it. I had, in any case, left Schalke being what I had always been from day one: the crowd favourite. And no matter where I had played henceforth, the fans had respected me, bar some radicals at Dortmund. In Milan, where I simply had not found my fortune, I had fared more easily by comparison, based on the fact that I had beaten their local rivals, Inter, with Schalke. The Italians had given me credit for my indelible heroic feat. But even in Dortmund, I ended up being celebrated occasionally – I had, after all, made my contribution to our winning the league and reaching the UEFA Cup final.

The fans do, of course, make you stronger than you already are, but at the same time, it is a damned fine line you are treading with them. More often than not, there is little more than a wisp between improvement and over-revving. I realised this on my long way to becoming Germany's number one. At away games, my relationship with the fans had always been shaped by this rivalry on the national team. I had always been the aggressive, insatiable number two who finally wanted to play and who would resort to any method. Fuelled by the comments coming out of Munich, I had stood there like the most unpleasant person. The only places things had come a little easier to me had been those where they could not stand Bayern.

I do not regret anything I said; I merely regret not having been clever enough to gauge the consequences. Today, I might be able to say that I never allowed myself to be bent out of shape, but my life would have taken some much simpler turns had I jumped through a few hoops or – plainly – kept my gob shut. But everyone makes their own mistakes, and you have to own up to yours. Besides, being the crowd favourite within a team is not all fun and games: everyone covets the place in the sun, and especially the weaker players envy the one who makes it there.

Today, these little games do not matter to me any more. Stuttgart, my penultimate stop, had greeted me in a great manner; the fans had welcomed me very emotionally. By the looks of it, everyone was happy to have a World Cup hero at their club, their very own piece of the *Sommermärchen*. Within the team, though, such matters of status no longer played a role. I was so much older than the rest that they all knew there was no need to argue with that Lehmann bloke as he would be gone soon, anyway. In any case, the clever players did not focus on my status but rather took a leaf out of my book for their own way into the fans' hearts, since the latter normally had a very good sense for the efforts of each player. By now, TV had taught them the pace with which the English league was playing every weekend. At home in their pretty German stadiums, however, world leaders in safety, family friendliness and quality of experience, they would occasionally see players trotting up and down the pitch in a monotone jog. This would prompt them to boo and hiss, doing so more readily than I have ever seen in any other footballing country. If you ask me, it was more than justified. Innumerable times, they would sit in the bone-chilling cold and a mangy drizzle, waiting in vain for a spectacular move. Occasionally, I still wish people would whistle more in order to force players to open the throttle. I keep telling young colleagues that, basically, it is easy to become the crowd's favourite: simply attack and defend at the top of your powers, sprint up and down the pitch at peak speed, play a few clean passes, and hey presto, you have the people on your side. Something the fans do not necessarily recognise at all times, though, is which player is actually important to a team. Naturally, they attach themselves to those players who are ever-present in public, who talk a lot, and who are portrayed as leaders by the media. The fact that those colleagues in particular hardly ever say a word within the team, however, and that the ones who at first glance appear reserved are often more important, is something spectators sometimes fail to see.

Over and over again, a debate would surface about whether we professionals should be role models and whether we could be at all. My answer remains unambiguous: I was a role model where most facets of my life were concerned; this is something I could not fight. Had I not behaved in an exemplary way over all those years, I would not be able to play on for such a long time. Even though my image was not always flawless, I always lived and worked in a highly professional, reliable and disciplined manner – something that came more easily to me than to many, many others – and the way I managed this did indeed make me a role model for our fans, their kids and my team-mates. No smoking, no drinking, no going out too much – all these are the basics for playing football successfully. Even nowadays, I know enough players who take liberties where beers and nightclubs are concerned. Fine, when you are young, you might still take it in your stride, but if you want to stay in the game for longer, this kind of lifestyle will make it even harder work. Towards the end of my career, I was still almost the only one who always stretched after training and brought his body to a state that would allow him to return to training without a problem next day. Most other players do not grasp the importance of this approach at all, which inevitably leads them to suffer muscle injuries. As a pro, however, it is your first and foremost obligation to be at your employer's disposal at all times, and that means being at the height of fitness. I have always tried to be commendable in this respect, and I managed to do so quite well for more than twenty years.

Just so I do not appear like an ascetical saint, I should mention that, of course, there were moments in which I did not live up to my exemplary ideal. Unlike a schoolyard wrangling, people remembered the details of the incidents in which I had been involved; after all, I had been tried for them. It might have only been the DFB court, but I am still on the record. Nonetheless, I believe that, for twenty years, I never crossed a certain line. Of course, I could get aggressive and angry on the pitch, but I was always able to get back in control, take a deep breath, and focus on the next move. On that note, I think there needs to be more sympathy shown for those colleagues who do lose their cool, considering how some fans go to work on some of them. The supporters, of all people, those to whom we players are supposed to be role models, often do not hold back at all. Terms like 'wanker', 'cunt' and 'bender' no longer faze me, but I do have quite some sympathy for a player losing his temper as a result of such slurs. It is important to remember that in a football stadium, spectators often stand no more than ten yards away from the pitch – you hear every word and see every dismissive movement, and every rude gesture. In reverse, in your home stadium, you build something of a personal relationship with the crowd behind the goal. At Arsenal's Highbury, the stand towered at my back not five yards away. Here, you would always see the same faces greet each other, even shake each other's hands. Besides, in England, you were often honoured unconditionally as soon as you threw yourself into the breach for the club. My status as supporters' favourite was confirmed when I smashed into former Spurs' player Teddy Sheringham in an early home game, lifting him off his feet.

The post-World Cup atmosphere did, of course, also mean that I was no longer able to move about as freely as I had done before. It had been easier prior to the tournament: in London, home to so many world stars from various sectors, no one cared about my private life. Back in Germany, though, not a day passed without me being in the media and the general public because of some trivial matter. Upon returning in 2008 I had thought that no one would recognise me after all those years in England, but I had apparently been rather naïve about that. In any case, I was glad that Bayern was now employing the superstar trio consisting of Klinsmann, Franck Ribéry and Luca Toni, as it diverted the attention away from me to some extent. For my final days in professional football, I made strict plans not to appear in the limelight as often and rather become positively invisible instead.

Occasionally, the fans forget that even we professional footballers are only mere humans, no matter how many slow-motion montages including our faces are shown on TV. Sometimes, you simply have weak moments, during which you do not necessarily correspond with your shiny image in the Panini album. This was especially noticeable during those two years prior to the World Cup. Oliver Kahn and I had been portrayed as machines fighting for the place in goal as if on autopilot, fuelled by a pure hunger for success. I was the aggressive number two in this battle, always attacking both in a sporting and verbal manner; neither of us were people of flesh and blood any more. At the time, my wife did and still does need to answer that clichéd question: 'Is he like this at home?' Of course she did not confirm the suspicions, but sometimes, just like every employed person, footballers take home their work. I was never able nor allowed to switch off completely or have a few beers to settle down. No, there was always training the next day; I had to be fit and stick to my routine. Although I never quite got rid of my profession, I have always been someone who could separate work from private life in conversation with colleagues. Whenever I joined a new club or met new team-mates, there would always be trouble initially, because people would only experience me on the pitch, where I was hell-bent on winning. Every day, I was ready to start an argument with someone, whether because they were not running properly or not marking their man. But as soon as we left the pitch, I would forget all about it and was able to go for dinner with that very same player, who was quite a nice person in private.

All of these are the tesserae that have contributed to my public image. I have always been portrayed as someone who does his job precisely, convinced of himself to the point of arrogance. And yes, I was and am an arrogant phenomenon, but that is what you need if you want to be up there. I had to signal to the other players that they could do whatever they pleased, but they were never going to beat me. They could perhaps score a goal against me at one point, but they would never truly defeat me. Considering this mind-set, you could be excused for thinking you were faced with a demoniac. Sometimes, perhaps, I could have benefited from having a PR person, but I would have probably forgotten their advice by the time the next match was coming up. I was raised in this macho world called football during a different time; it had taught me to forget everything around when on the pitch – a shaping characteristic.

I might be somewhat conservative or even old-fashioned in this regard, but I am a man who wants to be successful on the pitch, and so I consider men's football a sport for blokes. I do not know how to play-act nor do I want to be made to jump through hoops. Nowadays, many of those young, nice players are remote-controlled by their agents; I doubt that you could fight proper battles with them.

All in all, I do hope the fans have taken away one lasting impression: the fact that I always was a team player. Whenever we achieved great success with a team, I did not need to push myself into the foreground obsessively. Even after the Argentina game, I had not run to sing my own praises into every available microphone. In all my career, I never followed a mistake with the claim that a match might have been rubbish but that the next would be won by me alone. It would be a rather stupid thing to say; no footballer wins a game on his own.

At the end of the day, I can say that the fans have given me my due throughout the years. At the same time, I do not care about my sporting obituary, as that will fade into obscurity once the next top keeper turns up to mesmerise the masses. I myself know well enough how much I have achieved. There are many players who have won more titles than I have; I would never claim, either, that there has ever been a Lehmann era for the national team. Granted, I had been allowed to play two big tournaments, which both went so well that they changed the image of the entire side. Yes, we had made the national team cool and modern, and I had made my contribution, just like Klinsmann, Löw, and the other players – but a Lehmann era? No.

My own estimate is that there are few goalkeepers with a personal balance sheet that compares to mine. During my career, I got used to the fact that people often underestimated me and my performances; why should this change after I had retired? All I know is that I was one of the most complete and consistent goalkeepers to play the game. And what I am seeing is that almost all keepers are trying to copy my style of play – more or less successfully. To an extent, this does make me quite proud.

# Anything For A Headline: The Might Of The Media

'MENTAL CROSSOVER ARTIST', 'LEHMANN'S WORLD: HE OR I', 'THE problem keeper', 'The incomplete', 'All geniuses are crazy in some way', 'Goalkeeper in discord', 'From *libero* to titan', 'Lehmann scandal – the keeper at the end of his tether', 'Arsenal's keeper of the German flame – Jens Lehmann is part of the great eccentric tradition of German goalies'. This was only a fragment of the headlines I could have read over the last years, printed in various newspapers, journals and magazines.

But I did not. I did not want to know what they were writing about me. I experience everything myself, do I not – on the pitch, during training, in my life; what would I need with journalists telling me in black and white about how it all allegedly happened? Very early on, I told my parents never to tell me anything bad written about me – what I did not know could not hurt me. It is, of course, impossible to stick with this completely, because the media are omnipresent in football. Even when I intended not to read anything, a colleague would come up to me during training, saying, 'They cannot mean that thing they've written about you.' This, of course, would make me read the referenced article and, generally, I would get extremely irritated as a result – about the piece itself, and about the colleague who had told me about it in the first place. Although I have been in the public eye for more than twenty years, I can still say that I have remained relatively independent from the media. This can by no means be taken for granted as, naturally, television and the big newspapers exert power and influence over everyone in professional football. However, and this is my central experience drawn from all those years, they only ever hold sway over the weak. Weak manager, weak presidents, weak players – many of them believe that it will help them to be on the journalists' good side: you scratch my back, and I shall scratch yours. They are convinced that in exchange for disclosed internal information, the papers will print pleasant things about them, which in turn will ultimately lead to a better contract with their current club or a good offer from another one. What they do not consider is the fact that the really strong clubs do not reach their verdict about a player or manager based on what they have read in the papers, let alone foreign ones. Scouts at Arsenal, Chelsea or Real do not read *Kicker* or *Bild* to form an opinion about a player; if in doubt, they will watch them in person or enquire about them with reliable colleagues, who know their way around the clubs. Hence, the only people who believe that news outlets play an important role in this part of the game are weak officials and inexperienced players. It is they who grant the media that very same power about which they then complain. For this reason alone do some journalists occasionally manage to virtually write players into or out of a team. Generally, players and their employers turn themselves into the media's plaything.

In German football, great significance is placed upon the media's reception of any decision made. Be it a new manager or the signing of a new player, officials always think twice about how their eventual choice might be received and commented on by the public. Some might find it easier to get a new contract if they come off well or know how to sell themselves to journalists. But what else are presidents to do, those people with whom the final decisions lie? Most of the time, they are not experts on football but rather lawyers, business people or entrepreneurs – good at their jobs but new to the game. How are they to know what a player should be able to do on the pitch? Hence, they consult the papers to see which player is the flavour of the month, and in signing them, they set off a chain reaction of wrong decisions, all according to a rule-of-thumb estimate. Once, Hamburger SV tried to do it differently. They established a kind of findings commission like in a free-enterprise economy, who created a requirement profile used to check different candidates systematically: what kind of team do we have, what type of manager will we need for it, what is important for the club in general? I approved greatly of this approach, but since this process was very lengthy, the officials would have their legs pulled by the media for weeks on end. Football, after all, is very protective of its structures, and as soon as someone has a try at an innovation, others will take the piss. Evidently, though, Hamburg allowed themselves to be swayed by this: in the end, they signed Martin Jol, who got the side to be top of the league for a while at least, which had not happened in years.

The media have virtually no influence on strong personalities, which is noticeable in the fact that, despite all cries of the naysayers, the really good players and managers stay at the top for years and decades, even though they have been written off repeatedly. My case is similar: I cannot remember how many times and for what reasons I have been bashed, written out of teams, and supposed to be prevented from playing in big tournaments. But whatever was written there, I always knew that I could rely on my qualities as a player. It was one of the things for which I had trained obsessively: do not open yourself to any attack from anyone – not from managers, not from colleagues, and definitely not from the media. I made mistakes just like many others – conceding savable goals, misjudging shots – but compared to my peers, those mistakes were rare. Had they happened to me over and over again, I would have been out of the picture long ago. However, if you consider all the years of my active career, I was never out of the game for more than a few matches. In the long run, I was always there, and no ever-so-sensational headline could have changed that.

The most powerful medium in German football is *Bild*, simply because it is published daily and everyone can find out in a matter of minutes the good or bad things written about them. Some may consider television the more influential institution, since it provides the majority of monies off which all the industry lives. But despite third-division matches and God knows what else being broadcast these days, football is not readily receivable everywhere and any time. Besides, in comparison, television does not report as much on the internals of teams or clubs; they predominantly show the games. If I do not turn on a specific channel at a specific time, TV will never tell me what blunder this player or that manager has allegedly made this time. No, this information is supplied by *Bild* and is readily available, whether I am sitting in the doctor's waiting area, at the hairdresser's, or on the train. Furthermore, there would always be a copy lying around at the training ground. I do not even know who keeps buying them and bringing them in, perhaps players or club employees. In any case, *Bild* would always be around.

After my departure from Arsenal, I had to change my thinking with regards to publicity. In London, that metropolis, I had been one among a plethora of players at a number of top clubs; in Stuttgart, I was one of the best-known players in a manageably sized town with only a single big club. Suddenly, even journalists from out of town showed an interest in the most remote things in my life: my holey jeans, for example, which car I had taken to training, me having been to the cinema one night and whether or not I had enjoyed the film. This focus on my humble activities was, of course, also to do with the fact that, at the time, there were not many players left with a mind of their own and grand sporting merit.

Had I known before my return from England how the German media were focusing on fewer and fewer individuals, especially in sports, and particularly football, I probably would not have come back – every bit of trivia beyond the pitch was being remarked upon. However, on the pitch, too, each one of my moves was being eyed critically. When, for example, I once threw behind me the boot that Hoffenheim's Sejad Salihović had lost during the game and it accidentally landed on top of the net, they immediately dubbed me 'the stinker of the league'. That might sound a funny name but, for me, this trifle almost had serious consequences for me. Apparently, I had broken the netting, for suddenly, the referee chipped in with his evaluation, and the DFB's supervisory committee genuinely considered investigating me. Somehow, the relationship had cracked. Every little thing that happened to me would at once be labelled a 'tantrum' or 'lapse'. Did my getting booked for a small jostle really constitute 'going mental'?

Even on the occasion of my fortieth birthday, most journalists were more excited about dragging skeletons from the cupboard I had been filling for 23 years. The pleasant things, in contrast, did not get too great a mention. It is not surprising, then, that we Germans are at times characterised as a nation of grouches and sourpusses if this impression is reinforced on a daily basis by the national press.

Among the many experts in German football, there is one who embodies something of a last resort during the assessment and evaluation of players and events, and whom I will defend rigorously: Franz Beckenbauer. Despite his time as outstanding player being long over, his word still carries a certain weight. He has won the World Cup both as a player and manager, and in making Germany host of the 2006 tournament, he has brought so much to the people that they simply listen to what he has to say. In addition, he has always remained an incredibly polite, courteous and correct man. I could count on his help during moments when the media had appeared to have it in for me. Beckenbauer did not consider the whole thing to be all that, and so it was overcome. Thanks, Franz.

My advice in terms of working with the press, advice that has always worked out well for me, is simple. Focus on your skills, and do not pander to the media; it will make sure you stay independent. In the long run, less will be more, especially with regards to public presence. Also, no one is obligated to give their phone to journalists to be constantly available. Professional cooperation with the press at certain times is important, but never ask anyone a favour – owing the wrong people can turn unpleasant, both in football and in life.

In England, the distance between players and reporters appeared to make journalists focus more on the essence of the game. *Sky*, for instance, who broadcast most of the league fixtures, had an array of journalists and ex-players who knew how to analyse the match, the paths, the tactics, and the quality of individual players. Unlike their German counterparts, they were not polemic and resentful, either: when a player made a capital error, they genuinely suffered vicariously with him and could therefore be happy for him when he played a great pass a few minutes later. In Germany, you were 'off form' straight after your first misplaced pass, and even if something went well later on in the game, all they would say was that you had compensated for your mistake but that, at the end of the day, your performance had been quite disappointing.

This negativity is a very German phenomenon indeed. If I had had a say in this country's football broadcasting, I would have built on Reinhold Beckmann's *ran* programme at *Sat.1*, who used to show the Bundesliga matches at the time. They had begun to show the game in a great light – after all, that is what people want to see on a Saturday evening: something pleasant, not two hours of misery.

They want to get excited about commentators and presenters who are just as spellbound by the game as they are. Over the course of my career, I learned that the inner circle of presenters and pundits did not take too well to someone being overly positive. Why do things have to be like this? Are people not allowed to be a little sympathetic if it is not going as well on the pitch? After all, at the end of the day, it does not matter what standing a presenter has among his colleagues; all that matters is that the public like to tune in. If television managed to find a new, positive tone in this popular field, it could create a pioneering culture far beyond the game, in which the glass is half full instead of constantly half empty.

By means of such an attitude, you can turn an absolutely awful match into something worth watching. Take those international dead-rubber friendlies, for example. The 0–1 against Norway in early 2009 had been our first home defeat to the Scandinavians in seventy years. In all probability, this should not have been possible, because every single German player was of better quality than his Norwegian counterpart. The only explanation given on TV was that effort and commitment had not been sufficient, which was exactly wrong. I am sure they had been giving it their all; no one loses any game voluntarily, let alone one for your country. But let us, for argument's sake, take a look at a scene from the match: the Norwegian goalkeeper came out of his goal to greet a German cross, missed the ball, and Mario Gómez managed to head it past the goal. What, then, did the commentator have to say about this? 'Another mistake by the Norwegian keeper.' No. If the goalkeeper comes out, it should result in the ball being put past the line, giving us the lead and an eventual win. If you read from the results, then, the goalkeeper had done everything right: had he stayed on the line and Mario had managed to reach the ball undisturbed, the latter's header would have been unstoppable. Due to the keeper bolting out of his goal, however, Mario lost focus for a moment, relinquishing control over the ball. In considering such a situation, you should always ask for the alternative to the mistake. From the goalkeeper's view, the alternative would be catastrophic: staying on the line and conceding.

Something quite similar happened to me during that infamous international against Austria in February 2008. True, eventually, we won 3–0 and I had secured a national team record without conceding, which I would eventually stretch to 681 minutes. Yet later on, every report said I had not looked good. At one point,

I had come bolting out of my goal towards two opposition players without really reaching the ball – in the end, the shot hit the bar. 'Another Lehmann error,' the commentator had cried out. But what would have been my alternative? Had I stayed put, the opponent would have managed to reach the ball unchallenged, putting it over the line. 'Nothing he could have done about that,' the supposed pundits would have said. For me, however, it would have been the ultimate punishment, because I would have been unable to confuse the opposition player in such a way that he would not have scored. And that is exactly where I see opportunities, potential and possibilities for journalists: instead of plainly criticising what has not been done well, they should use the analysis to demonstrate how to do it differently, perhaps better, and present players with alternatives to their mistakes.

# From The Bench To The Final: The 2008 European Championship

AS THE FIRST NOTES OF THE NATIONAL ANTHEM SOUNDED, MY EYES searched the upper stand for the Chancellor. During such an important game, the final of the most technically demanding tournament in the world, she was simply the embodiment of my fatherland. There she was, conspicuous in her orange suit coat. While we were all singing about unity, justice and freedom, it occurred to me that this was probably going to be my last match for the national team. It could be worse than finishing on a final, I thought. The only thing missing as a crowning achievement was a win.

Yet, a few weeks previously, things had seemed very different. In February, we had been due to play a friendly against Euros host Austria. Around this match, several PR events had been arranged; among others, Bryan Adams had photographed us for German designer line Strenesse. I probably should have enjoyed that, but somehow, it was one of those things that never really agreed with me. Adams really was a great bloke and a very good photographer, but I always tend to sneer at little at these corporate stunts. To people who only knew us from TV, it might have looked like something from another planet, but being quite ordinary, I kept feeling out of place. The one thing that has stuck with me from those shootings is that they would rob me of my siesta.

All the trappings had led to us subconsciously not taking the Austria game very seriously, and that was why I ended up making a mistake for the first time in ages. In the first half, the Austrians had been very aggressive, putting us on the spot again and again. At one point, I misjudged a through ball – bored as I was, I had tried for a good move and left the confines of my goal. The forward ran past me, having to zigzag a little, and ended up being deterred on the line by Per Mertesacker. During the subsequent two corners, I was just as lucky not to concede. I might have saved everything else for the rest of the game, and we might have won 3-0, but thanks to three awkward situations in ninety seconds, the media had finally been supplied with fresh debating material. The commentators at *ARD* condemned me in public, and most of the other journalists could finally bring forth my lack of playing practice as a reason to call me into question. The fact that I had played more domestic games in the previous weeks than all other German players was conveniently overlooked, as envy, resentment and malice apparently needed to be expressed at all costs. Even Bodo Illgner, Toni Schumacher and Uli Stein, some of my predecessors, felt compelled to discharge their opinions about my situation in the German goal. According to them, my nomination was 'unfair towards other keepers who were playing every week', because I had only been sitting on the bench this whole time. After my return to England, however, I had played against Manchester United and Milan – teams of a calibre to which none of my German colleagues even came close to encountering. And yet here I was, the main topic in the German media landscape.

Following the Austria friendly, all manner of people laid claim to my goal. Frank Rost, for example, whose Hamburg side had played a great game against Leverkusen, maintained he had always said he wanted to make it into the national team. This was the same Frank Rost who a year previously had asked his agent to call me and ask whether I could get him a new club in England. At the time, comrade Rost had only been number two behind a still very young debutant, Manuel Neuer. Unfortunately, I had not been able to help him, but his asserting a claim to my position at the first opportunity clearly showed me that neither loyalty nor restraint were his strong points.

Example number two was Tim Wiese. Initially, his Bremen side had lost against Bochum, but he had then saved two penalties against some Portuguese team in the UEFA Cup. Even though he had announced his resignation from the national team a few months before, he was now coquetting with the idea of having earned a chance, seeing as he was, apparently, 'Germany's best keeper'. Example number three was Timo Hildebrand. His verbal stalking up to the much-coveted spot went as follows: after two qualifiers – 1–1 in Cyprus and 0–3 to the Czech Republic, as well as a number of mistakes at his new club, Valencia, he had modestly spread the notion that the current ranking in the German goal was Lehmann at the top, followed by himself and Enke. After my error-strewn Austria game, however, he made it quite plain that he would like to play – remarking dismissively that he 'did not want to make a great big fuss about it all'. Following a fantastic game in the Spanish Cup against Barcelona, he announced: 'I would like to play at the Euros.' Now, I am not one to be contemptuous of anybody aiming to play regularly. It is the way of the world; I had just the same attitude. It does, however, depend on the manner and time you choose to put forward your claim. My advice to everyone would be not to raise your claim until you are sure that you are perpetually going to be better than someone else – otherwise, there will be a rude awakening if you make even the tiniest of errors. Additionally, you will earn more respect by not piping up at your rival's first mistake. Everyone will have seen that mistake, but will they see clearly that you are truly better? It is something on which you should work.

How, then, does one judge a player's quality? Football is no science; it is an art form, because tastes differ. Some like that player with the elegant running style; others prefer the one with the swift movements. It is impossible to determine which is 'better', just as is the case in art, although some things are indeed comparable if considered on a high standard. At the end of the day, all that counts in football are results. And in spite of it all, mine were much better than those of my colleagues.

I finished the Premier League season by coming on for the last twenty minutes of a 1–0 win over Everton, with the Arsenal fans at the Emirates giving me a very emotional send-off that moved me to tears. For some time after, supporters would approach me in the street to thank me for what I had done for them. Not having experienced anything like it in Germany, I was flabbergasted at the respect and recognition with which I was confronted in those moments. Now the anticipation for the Euros was on the rise. Since the kids were still at school,

I stayed in London for a week after the season had ended, training three times a week with goalkeeping coach Gerry Peyton so as not to lose my rhythm. At the weekend, my family and I staged our farewell party in London; it was to be my last evening in the English capital for a long time. We had invited twenty of our closest friends, who gave us a very emotional goodbye. Only then did we realise just how significant this period of our lives had been, a period we were about to leave behind.

The following Monday, I flew to Frankfurt to meet the national team. The first thing we did was get kitted out – new suits and a leisure collection were needed. Upon arrival at the hotel, I noticed that the members of our care team now all looked like mechanics working in a garage, thanks to their dark, jumpsuit-like clothing. When it was my turn, I said hello to some Strenesse employees – players and officials were usually acknowledged with an athlete's greeting, strangers with a regular shake of the hand. Suddenly, a weedy-looking chap approached, surely a Strenesse bloke, and offered me the athlete's greeting, and plainly said, 'Hello'. I looked at him, a little puzzled – who the hell was that? Uli Voigt, our head of media, joined us and started to laugh. 'Do you know who that is?' Uli asked as we watched the little fellow walk away. 'No,' I replied, 'he has not introduced himself.' 'That's Mönchengladbach's Marko Marin.' I had never seen him before. For years, my colleagues on the national team had been teasing me about my constant failure to pin down new arrivals. This was certainly based on the fact that many of them were already invited after a few fairish games and that, in England, I had never had the opportunity to become aware of them. Perhaps Marin was too shy to introduce himself by name – or perhaps he had been brought up poorly. To this day, I introduce myself to strangers by name, as I do not expect them to know who I am. But I suppose times do change.

In the afternoon, we flew to Majorca to set up camp at Son Vida hotel. I knew the place like the back of my hand, since I had often come here with my family to relax for a day or two. It was the perfect location for a Euros training camp. We trained very hard under the supervision of Mark Verstegen and his fitness coaches, just like we had done during World Cup preparation. By combining short, intensive strength sessions with tactical schooling and training on the ball, it took only a short while for us to become fit enough again to play in this excruciating tournament. I was informed about my level of fitness two days before the first warm-up game against Belarus, to be played in Kaiserslautern. On this day, we completed two units; the first in the morning with goalkeeping training on the pitch, the second in the afternoon with sprint training and a special test in the weights room, where I went with Christoph Metzelder and Per Mertesacker. In there, I made the acquaintance of a rather peculiar device: standing upright as if on a climbing frame, you had to move arms and legs simultaneously against the drag of the machine, six reps for fifteen seconds and five reps for ten. To be sure that we had a specific minimum in terms of fitness levels, we needed to reach a certain number of points on the device; the exertion was greater than it had been during the entire season. In addition, we were connected to a heart-rate monitor, which prompted a panting Metzelder to note that I had to be rather fit: compared to the others, my pulse did indeed remain fairly low. As a result, I was quite certain that I was in very good shape, despite having barely played 25 games throughout the season.

On the way to training the next day, my legs were still heavy from those tests, and I sensed that the Belarus match would not be an easy one. Everyone else felt the same, and we were to be proved right. Floppy from the rough training, we gave away a 2–0 lead in the closing stages, ending up drawing 2–2. I had been unable to hold on to two or three balls; the shot that sealed the final score had been one of them: suddenly, it had fallen to the ground in front of me and was behind the line in the blink of an eye. Promptly, Germany had a fresh goalkeeping crisis. I had too little playing practice, they all said, and besides, I was too old anyway. There was a silver lining to the discussion, though: at the next game, I was under a fair amount of pressure again and, as mentioned before, pressure has made me reliable. The only thing that bothered me was the realisation that, once again, we players were faced with journalists who unfortunately were unable to dispute with us and our game on an objective and expert level. Sneering comments were being made all around, tied to the suggestion that either Robert Enke or René Adler, the plainly younger substitutes, should be playing instead. Certainly, this excessive criticism was – among other reasons – the result of my prolonged, twenty-year refusal to favour any single journalist. On occasion you would, of course, give preference to one medium or another: whenever I had something important to say, it was only logical for me to say it to *Bild* or *Kicker* rather than some small local papers. But I never bestowed a privilege upon individual journalists, which was probably why I now had to live with the fact that they wanted to suss me out properly until the very end. From my standpoint, the second test went quite well; self-assured and relaxed, we beat Serbia 2–1. Metze was made responsible for our conceding, even though the midfielders had been predominantly standing poorly. The winning goal was scored by Michael Ballack, who had only joined the team a day before – after losing the Champions League final with Chelsea against Manchester United on penalties, he had been on a four-day holiday. This took me by surprise – two years previously, I had been with the team already two days after the Champions League final. Quietly, I wondered whether Michael was fit enough for such a tournament this time.

At the end of the preparation period, one thing in particular was clear: the expectations among the media and the public were no longer as high. The tournament had not even begun yet, when we were already being lambasted – a typically German fad. Perhaps, though, that is exactly what we need, so that we may rise like a phoenix from the ashes and fly all the way up to the Mount Olympus of sports. The English, in contrast, already get high on their team even before the start of the tournament – they probably fancy a feeling of elation at least before the games. We Germans prefer it the other way around.

Following a short relaxing holiday at home, we set up shop at the official Euros headquarters in Ascona. Initially, the weather was dreadful, with rain and low temperatures. Not until the second day did the mountains become visible, even though they were only an average 500 yards away. Ascona itself did not offer much entertainment, either. The small lakeside promenade might be very pretty, but every 200 yards we would bump into all the journalists who were reporting about us and the tournament. After a short while, they complained to our media officers, Harald Steger and Uli Voigt: 'There's nothing going on in this dump; no birds and no scandals around the team. Properly boring.' We players sat in our golden cage at the hotel; any contact with the opposite sex would have probably been printed in some paper the next day, so no one was tempted to think about it in the first place. The journalists, on the other hand, had no problems spending their leisure time however and with whomever

– it was not as if they were reporting on each other.

Eventually, a small scandal was crafted artificially, involving someone I knew quite well: Toni Schumacher. A tabloid had chosen him to test the playing device I had labelled a swirling ball, and a number of rather frightening journalists were now taking shots at his goal. Before the final effort, Toni gave his verdict; he did not think the ball did swirl. Evidently, he had not paid attention during the last shot, because he rounded off the exercise by coming into our hotel of all places to have his finger treated by our therapist. The diagnosis, though, a dislocation, did not deter Schumacher from fighting boredom with his tabloid mates at the Seven bar, starting the same afternoon. When Schweini, Metze and I went to that very bar for some dinner that evening, we passed their table laden with beer and wine glasses. I spotted Toni and allowed myself a remark. 'Don't tell me the ball was swirling!' We went on to sign autographs for some fans, who told us that the group around Toni had been sitting there for a while, and that my great role model of old in particular had been raising his voice quite a bit after a few beers. Shortly afterwards, a girl approached our table asking for a picture. As we had already started dinner, we asked her to wait until we had finished, but she left and did not return. Apparently, though, she had ended up with Toni and his friends: the next day, Schumacher was quoted in *Bild* as saying, 'It really gets my goat when internationals consider themselves too important to give autographs. Who do they think they are?' A former close friend of Schumacher's told me a little later that Toni in particular had used to reject every request for an autograph so brusquely that even his friends had got embarrassed. He might have been my idol growing up, and I might have learned a lot from him in terms of attitude, technique and discipline at Schalke, but his ingratitude following our hospitality in London and the fact that he had preferred to talk Oliver Kahn into the German goal had got me acquainted more than enough with his undesirable side. By now, Oliver had retired, but evidently, Toni still believed he needed to annoy me.

Finally, however, the main event began. Our first opponent was Poland in Klagenfurt. Łukasz Fabiański, my goalkeeping colleague at Arsenal, had told me they were eager to take revenge for the World Cup defeat. We, the younger generation, are not necessarily aware of the fact that, due to the Second World War, matches against Germany are still something special for our smaller neighbours –

charged with a lot of intense feelings, none of which will be pleasant.

Jogi Löw and his assistants had prepared us excellently for the game. The goals we scored happened against an unorganised team standing too far to the front, just like the coaches had demonstrated. We did, however, have a little bad patch with less possession in the second half, which surprised me as I had expected a fitter German side. Poldi eventually put an end to that spell just before the final whistle – again, the Germans had won, and Poland accepted their fate: a match well played, but not well enough. For us, it was the first Euros win since Oliver Bierhoff's golden goal in the 1996 Wembley final. The victory relaxed the team – a little too much this time, apparently. The regulars did not train again until the Croatia game four days later: according to the doctor, some of them were on the verge of tearing a muscle, so the manager cancelled the planned programme due to the physical strain being too high. During regeneration training, I noticed that Ballack and Frings were a little tired, telling fitness coach Oliver Schmidtlein curtly they thought weight training after the matches was far too much. For the first time, there were discrepancies in terms of the programme. Following the stretching exercises, I got up and pointedly approached the machines to work through my training. The others followed suit, and soon they all participated.

The next day, which had been placed exactly between match days one and two, I shortly discussed the programme with Andy Köpke. Normally, this day would have been perfect for regeneration, since everyone was quite tired – at least, that had been the rhythm we had followed at Arsenal. During a tournament, however, this was a little more difficult to implement, as the games were played with three or four days in between. As a result, I trained sharply and on a high level for half an hour, while the other players trotted up and down the pitch, without any particular physical strain.

The day after, I went through my usual final training: one hour of shots on target, crosses and passes. There was no proper match; the outfield players merely amused themselves a little playing five against two. 'No strain' appeared to be the name of the game. Following the session, we flew to Klagenfurt once more. On the morning of the match, Mark Verstegen gave one of his popular barrack-yard motivational speeches again. He had written the word 'focus' on one hand and was now showing us the individual letters one after the other. Entranced, we listened to him link each finger to a specific requirement. On the morning of the match against Croatia. Unfortunately, it did not go well: before we had woken up, we were already trailing 0–1, moving about the pitch like lame ducks. At half-time, most players talked wildly over each over; some even hurled abuse before we had to go out again. The second half went just as the first had done; half an hour before the end, the score was 0–2. Even Poldi's goal, which closed the gap fifteen minutes later, was not followed by the usually feared German comeback. The Croats' songs of victory after their 2–1 win were getting on my nerves, but I could not get them out of my mind. Let's just see where they end up if they're already celebrating like they've won the whole tournament, I thought, convinced we would be more successful than them.

First, however, we needed to be concerned with ourselves. Apparently, during the game, a few players had continued abusing each other, something that I had not noticed back at my end of the pitch. I only heard about it after full time, when I was told to organise a team meeting that was supposed to weld us together and clear up any disruption in the side's atmosphere. Hans-Dieter Hermann, our psychologist, took me aside and asked me to head the meeting with the team in mind. As I had heard that it had been the captain who had come to blows with a few players on the pitch, I was not all too surprised that I had now inherited what was really his job.

As a general rule, a debate like this can always be considered a success if both sides tell each other their opinions without being insulting and, more importantly, if the next game is won. Eventually, the meeting ended with a rallying cry for the final group match against Austria. As we knew that the Austrians were not as used to these pressure games, we finally picked up the pace in training again. This time, those two players who had cursed the whole side into exhaustion-based inaction before the Croatia game were no longer able to influence the sessions' intensity.

We departed for Vienna, the place where my international career had taken a turn for the better during that first match under Jürgen Klinsmann. I was surprised when I saw the Austrian line-up; there was only one forward, and he was a little one who was not predestined to hold balls. He was not fast, either. Good, I thought, we won't have much to fear. And I ended up being right: the Austrians did not have a single chance and were entirely dominated by us. Unfortunately, we did not score any goals and so went into the break on a 0-0, where I was taken aback to see assistant coach Hansi Flick give the half-time speech. 'Where is Jogi?' I asked Arne Friedrich, who was sitting next to me. 'I think the ref's sent him into the stands,' he replied. I had not witnessed this banishment, but that was a good sign; it meant I was highly focused. 'Keep going, we need to be patient and stay well organised,' Hansi was saying now, 'we'll get our chances.' And we did. A short while into the second half, we were given a free kick in a central position and, with breathtaking speed, Michael Ballack lifted the ball into the right corner. It was a fantastic shot and an equally fantastic reaction to the events of the previous days by the captain.

The Austrians were simply too weak to put us under any pressure; they would have had to score two goals, something with which they had evidently struggled. We, on the other hand, had reached the knockout stages, albeit in second place behind Croatia. Jogi was allowed back into the dressing room and was rather relieved about it; he too had experienced the Austrian match as a pressure test. I had not been following the press as closely, but following the game a rumour made the rounds at headquarters saying Jogi would have been history in case of a defeat. Apparently, there were critics even at the DFB who were waiting for just that scenario to take place. For me, this was quite incomprehensible, especially considering our development over these last two years after the World Cup. We had played a very strong qualifying campaign and some great football, but apparently, after the Croatia game, not much backing had been offered to the manager. DoF Matthias Sammer was being strangely quiet on the matter, especially considering the fact that he normally put in his tuppence-worth on a constant basis – it was rumoured that he wanted to become national team manager himself.

Our next opponent, Portugal, was on the agenda three days later. They had marched through their group at ease and could even afford to have their second-string side play the final game against Switzerland. This had given their first team six days to regenerate – twice as many as we had. During our preparation, the notion of a 4-5-1 system cropped up, of which I approved as I was able to contribute my experience from England. At Arsenal, we had always used to play

4-4-2 in the Champions League, both at home and away. Especially on foreign pitches, however, we had conceded many times, and only once Arsène Wenger switched to a 4-5-1 had we kept a clean sheet until the final. Wenger had, however, had the system practised again and again in training. For us Germans, it would certainly be an advantage against the Portuguese with their strong midfield around Cristiano Ronaldo. We would be able to disturb their flow of play, which was based on short passes through the midfield: with five midfielders, we would be better able to block the interfaces for the vertical passes. Another thing Michael Ballack and I could tell the team was how best to play against Cristiano Ronaldo. He had to be blocked already during our own attacks, because he liked to offer himself as an open man after parried shots. If you caught him there, however, urging him towards the middle, he would lose much of his ability to carry the ball to the front sprinting along the wing.

The tension before the quarter-final was immense. We were no favourites and knew all too well the strengths of the Portuguese, but it is this tension, mixed with slight doubts whether it was at all doable, that allows you to deliver your best performance. And indeed, we played our best game of the tournament amid the great atmosphere at St Jakob Park in Basel. Following a fantastic combination, Schweini made it 1-0 in his first game after being suspended. Poldi had put the ball precisely into the box, where Schweini emerged victorious from a challenge by two Portuguese players. At this point, only 22 minutes had been played. Portugal never really found their way into the game, because Simon Rolfes and Thomas Hitzlsperger complemented each other perfectly in midfield. The victim of this adjustment was Torsten Frings, but he was not yet fit after breaking his rib and hence would not have been able to give a top-level performance. Four minutes later, Miro Klose made it 2-0, taking ice-cold advantage of a misunderstanding between the Portuguese keeper and a defender. Now, the match had everything that marked it as great: suspense, fighting and goals – but unfortunately, mistakes too. At one point, we had been defending in an unorganised manner during a Portuguese counter-attack, and suddenly Ronaldo stood before me, completely open. I was able to parry his shot, but the rebound by Nuno Gomes went through Metze and me and into my goal. Just before half-time too – bugger. During the break, we tried to rest a little and focused again on the instructions given to us once more by Hansi Flick, seeing as Jogi Löw had been suspended for this match.

In the second half, Portugal created superiority in midfield, their passes, crosses and shots now being more dangerous. Our defence around the penalty area, however, was still good, and towards the middle of the second half we managed a clearance. When a free kick sailed into the Portuguese penalty box, Michael Ballack pushed his counterpart slightly and headed the ball past the again poorly positioned Ricardo to make it 3–1. The atmosphere in the stadium was now beyond description; the German fans could barely believe it and turned St Jakob Park into a bubbling cauldron. Portugal, however, had not yet given up. Once more, they increased their passing accuracy, which barred us from making any mistakes, or we were going to be punished. To our credit, we did last until the 88th minute, when Petit reached the ball on the right wing and lunged for a cross. 'Deeper, behind you, come back, come back,' I shouted at Per Mertesacker, and wondered for a second whether to leave my goal. I knew Petit was too far away from me; I would never get to the ball in time, and neither would I manage to block it while it was at head-level. Hence, I stayed on the line, watching the cross come in precisely behind six-foot-tall Mertesacker. I reacted when the ball had reached Hélder Postiga's head, but it struck underneath the bar – 3–2. Again, the notion of the alternative to a mistake crossed my mind: sometimes, I simply had to go out fully conscious that I would not reach the ball. It might look like a mistake, but leaving your goal confuses or hinders your opponent easily, preventing him from kicking or heading the ball unchallenged. The alternative to a mistake, then, would be conceding.

Six minutes left, including stoppage time. Later, during repeats on TV, I could see that the German fans had buried their faces in their hands every time Portugal had attacked. To some extent, this maximal pressure was mirrored on the pitch: I was yelling, fisting away balls and organising the other players, who were only ever watching the ball instead of including the opponent. In the middle of injury time, I intercepted a long ball and received a dead leg in return, forcing play to be interrupted for a short bit of treatment. 'Come on, big man; get up,' Ronaldo challenged me. Fine, I'll get through these final two minutes, I thought, hitting the ball towards the front. The whistle sounded, and again, it was a great win for us, accompanied by a fantastic atmosphere, just like at the World Cup in Germany.

My joy, however, came to an abrupt end when Andy Köpke and Oliver Bierhoff approached me to tell me my wife had collapsed in the stands. I ran towards the exit and up along the rows of seats, where I saw the other WAGs, my friend Niklas, our team doctor Sepp Schmidt and two paramedics. Conny was lying across the seats. She was conscious but quite pale. 'It's okay,' she said. The shock had gone under my skin. We supported her all the way into the medical room next door to the German dressing room, where Tim Meyer, our internist, joined us to check up on her. She should eat and drink something, he recommended; it would make her feel better quickly. Finally, I could enter the dressing room, where I found Poldi dancing yet again to 'Viva Colonia', joined by the rest of the team and officials. Nothing could replace this kind of post-match atmosphere. When we arrived at our Ascona hotel at two in the morning, the staff were holding torches, forming a guard of honour. Accompanied by a small band playing music, a perfect evening drew to a close. The first thing I got to hear after the match was that Michael Ballack's agent had sold the change in our tactics to *Bild* as his client's brainchild – a fancy that once again presented an unnecessary disruption, bringing unrest to the team.

What followed was the most pleasant time of Euro 2008; we had six days until our next match. Before regeneration training the next day, my now fully recovered wife and I drove up the valley along the River Maggia. We wanted to sit in the sun on the stones by the bank, so we parked the bikes, and I led the way across to reach a nice spot. Turning around, I saw Conny lying in the water – she had slipped. 'Seems you're having a bit of an unlucky streak since last night,' I laughed. We sat down on a hot stone and put our legs in the water until her clothes had dried. That afternoon, I told Mark Verstegen about the stones by the river. He promptly decided that everyone who had played was to ride their bikes along the river to our spot for regeneration. There, we sat and stood in the cool water; finally, we were able to enjoy the area. On the way back, Metze was cycling next to me and said, 'Mental, these matches are so much fun; I'm still filled with adrenalin.' How right he was. Before long, I would miss these games. In the evening, there was a barbecue in the hotel garden, during which we watched the second quarter-final between Turkey and Croatia. Once again, the Turks won by flipping an apparently doomed match in the last moment. They were now our opponent in the semi-final, a fact which, of course, rallied Germany even more, considering the country's large Turkish population. The staff at the large car manufacturers, with thousands of Turks among them, would witness their second summer's tale: their shift during which the match had been scheduled had unceremoniously been cancelled. Reduced hours because of football – something of which everyone should dream half a year later, when a crisis befell both the car and financial sectors.

After two days of leisure, preparation for the semi-finals began with hard work and setting the mood for the opponent with the use of videos and meetings. No one quite knew whom the Turks would be able to field, as many of their players were either injured or suspended. Inevitably, we were favourites for this game, which again did not do us good. The venue was Basel once more, where we virtually slept through the first half. Limp and taken by surprise by the Turks' dangerous moves, we eventually saw them take the lead in an almost clichéd manner. An unsuccessful shot had bounced against the bar in a high arc and fallen at the feet of a Turkish player, who did not hit the ball properly, causing it to wobble entirely uncontrollably through my legs and into my goal. Luckily, out of the blue, Schweini managed to level four minutes later. The Turks had probably also heard of that typically German ability to make something out of nothing; it was very important that, apart from ourselves, our opponent believed in it too. In the second half, we finally gained some more control. While not much happened at the front, our defence was standing much more securely. A good ten minutes before the end, we took the lead, again out of the blue. After a cross, Turkish keeper Rüştü had come out of his goal rather aimlessly, allowing Miro Klose to head the ball into the empty net from ten yards. Was the final on the horizon?

Apparently not. Just before full time, we had to learn how negative psychology could turn on us. The common thought among the team seemed to be that the Turks would not manage a comeback this time. Unfortunately, the subconscious is unfamiliar with the word 'not', and so Turkey equalised one more time four minutes before the end. For all intents and purposes, the angle was impossible, but before I could pick up the seemingly safe ball, Semih Sentürk had put it past the line. I could not believe it. The Turks were on a high, which, really, was lucky for us, because this way they allowed Philipp Lahm to play a double one-two with Thomas Hitzlsperger – a moment of brilliance, crowned by Philipp with a curl into the near corner, granting Germany yet another deciding match.

Even though we had reached the final, we were unable to enjoy ourselves properly; we simply had not played well enough. All the drama might have only arisen due to our shortcomings but, at the end of the day, we had yet again achieved great success. Reaching an endgame was in itself a triumph, no matter how it had been done. Nonetheless, we needed to be vigilant, as anything could happen in a final. There, more often than not, the difference between victory and defeat would be made not by a team's quality but rather the form of the day or even one player's single moment of genius.

Some nations never reach a final, despite perhaps playing a more beautiful form of football. Whenever they fail, they ask themselves why we are successful while they are not. I believe our sustainability over the years could be explained by our mentality, which blends great self-confidence with an excessive tendency to criticise everything – the 'Yes, but' phenomenon. I am not sure from where this stems, perhaps from our ability to work hard and thoroughly. Additionally, we did not ordinarily lose the ground beneath our feet whenever we would achieve partial success. For us, there was no such thing as unconditional success: the typical German post-success comment was, 'Yes, we might have won, but this and that was poorly done, too.' It is the piece of lead strapped to our feet which prohibits the mere notion of taking off or even flying.

To me, intelligence also means turning potential into success – a clever turn of phrase I have learned from Arsène Wenger. Evidently, German teams are especially intelligent, seeing as they often manage to turn even the most restricted potential into maximum success. But would Spain this time, in the final, be the cleverer side? Their potential was great, and they had been playing the most beautiful and effective football of the tournament so far. This final, however, would be their first in almost half a century; how would their intelligence hold up? In my eyes, manager Luis Aragonés was a smart bloke, who had drummed into his team the motto that winning was everything, and losing was nothing. While he was considered a good psychologist, he was also a disgusting racist. Once, he had egged on my former team-mate José Reyes with the words, 'You'll have to polish off that nigger at the front if you want to play.' He had been talking about Thierry Henry.

Now, the Spanish surely had respect for us, and in all their previous tournaments, respect for an opponent had always turned into fear very quickly – a question of mentality, apparently. If, however, you gave them free rein, they were fantastic, so we needed to try to hurt them somehow.

For Germany, Euro 2008 was the sequel to the 2006 World Cup. Again, the country was allowed to continue the party until the end; again, there was public viewing; and again, match days meant time off from work and suspense from start to finish. It was just the right mix for a lovely summer. As a player, this attitude had already seemed strange to me after the World Cup. We had always been celebrated whenever we merely achieved more than we had been trusted to do. Did the nation not believe that we would also have something to celebrate by the end? This was no optimal preparation for this final, I thought. Even within the team, voices were raised expressing relief that 'the great pressure' had gone. I considered this approach completely wrong – the pressure needed to be as high as possible in order for us to deliver a top performance. We could not afford, then, to be satisfied this early on.

Once more, we played the 4–5–1, unsure whether it would be the correct system against Spain. As a manager, you struggle to find the perfect line-up for such a game. With five players in midfield, for example, we would be able to disrupt the Spanish flow of play, but with two forwards, we would apply more pressure to their build-up play, potentially unsettling them. Prior to the match, though, a long-known body part had come into the focus of public interest once more: Michael Ballack's calf. It had closed up, cramped up, or simply calloused. The captain's calf appeared to have a mind of its own. Among the national team, the cursed thing had been well known since the World Cup, where Michael had missed the opening match because his muscles had closed up yet again. Now, another final was looming; again, Michael had been unable to train, but this time he was allowed to play. Was that a good idea? In any case, he was now standing next to me in the row at the Ernst Happel stadium in Vienna, singing the national anthem. Roberto Rosetti blew his whistle shortly after and the match began. We had begun well, with the Spanish not finding their way into the game. While we played fluently towards the front, no forceful opportunity presented itself. After around twenty minutes, however, Spain began to make combining moves despite our five players in midfield, resulting in exactly the situation we had wanted to prevent. The Spanish shifted play to the right for a short while, then back into the middle via a vertical pass to Xavi. He turned on the spot, playing the ball through Lahm and Mertesacker into the penalty area. Recognising the danger, I ran out of my goal. Philipp saw me do so and slowed down, making himself unable to intervene. Fernando Torres was fast – I knew that much – but would he be fast enough to play the ball past me purposefully? I had almost got to the ball, when his leg extended like a telescope. Reaching it before me, he lobbed the sphere, forcing me to calculate its trajectory within a millimetre. The angle should be sufficient, I thought – perhaps the ball would hit the post, or maybe a defender would clear it on the line; it was not coming very fast, after all. Unfortunately, it appeared that the stadium's groundsmen had not done clean work: the ball bounced and turned towards the goal, crossing the line. I could not believe it; I should have done better.

Our reaction was nothing in particular; until half-time, we did not have any real chances. The break was filled with the usual rituals, but the second half saw the Spanish again as the ones who played better towards the front. They had several chances to decide the game but did not use them. Nonetheless, we were still merely running after them. By now, Mario Gómez had been brought on, with eleven minutes left to play. Perhaps he was going to have his happy end at this tournament, after all. Well, he would have done, providing Mr Rosetti, the impartial third party, had done his job according to the description. Instead, however, the way he was officiating this game gave me the impression he had been overlooked during muck-out after the Italian refereeing scandal. He did not, for example, punish a clear clout by David Silva, despite standing immediately next to him. A few minutes later, we sent a cross into the Spanish penalty area, where the ball suddenly flew up vertically. During an attempt to clear it, Puyol jumped into Mertesacker in such a way that anyone other than our giant defender would have fallen over. Nevertheless, Per managed to get the ball to Mario Gómez, who was suddenly standing in front of the goal, completely unimpeded and not offside. 'Do it,' I screamed from the back, not that he would have been able to hear me, but I still wanted to transmit some energy. Suddenly, though, that strange referee blew his whistle, granting Spain a free kick. This, of all things, was taking the piss. Mertesacker had not done anything; on the contrary, Puyol had jumped into him. And yet, this arse – excuse my language – was working against us. Something was not right here; there was no other explanation. In the opening match, he had already refused Switzerland a clear penalty for handball against the Czechs, and yet he had been allowed to officiate the final.

Shortly after, it was full time. Game over. What a disappointment. We had not been Germany in this game; there had been no rising up or any boundless will to turn the match around. I was leaning against the post of my goal, incensed. My anger was directed at the Bundesliga, because it kept sending players to the national team who were not educated well enough where tactics were concerned. During the Euros, there were few players on which we could rely to be drilled in the correct techniques. While the three weeks of tournament prep had been used for some defensive practice, there had been no time for attacking solutions. All managers, whether on the national team or in the league, were going to be challenged with finding the latter over the coming years, since some countries were as much ahead of us in that respect as Spain had been. In future, we were going to have to close this gap, or we could goodbye to any more big wins.

When we attended the presentation ceremony – well, the losers' ceremony, really – the Spanish formed a guard of honour; my Arsenal team-mate Cesc Fàbregas high-fived me. What a fantastic success, European champion at 21 – richly deserved considering the team's way of playing across the entire tournament. The last thing I recall from inside the stadium that day is the awarding of the medals. What I had failed to notice was the fact that, apparently, Oliver Bierhoff and Michael Ballack had had quite the row after the match. According to reports, Ballack had said that considering the mistakes that had been made, no one should have been surprised by the defeat. It infuriated me; you should always look for the fault in yourself.

The DFB had hired a Vienna club for the farewell party, so we drove to the hotel, got changed and set off. At the party, Conny and I took our seats and listened to DFB president Theo Zwanziger give a speech. 'Well done' appeared to be the tenor yet again – the association, too, seemed to be focused on the

Olympic motto. Taking part was everything once more. Of course, Zwanziger would have preferred to be standing before us with the trophy in his hands, but his world was not ending. It was for me, however – after all, this had been my last chance to win a big title. Initially, my mood was accordingly reserved, but after a few beers, I told myself that I simply wanted to enjoy this provisionally final evening among the national team, regardless of the score. Eventually, the singing and dancing commenced. Our women were in high spirits anyway, as the holidays were coming up, which meant we could finally be with them. It turned out to be a great night that seamlessly merged into morning; shortly after 7 am, I left the party with my wife, and we were not the last to go.

The next day, we all flew to Berlin one more time, where thousands of people stood in front of the Brandenburg Gate, celebrating us and themselves. They were right to do so, since it had been a pleasant time for us and our spectators. After the World Cup, I had found it a nice gesture to show gratitude once more to millions of Germans for their support. This time, no one complained about the journey to Berlin that had, after all, meant a detour for almost all of us. Now, the Euros were well and truly over and, for me, a new stage of my career – presumably the last one – was about to begin.

# Always Leave Them Wanting More – International Goodbyes And New Beginnings

'OKAY, THAT'S IT, THEN.'

With these four succinct words, my career on the German national team drew to a close. I had arranged an appointment with Jogi Löw and Andreas Köpke to discuss my future. It was July 2008, a few days after the Euros final, and we were meeting in a Stuttgart hotel. I had not wanted to settle on a clear-cut strategy for the conversation; there was only one thing of which I was sure: I no longer wanted to make those journeys to Azerbaijan or Finland for some qualifiers. I would have liked to be part of the big games, but I could no longer picture myself going to places like Almaty. Hence, the dice was cast already, as it was clear to me that the boss would not allow me to cherry-pick, which was exactly what the two ended up telling me. I was either in or out, so I was left with no choice but to utter those four words.

'Okay, that's it, then.'

The phrase might sound succinct, but it was an emotional step, because over the years the national team had been one of my decisive motivators – to be the best German player in my position and to play for my country. Like a common thread, the national team had run through my various clubs, and for its sake I had made my only big mistake: had Erich Ribbeck in 1998 not made me choose between playing for Milan or not be invited onto the national team again, I probably would have stayed in Italy for longer and my career would perhaps have gone completely differently. So, I had gone to Dortmund for the sake of the national team – a move which brought a lot of trouble with it; but seeing as I had fought so long for my spot on the team, I was going to do everything to hold on to it. Especially when you are playing abroad, the national team is the only professional contact with your home country and an opportunity to come home for more than a day at least from time to time on the occasion of home games. Especially during my time in England, the team had become even more of a point of reference. Team doctors Dr Müller-Wohlfahrt and Sepp Schmidt; therapists Klaus Eder, Wolfgang Bunz, Adi Katzenmeier and Christian Müller; kit managers Manni Drexler and Thomas Mai – for many years, they had been my footballing family, and saying goodbye to them was not going to be easy.

Jogi Löw and Andreas Köpke did not try to change my mind during our meeting. They were, I think, quite glad that this would clear the path for a new beginning. The older you get as a player, the more dominant you become, and you make no secret of your superior knowledge of the game, either. Eventually, managers will not be upset to see new faces as well as players who develop. I would have quite enjoyed some rivalry with the youngsters – as long as I was still playing, I remained a competitor. After all, that was my raison d'être in football; without it, there would be no thrill. While I simply could not be bothered any more with the parameters of said thrill, I knew that the manager would not be able to give me special treatment. Based on this, I was not offended by their readiness to accept my decision. At the time, I was 38 years old; I was not going to be upset by anything in football any more. Three years previously, before the World Cup, I would certainly have taken the whole thing more personally. Yet one thing that was never acknowledged was how valuable it could be to have someone experienced and reliable at the back.

By the end of 2009, among the national team, especially following the death of Robert Enke, it was still unclear who could really be trusted with the role of number one. Already a year previously, I had planned to consider the 2010 World Cup after all; I had even phoned Jogi Löw to tell him of my idea. I had not expected an answer, but he was supposed to know that he could count on me. When I eventually had made my thoughts public, there had, of course, been a lot of head-shaking. What did the old geezer want now? Oliver Kahn of all people had given me the idea in December 2008. On the sidelines of a TV show, he had told me how the current keepers were playing so poorly that he could march into goal without training. As a result, I had another look at the statistics of Adler, Neuer and Enke, and noted that the result really was rather average. During the second half of the season, Adler and Neuer had made so many mistakes that their clubs slipped from upper-table spots into mid-table obscurity. Besides, while I had at least been playing in the Champions League with Stuttgart, neither of them had had any international experience.

I might not have said anything further had I departed the national team wholly officially. However, even though the manager had briefly raised my hopes for a testimonial, it never happened. It had been his idea to possibly call me up for the Berlin friendly against England in November 2008. Of course, I had thought this a great thing, but had said immediately that it would be down to the team leader to sell the notion to the public. So, they had leaked the plan, but as the date was coming closer and closer, those in charge were backing away from it further and further. When I had eventually not been put in the first XI, the public picture suddenly looked as if the whole thing had been my idea, as if I had arrogated something to myself that had not been due to me. Of course, I had not been against the initial notion; I approve of the attempt to allow for a worthy goodbye for fairly merited players. It had not been about my playing another sixty or eighty minutes but about acknowledging history. After all, within the commercialised world of football, the national team had still been a small enclave that set great store by symbolic values, honour and identification with the fatherland. A gesture such as a testimonial would have expressed and elevated this identification, something I had written in a letter to DFB president Theo Zwanziger. Such a farewell would not mean much trouble for the association, especially if it took place in the context of an international match: a bunch of flowers, an announcement in the ground, done. For a player, however, it would be of great importance.

Jogi Löw had called me and said that considering the planned fresh start, my renewed appearance would equate to a lost game for the others. He had added that I was still warmly invited to come down and say my goodbyes to the team, but

I had declined gratefully and had not driven to Berlin. Seeing as they had got rid of those official farewell games against some random old-age teams after Oliver Kahn's retirement, I had exited the national team entirely unsung. I consider this a loss of tradition. For the sake of future generations, you have to hope that those in charge eventually understand that, occasionally, tradition is more important than rigidly organising an annual calendar.

At the end of the day, my resignation from the national team had been a compromise with my wife and children. Professional footballer is not a particularly family-friendly job – you are constantly on the road; you cannot focus on the kids' upbringing, and you can barely maintain social contacts. The old German trade unionists' saying, 'On Sundays, Daddy belongs to me' was evidently not made up with us in mind, on the contrary. Based on this, footballers should really start a family as late as possible, but of course, this is something over which you do not always have decisive power. In early 2008, I had considered whether I should not retire from football completely after the Euros. My contract at Arsenal was about to expire, and other offers, such as from Hertha BSC and Aston Villa, were not quite worth considering. So, after some toing and froing, we decided to move close to Munich from London.

In May 2008, when the Premier League season was nearly already over, I received a phone call from Horst Heldt, the DoF at Stuttgart. I had played alongside him across the youth national teams, and we had kept in touch. A year and a half previously, he had called me once before, at half-ten in the evening, when I had been in bed already. 'Horst, do you know what time it is?' had been the first thing I had asked him. 'I do, but it's not like you're sleeping,' he had replied. 'We need you; we're looking for a goalkeeper.' At that point, however, I had already extended my contract at Arsenal by a year and had been forced to stave him off. In the end, Stuttgart had signed Raphael Schäfer from Nürnberg, with whom they had not become very happy. This had been the reason Heldt was now calling again, a few weeks prior to the Euros. 'Thanks for calling at a civilised hour this time,' I said, before we got down to business. Eventually, we met in Palma on the sidelines of the pre-Euros training camp in Majorca, and once more in Dortmund later on to negotiate the details. Heldt briefly outlined the Stuttgart squad and said they needed someone like me, who could work in a success-orientated manner and bring a winner's mentality to the team. It all sounded good enough; there was only one thing that took me aback a little. Heldt had taken care to emphasise that his recent signings had been approved by experts as well as the media. Straight away, I caught myself thinking once more that German football attached great importance to making sure that everything was received well by the public. For now, however, it was all the same to me; I had merely one condition: I was not going to come all the way to Stuttgart for regeneration training the day after a game – that bit of stretching, massaging and cardio could be done at home. That was not going to be a problem at all, Heldt said. I decided to take a small flat in Stuttgart for those days when I would definitely not make it home. My wife imposed another condition: as, initially, she would be moving to Starnberg near Munich practically on her own, I would have to pass on the national team. I understood this wish and respected it eventually. On the downside, my children were upset by this step, asking why their Dad no longer played for the national team.

In addition to the rational assessment, Stuttgart gave me a reassuring gut feeling. The board around Erwin Staudt made a good impression, just like the coaches and players, among whom I knew Mario Gómez and Thomas Hitzlsperger from the national team. This instinctive sensation was very important – if I had not had a good feeling about the matter, I would be affected as a whole – not to mention my wife and kids, whose lives I was about to steer in a completely new direction. Initially, my decision appeared well made. It was a pretty town with pleasant people, and after five years in England the Bundesliga would be a new stimulus, something that is simply needed every now and again. Besides, the most recent intense impression I had taken away from Germany had been the great mood around the World Cup, of which I hoped a little had been preserved – after all, the stadiums had remained the same. Of course, all the driving to Stuttgart was annoying – two hours there, two hours back, at least three times a week – but I eventually got used to it, and it did not spoil my enjoyment of football. The game was simply what I knew best, and as a result I was willing to put up with a lot. Moreover, since I did not always drive myself, I was able to work or rest in the car.

However, merely having a nice time in Stuttgart was not going to be enough; I wanted to win titles. After all, the team had won the league title a mere thirteen months before my arrival. I knew they played the kind of football and had the euphoria as well as the energy I had absorbed and learned to value at Arsenal. I had a short chat with Thomas Hitzlsperger – he was the realistic type, who would list soberly all the things good and bad about the club. I did not want to know too much up front; it is always better to make your own judgment and not to approach a new task laden with too many prejudices.

Initially, there was the great disenchantment: the mood around the country was no longer as effusive. And why would it be – while the World Cup and the Euros had been a celebration, I was returning to find everyday life back in place, not aided by a worldwide economic crisis during which more optimistic nations than ours had slouched their shoulders.

However, the sporting side of things did not take off at first, either. To me, the team under Armin Veh was a mystery. Already during pre-season prep, I had been confused by the fact that only three players had said decidedly that they wanted to win the league, while the rest saw the team finishing somewhere between third and seventh place. I did not understand this – why should we not want to become champions? The squad did not look much different from their successful year, and there were no superior teams in the league from whom we would have to hide, not even Bayern Munich. Then, however, I quickly realised on what this universal humility was based. Due to the most basic mistakes and pure lack of concentration, we lost a number of games at the beginning of the season in such a stupid manner that I was reminded of my worst period at Schalke. Often, I had to re-watch the games on TV in order to genuinely believe those gaffes. How had this lot won the league, I wondered; just how poor must the others have been? The players simply resigned themselves too easily to things that did not run properly – not out of convenience, either, but because they were perhaps too nice to come to blows with their team-mates. In any case, no one really revolted against the downward trend, and it was not getting us anywhere.

By now, I had understood what those in charge were expecting from me. Heldt knew I was a strident person on the pitch, and that was exactly the individual he had been after, as his team was simply too gentle. I was not overly fond of this role; it was rather stressful to keep telling my young colleagues to 'do this, do that, come here, behave more professionally', and so forth. But if I wanted to be successful, I had to say something every now and again, despite not being captain. Stuttgart might have been my last station, but in no way do I consider this time to have been a kind of sanctuary for an ageing veteran. When I played, I harboured ambitions, which was why I could not care less whether some colleagues took umbrage with my role or my contractual privileges. Everyone negotiated their contracts as well as they could, and at the end of the day, your role on the team is decided by your performance and your willingness. That is how things are done in an achieving society. During my entire first season at Stuttgart, I only missed four days of training, not giving anyone reason to complain.

I was keen to see how the league had changed in the years since my departure, but after only one week, I had to learn that the trappings had retained their usual charm. I still had to sign autographs for two hours directly after training, which was counterproductive for the body and would have been utterly unthinkable in London. Organisation had not changed, either. On the way back from my very first game for Stuttgart, a friendly at St Pauli, the plane became inoperative for some reason. Instead of chartering another, we travelled by rail for seven hours, until we ended up on a regional train with a bunch of drunks at one in the morning, going from Karlsruhe to Stuttgart. Arsène Wenger would have fired his travel manager the very next day. Mind you, if they are rare, such gaffes are quite amusing, just like the Swabians' habit of taking two packets of maultaschen to every away game, served in beef broth before the match. But pleasant did not necessarily mean professional. The Stuttgart dressing rooms were so antiquated that I was reminded of the very beginning of my career. The floor was in such a disgusting condition, I feared even the two-inch soles of my flip-flops would not protect me from all the germs. What would have been considered highly modern thirty years ago appeared to still serve its purpose in the Swabians' eyes. When I eventually extended my contract by another year, my only condition was that the dressing room be renovated.

Following the first few defeats, the club officials apparently got the impression that top coach Armin Veh was not very motivated any more. After the 1–4 loss in Wolfsburg, Horst Heldt insisted I come to training the next day, despite it being my day off. When I walked into the conference room the following morning, everyone was there: the squad, the physios and second assistant manager Markus

Babbel – the only one missing was Armin Veh. Khalid Boulahrouz was standing nearest to me, so I asked him where the boss was. 'They've just fired him,' came the reply. My word, I thought, would you look at these Swabians; they had not said a word all this time and, before you knew it, the manager was history. Hard as nails. It was especially brutal if you considered the fact that we had initially been in the lead against Wolfsburg and had only conceded those four goals due to unsuccessful tackles. How could the manager alone be at fault for that?

In any case, his dismissal was now followed by the sudden promotion of my former national-team colleague Markus Babbel – from third in line to the pole position overnight. With his positive speeches, he did indeed bring a breath of fresh air into the dressing room, albeit he could not get rid of the niff accumulated over thirty years. Even against Bayern, we turned around a 1–2 in the last minute to walk away with a draw. By the winter break, we were eleventh in the table, eleven points behind miracle side Hoffenheim. The fact that they had managed to top the league by Christmas not only said something about their strength but also spoke volumes about the weaknesses of others. Future champions Wolfsburg only ranked two spots above us.

After the winter break, the club repeatedly enquired whether I wanted to extend my contract by another year. Time after time, I delayed the decision – I did not want to inflict such a poor season on myself again; eleventh in the table was pure mediocrity. In the back of my mind, however, there stuck a remark by Jochen Rücker, our team organiser, who once, out of context, had told me during training, 'You can't leave things like this.' So, I set myself a final goal: the championship. And it had remained set by the time we were asked to formulate our ambitions for the season during training camp in Portugal. Some of my team-mates, Ludovic Magnin in particular, dismissed me as out of touch; others mocked me behind my back. For them, positions five to seven were the height of pleasure – typical mediocrity. I retorted that there were still 51 points left to be distributed, three in every game. Why, then, should we not consider each match on its own and win them all? No team who had played us had really been better than us, apart from Wolfsburg, who had beaten us deservedly. By the end of the debate, positions three to seven had been established as the official season aim.

Apparently, for some of my colleagues, it was no picnic to have to play alongside someone like me, someone who only defined himself through successes. As long as they arrived, I was considered a 'booster and great professional' on the pitch and a pleasant, affable bloke off it. As soon as things did not go that well, some colleagues regarded me as 'the difficult type', who turned into a completely different person on the pitch. Of course, such things were never said to my face. Instead, they were slipped round the back to some journalist, along with the complaints about my 'special treatment' – in the hope to come off well in the coverage. I had seen these types before in Dortmund, but here, it was above all Ludovic Magnin who fell into this category. While almost half of all goals scored against us came from over his side, he spent his time telling the press internals from the team and complaining about my days off. That was the way of things: whenever players like that feared losing their place on the team for whatever reason, they would become political. After the winter break, we bowed out of both the domestic and the European cup competitions, but there was no beating us in the Bundesliga. And because the other teams were putting on their trousers one leg at a time, just as I had expected, we climbed the table bit by bit. In March, on the back of this momentum, I sat down in the office of Horst Heldt and Jochen Schneider, the club's managing director. They wanted to hear once again my assessment for the course of the season, or rather, for what was left of it. At this point we were seventh, so I said we would definitely get into Europe, perhaps even the Champions League. The only tricky matter would be the championship; Wolfsburg were simply playing too well. In the same breath, however, I pointed out that the greater challenge would be the following season: Hoffenheim would be continuing their stabilisation; Leverkusen, Schalke and Hamburg would also be doing everything they could to finally play at the top alongside Bayern Munich. Heldt and Schmidt listened to all of this and offered to extend my contract. I, in turn, consulted my family. My wife made the case for the end of my footballing career, but my kids wanted me to play another year. Eventually, I signed the contract, in which, aside from that dressing-room refurbishment, I sought assurances about continuing regeneration training at home. A few weeks later, we actually made it far enough to stand a chance of winning the championship on the last match day, the only condition being that Wolfsburg lost to Bremen, and we won at Bayern. In the end, Wolfsburg won 5–1 – a tight score indeed – making the numbers game redundant.

The first matches of the 2009/10 season did not go all that well for us as a team in general. On the bright side, a poll was conducted asking for the best goalkeeper in the league, and I took the lead with 32 per cent of the votes, ahead of Manuel Neuer, who got 12. Evidently, people were still putting their trust in me. Having said this, now Oliver Kahn seemed to feel appointed to do his own rating of the nation's keepers. The fact that he was doing it in *Sport Bild* of all places did not surprise me. The only thing that puzzled me was the result of his analysis: he considered Tim Wiese the best, probably because the Bremen man had once said Kahn was his role model. By the looks of things, Oliver had still not understood what constituted a quality goalkeeper – merely being strong on the line was not enough. Wiese still had deficits in terms of dominating his penalty area, Kahn admitted, but this could be remedied easily. Funny, I thought, some never learned that over the whole course of their careers.

Unfortunately, however, we were now no longer fetching positive results in the league. When we lost at home to FC Köln, I was reminded of situations at my former clubs: whenever a team, with supreme effort, had managed to achieve a season's aim after all, there had immediately followed a nadir, a breathing spell, during which the most preposterous goals were conceded. This was football imitating life – breathing deeply after the great strenuousness before carrying on successfully. Hence, I did not think anything of it when, after the Köln defeat, I accepted an invitation to go the Oktoberfest. Wearing lederhosen and accompanied by my wife and a few friends, I drank half a Radler and drove home just before midnight.

The next morning, I received a call informing me that due to our sporting crisis, the training camp scheduled before the cup game against Lubeck was to begin a day early. It was a pure case of doing things for the sake of doing things, in order to demonstrate to the public that everything was being done to combat the aforementioned crisis. The squad was to sit down together 'to talk and evoke the team spirit'. There was no mention of an opportunity to compile things that would finally help us advance on the pitch. But even before I had arrived in Stuttgart, Markus Babbel called me with a bollocking in mind. 'How could you be so stupid as to be photographed at Oktoberfest after a defeat?'

I did not quite know what to say; it did not say anywhere that I was not allowed to spend my free time at a funfair. 'And what do we do now?' I asked. 'I know you've heard from your wife that I'd gone home by half-eleven.' I had met Silke Babbel in Munich; she had been setting off into the nightlife with a friend. 'You're coming to Stuttgart, and you're going to train,' Babbel retorted. In plain terms, that meant no training camp and no cup game in Lubeck. It had taken forty years, but I had finally been suspended by my club for the first time. Players getting banned was nothing out of the ordinary, but where others had theirs acknowledged with a shrug of the shoulders, my suspension triggered yet another media avalanche. It even stretched all the way to England, where the *Sun* used the opportunity to take the piss. Luckily, the rest of the team won in Lubeck – without me but with some effort – and after a clarifying conversation with Babbel and Heldt, I was allowed to play the next league match in Frankfurt.

This just went to show that the way clubs handled their stress management always went according to the book: one or several players were chosen and punished in one way or another; it was their way of demonstrating stoutness to the public. In most crisis situations, I simply continued to do what I deemed correct and important for my performance capability. Unfortunately, there was no experienced sports psychologist at Stuttgart to clear any mental blockage in the minds of some of our insecure players. Wistfully, I recalled my time at Arsenal, who during the week would do everything to relax the players and enable them to focus on training as intensely as possible. Spectators were categorically not admitted to the training ground, and the press were only allowed to come round for interviews once a week. TV journalists were only allowed on the pitch on Champions League nights, for thirty minutes before the matches. This way, players could concentrate wholly on their profession without being followed around by cameras at every turn.

I never quite understood the reasoning behind public training sessions. A good manager would be stupid to let his work be observed. His training methods were his expertise and therefore depicted his value; why should he pass this on free of charge? It is not as if the engineers at Mercedes, for example, let themselves be watched as they developed their vehicles, so that Toyota might copy everything they did. Or did managers and clubs have so little respect for their own work they

THE MADNESS IS ON THE PITCH

thought they had nothing to hide? Evidently, clubs were afraid to get bad press if they shut out the public, but did they not worry they would be booed by 60,000 people in the stadium if things were going poorly? I have no objections against a few open sessions – especially during school holidays – but they should be the exception, not the rule. Obviously, though, it was going to be a while until this view took hold in Germany.

Our sporting decline continued, and on the evening before our cup game in Fürth, Horst Heldt took the team to task. 'If you lose tomorrow, I will have to fire the manager,' he announced. 'We won't be travelling as comfortably any more, either; it'll be the bus for every journey. And you can kiss goodbye to those single rooms, too.' In the end, we lost 0–1. Hardly surprising: the pressure had been so immense that Alex Hleb had picked a quarrel with the manager during the game and had even come to verbal blows with our dear team doctor, Heiko Striegl. Utterly frustrated, the management were sitting in the chamber next door to our dressing room. 'We'll sort this out,' I said, 'we'll talk it over, and we'll fight our way out together.' I then addressed Horst Heldt. 'What is the manager supposed to do if you sell thirty goals before the season without providing compensation?' Thirty goals, that was Mario Gómez, who had moved to Bayern for 30 million euros. Pavel Progrebnyak had been bought as his substitute, a completely different type of player compared to Mario, someone who was able to keep the ball at the front and put others at the centre. He needed some time to acclimatise to a new league and a foreign country. Hleb, the other new signing, had not even been properly fit on arrival, and despite some good matches until winter, he had been unable to make up for this physical disadvantage.

Before I returned to the dressing room, press officer Oliver Schraft asked me to repeat that sentence about fighting together to the press: 'just without the thirty sold goals, that would help us'. No sooner said than done: I stood before the press and told them a managerial sacking would not help matters. Markus Babbel remained in office and, for my pains, I was made the bogeyman as soon as the crisis deepened. Very rarely the whole team or the club management were criticised. Instead, everyone preferred to take shelter behind one of those media-hyped stories circulating about my person; this way, there was no need to talk about the real roots of the crisis. Following the defeat in Fürth, our single rooms were indeed axed – an absolute nonsense, as this was definitely going to damage our performance. How was I supposed to regenerate if my allocated room-mate – yes, we were even assigned room-mates – wanted to watch TV until midnight? If he slept until nine the next morning while I was up at seven, was I supposed to sit in the dark for two hours?

I ended up alongside Alex Hleb, my former Arsenal colleague, who shared my opinion that double rooms were an absolute no-go. So, in secret, we tried to book an additional room before the next game, but ended up getting caught. Eventually, Alex asked a friend to book an extra room under his name, to which he snuck in the dead of night like a thief to ensure our peace and quiet. After the Champions League match in Seville, he slept in one room with his wife, who had simply checked into the same hotel. It was such rubbish, and it did not end there. Markus Babbel began his pre-match address before one of the most important games of the season by getting in a lather about the secret attempts to obtain single rooms. Mind you, after we had won a point in Seville, said single rooms were suddenly back.

The crisis reached its peak after a draw at home against Bochum. The outcome of the match led to what fans usually called an 'uprising'; in reality, it was quite the turmoil. Already before the match, around a hundred of them had veritably attacked our bus and lit a smoke bomb. After the certainly disappointing match, during which we had only conceded the equaliser shortly before the end, a few supporters ran riot in front of the stadium. Never before had I experienced fan unrest as extreme as this; in the end, arrests were made and supporters as well as police suffered minor injuries. Bowing to the pressure exerted by the fans and confronted with poor results, the club management decided to let Markus Babbel go the next day.

Babbel's last decision before the Bochum game had been the public, 'heavy-hearted' dropping of Thomas Hitzlsperger as captain and the cancelling of my regeneration day at home. He had justified the latter by saying he was merely following the wish of both the board and parts of the team. While I knew there were one or two players who were vexed by my training arrangement, the board had stabbed me in the back – it had been them with whom I had made that very same arrangement in the first place, and their inability to tell me their decision to my face made me very angry indeed. I contemplated going to the president but then abandoned the idea, because I was too annoyed by this child's play and could not be bothered with any more conflicts.

After Markus Babbel was fired, I gave an interview in which I traced the background to his dismissal back to the pressure from the streets. The club reacted promptly, imposing a €50,000 fine. I did not accept this enormous sum, only for the president to tell me during the ensuing discussion that the measure of scrapping my regeneration day had been explicitly requested by the manager. Again then, I of all people was being exposed to public ridicule, despite having helped both the manager and the club after that cup game against Fürth. Eventually, I did agree to pay the fine after all, but I gave the money to charity – this way, I could at least have the joy of doing something good.

I did not assume our new manager, the Swiss Christian Gross, would reinvent the team in the two training sessions before the next Champions League match and, really, it did not matter to me. I wanted to win at all costs, or this game against Romanian champions Unirea Urziceni would have been my last ever fixture in European competition. I could not allow my departure to happen like this. Perhaps these historic dimensions were the reason I was nervous, something that usually did not even happen before big games. There was no need to worry, though – whatever had got into the team that evening, the match went perfectly. Apparently, the new manager had magic powers. One thing, of course, did not change even after this immensely important win: I was once more the centre of attention.

What had happened? Well, towards the end of the game, I had noticed that the jockstrap I always wore to play had been shifting. What was I to do, drop my britches in front of 40,000 people to sort it out? No chance. So, I chose an opportune moment to hop over the hoardings behind my goal, where I perched and put things in order. No one would have become aware of it had there not been footage of the scene. Even the people standing directly behind my goal had not noticed my short and not-quite-proper excursion. The next day, however, barely anyone spoke of our reaching the last sixteen in the Champions League contrary to expectations; instead, the main topic was my alleged 'wee-wee pause'. This way, all involved once more saved themselves the trouble of properly analysing the actual athletic events, and when I was sent off during the game in Mainz a few days later, speculation arose whether I was going to be released. This showed just how irrational the coverage of me had become – why should the club be able to dismiss me? Players stepped on their opponents' feet a dozen times per game, after all.

After the seventh sending-off in my career, Oliver Kahn piped up again in two tabloids: he considered my behaviour on the pitch to be 'beyond belief' and 'bizarre' and effectively challenged me in all seriousness to retire. Evidently, the acrimony about my ousting him at the World Cup still ran deep. In hindsight, his gesture of offering a handshake before the penalty shoot-out against Argentina should probably be judged differently, too. To me, those tabloid comments mirrored what had always characterised his statements ever since I had met him: fear. The fear of not achieving something, of having to surrender something, of losing something; and the fear of telling someone an uncomfortable opinion to their face. In his years as national team captain, he had never once addressed the squad directly. Instead, he had always spread his opinion via the media, and this tactic had not changed.

In Stuttgart, however, things were suddenly going uphill, and fast – similar to the development that had followed the previous year's change of manager. Christian Gross had a clear plan how to save us from relegation, and he put it into action quite effectively through good training methodology and fine-tuning during discussions. It quickly transpired that he was really quite well-spoken; in some team meetings, he would resort to speaking five languages in order to illustrate his vision of football to every player. Unfortunately, as a result, the meeting would sometimes take twice as long. On the downside, he got me to agree that I was only going to be allowed to regenerate after we had won a match.

Meanwhile, the World Cup was six months away, and during this decisive time the three national goalkeepers were beginning to make mistakes. Jogi Löw declared René Adler number one quite early on, probably in an attempt to take away a kind of rivalry pressure to which he could not yet measure up. Manuel Neuer was in a similar position; he was playing good matches, but his performances were regularly interspersed with errors. The third component was Tim Wiese, a miscast who had no feeling for the game, the space or the ball. Even if opinions differed, the fact that no club other than Bremen wanted him spoke for itself – the market had always been the clearest gauge when it came to assessing players.

The last highlight of my career was certainly the first leg of the last sixteen in the Champions League against Barcelona, a match which ended 1-1. It was one of those games during which you were not allowed to lose focus for even a second; organisation needed to be perfect. You only get a chance against one of the world's best clubs if you use aggression to put them under pressure. We nearly managed to do exactly that – almost. After Cacau's opening goal, we should have got at least one penalty, but once again, the referee was not on our side. As they needed an away goal, Barcelona played more aggressively in the second half and were rewarded. It was a quite ordinary goal, one you do not want to concede: a long ball towards the front, a flick-on after a lost aerial duel, and there it was. A team like Barcelona was always bound to make use of every chance, no matter how small. The goal was scored despite the manager setting us up well and explaining the paths. To his credit, each player knew what to do – and they did it.

The return leg in Barcelona became a lesson for us. Contrary to some observers' opinions, however, our defence was not the reason for defeat. During the first two of four goals conceded, the tactical order in the attack got lost for a moment. In addition, loose passes were played time and again, while Lionel Messi was outstanding as ever – as a result, we were hit on the break on a foreign pitch. How, then, do those situations arise? It is not enough to play one against one; our midfield should have tried to block their counterparts in such a way that no gaps could have opened up. However, we did not manage to outnumber Barcelona, and since even their defenders were great footballers, they used every chance for combinations at once. We had not succeeded in taking away their time to look around, to think twice, or to pass, and so they exploited the space perfectly. It was clear to everyone, of course, that we had lost against an absolutely world-class team, and yet my disappointment was great: for me, the lost game was a sign: the end of the season was going to be the end of my career. I was part of a team who had been utterly dominated by their opponent, and I did not want to do this to myself any more. After all, I had played on teams with wholly different aspirations; if that was no longer possible,

I thought, I might as well put an end to it.

Again and again, I have been asked what I considered the decisive difference between German, English and other international top teams. In my time, it surely was not the quantity of training. Compared to Germany, the English did not do as much, never more than one session a day. Twice a week, however, training was awfully hard, focusing on pace, explosiveness and sprints – over and over again. These sessions were followed by regenerative days, so that you never really felt tired. There were phases during which we had to play four, five top games in ten days with Arsenal: Chelsea, Liverpool twice, and Manchester United also twice. The strain and tension might have emptied our minds, but our bodies would still work. This intensity did not exist in any other league in the world, which was why the French, Italian and Spanish clubs struggled to keep up with the English in terms of speed; it was not a problem exclusive to Germany.

Do not let anyone tell you that the only reason for this was the English clubs having more money at their disposal. The example of Manchester City showed that money was by no means everything. The sheikhs from Dubai might have bought anything for the club that was considered good and expensive, but the team took a long time to gel and achieve sucess. There was the misbelief that a particularly expensive player would make particular efforts, but the opposite was true. Long since, transfer fees had become arbitrary numbers; who could say whether Cristiano Ronaldo really was worth 120 million euros? Did this mean he had to score forty goals a season? Did one or two million shirts with his name on the back have to be sold to finance the deal? Had someone offered 110 million euros, resulting in the next club having to pay 120? In any case, the mighty sum did not put the player under any pressure but rather in a relatively comfortable position: he was guaranteed a place in the starting line-up, because no one would dare bench such worth, as that would indicate an erroneous purchase. And that is always the club's responsibility, never that of the player. At the end of the day, the star always had the upper hand. How, for example, was he supposed to be sanctioned if he had been late for training or out for the night? You could not bench him while paying him ten million euros a year.

At the end of the day, a modern football team needs four things in particular in order to be successful. Firstly, technically outstanding and intelligent players.

With its rapidly increasing pace, football has almost become a kind of mental exercise that demands rapid perception and understanding for complex systems. I used to keep telling my colleagues to play with their teammates in mind: when they passed the ball, they already needed to be thinking of the next move. Secondly, a good physique with an emphasis on pace. If you want to enforce your game upon your opponent, you constantly need to have at least three players near the ball; this takes a high physical toll. Thirdly, intelligent training that not only backs strength, stamina and endurance but also sprightliness and tactical skill. According to a study, 70 per cent of managers overtrain their team; constant, slow and sustained running increases the risk of muscle and tendon injuries through so-called 'impact' – a perpetual and monotone concussion of the body. For this reason, Arsenal did not simply do the usual whole session after a game but rather left it at cycling and stretching. Fourthly and finally, a professional management who will create training conditions under which every single player can reach his optimum. After all, professional football does contain a great paradox: while it is an occupation for the player, linked with necessitation, it remains a game that demands freedom in order to be creative. Hence, a player must not lose the joy he takes in his work, or he will no longer be able to do it well. Pressure alone does in no way guarantee success, on the contrary. Especially before big games, the pressure is already intense enough; here, the trick is to reinforce the enjoyment of the game and to give the convincing impression that life goes on after the match, whatever the outcome. Some players need more pressure to give their best performance; others need less.

The optimal conditions in the workplace can be something as simple as the possibility of a proper meal at the right time, i.e. after training. I am not one for barracking players at the training ground all day, but often enough, you simply cannot seem to get away – be it due to treatment or some tests – and so it is important to find perfect conditions. At Stuttgart, they even served a post-session lunch, delivered to the dressing room – until it was scrapped: apparently, the Federal Tax Office considered it 'a countervailing benefit'. What rubbish! The thought did occur to me, though, that I was probably going to miss this kind of trifle once I stopped playing.

In the end, just like his predecessor, new manager Gross turned out to hit the mark: under him, we won match after match – even in Berlin and Munich, for the first time after nineteen and eleven years respectively. Gross's exercises in training and his plans for each game had brought about the turnaround. The board, too, was now relaxed once more, and the fans rekindled the kind of euphoria they had shown towards the end of the previous season. This way, I finally came to celebrate a joyful farewell.

# Now What?

WHAT, THEN, DOES IT LOOK LIKE, THE IDEAL EXIT AFTER TWENTY years of professional football? I do not know; I never worried myself much over it. At some point, your gut tells you it is probably time: once you no longer look forward to training, or once sorting out your bones in the morning takes up more time than you end up spending on the pitch. I was as little immune to this as any other professional athlete. At the same time, it was difficult to give any thought to it as long my performance ability and my bodily condition were greater than fifteen years before. In any case, I felt younger than I actually was. On the one hand, this was to do with the fact that I had constantly been involved with people younger than me – even my former manager Markus Babbel was three years my junior. On the other, I need to thank all the doctors and therapists with whom I have worked together over time. I have certainly benefited from the advances made both in terms of medicine and training methodology; had I been playing twenty years earlier, I would not have been able to stand on the pitch at forty. At the start of my career, training was merely another word for agony, an often senseless bludgeoning to the point of acidosis, because people thought a lot of work meant a lot of success.

Ever since my ligament rupture in 1992, I had paid much attention to the sustainability of my training. Over the entire course of my career, I was a regular in the weights room and always took care of my body off the pitch, too. Up until the very end, I would visit the weights room before every training for some exercises, jump-starting my muscles. This way, I managed to control most injuries and minor ailments; together with the appropriate therapy, I quasi-trained them away. According to new methods of measurement, I was able to resort to a very quick ability to regenerate: my resting heart rate was at 42 beats per minute, and even during top strain in training, it would not exceed 125 by a lot. In comparison, my young colleagues, some of whom were half my age, had a rate of 165 in similar situations. I was also able to come down quickly from stress situations during games, which, more often than not, were denunciated as 'tantrums'. On the pitch, then, I was still the spring chicken I had been years before. The lifeblood, really, was pace – I knew that once I had lost that, it would all be over, and this included mental speed. The fact that no one could prevent the ravages of time from gnawing away was demonstrated by Milan, where even the legendary Milan Lab was unable to forestall the bad patch of an ageing team. Whatever had been brewed up and concocted over there, it did not make the players any faster, which was why they were running after the English teams – and, in time, the German ones, too. As far as I was concerned, my tempo had remained the same as I could see every day in training, where I had to pit myself against people fifteen and more years my junior. Technically, the age barrier only exists in your head: eventually, even I thought it was enough at forty.

It was not easy, however, to catch the right moment. I had seen many other athletes struggle with this decision. At any rate, I had not picked out a role model of whom I could say they had managed it perfectly. For some time, for example, it looked as if Michael Schumacher had got out of the car at just the right moment, only to return a short while later. Evidently, he still felt fit and able to compete, and the initial results did show that he could indeed keep up easily with the youngsters.

I never dreamed of concluding my career at the height of my creativity with a final in which I made three great parries and saved a few penalties. For me, any game of football in which I was allowed to take part was a highlight. That still applied when it was certain that I was not going to extend my contract at Stuttgart. I was lucky to have always enjoyed my job in over two decades of professional football. There had not been a single moment when I had got the feeling that I had absolutely lost my hunger for the game. There are colleagues who never touch another ball after the end of their career, despite still being physically able to. Perhaps they had never loved the game as much before but had rather regarded it as a means to an end.

I was not under any illusion, mind you. Once I had finished playing, it would only be a matter of three or four months until all the work I had put into my body over a lifetime was going to disappear without a trace. As soon I stopped training, my body would tell me it was slackening because I did not feed it any more. In any other profession, investments in proper education and qualification pay off over an entire lifetime. My capital, however, was my body, and at some point it would no longer bear interest. Rather, it would irrevocably become weaker and weaker; such was the fate of a professional athlete. I did not fear this, though, on the contrary. It was going to be quite pleasant not having to listen to my inner voice any more but instead be able to finally relax. Besides, I had achieved almost every goal I had set myself. Of course, I would have liked to win one or two more finals, but measured against the dreams my twelve-year-old self had had on my parents' sofa during the 1982 World Cup semi-finals, I had been given plenty. That being said, I have never seen my statistics, so – bar a couple of official records – I do not know exactly how many parries, saved penalties, and minutes without conceding my personal balance might show. I never counted my mistakes, either; perhaps a list of those would have surpassed the length of this.

Considering, then, that I had initially 'merely' wanted to become a Bundesliga player, I have come quite far in the end. And even if my body will not allow me to update the aforementioned balance, I have definitely retained my collected knowledge of the sport, which can certainly be considered a great treasure. In addition, there is the exact awareness of my mental strength: the ability to torture myself for a certain target will survive the rest of my life. I can be sure to accomplish any realistically set goal, because I have learned to work for my dreams with motivation and discipline. It is what the football gods have taught me, and it is something everyone can do: turning potential into success. The Lord has given everyone some sort of potential alongside the means to make something from the opportunities. You merely have to muster the courage and the confidence to trust and invest in your talent. I, for example, could never become the next Picasso, no matter what energy and will I put into trying – my artistic gift simply does not suffice. But as is the case for anyone else, there are other areas left in which my ambition can be put to good and sensible use. And no matter what I set about doing in the end, I can always rely on a specific talent gifted to me by God: the ability to reliably deliver my performance especially in stress situations if I have worked for it hard beforehand.

Speaking of stress – several studies have found that football is the most stress-intensive type of sport after F1. We might not put our lives in danger, but the game depends on so many factors – opponents, readiness for tackles, supporters, the unique coordination of mind and foot, even the weather – that you can easily lose your inner calm and peace. In retrospect, my time at grammar school and university must have been a great school to my power of concentration, and it must be from whence my stress resistance stems. The latter never left me, apart from that short period at Dortmund, when a few lunatics had even insulted my family in their hatred of me, leading to my making grave mistakes in four consecutive games that resulted in goals against us.

Now, I was faced with the challenge of finding a substitute drug for all the adrenalin that had been released reliably during almost every match. Like an addict going through withdrawal, I was going to miss these physical states of exception that had reigned, especially after Champions League games and internationals. On this, then, drew the inevitable question of whether I was ever going to be as good at something as I had been at football. I had no idea. It was rather unlikely that I was going to be absolutely world class at anything else ever again. A substitute drug would be to simply stay in football, perhaps as manager or director. It would mean I was still part of a team and would probably feel the same kind of suspense as before upon walking into a stadium. Actually, I had already become a manager – on the silver screen, at least. Big John was my stage name in a film called *Themba*; it told the story of a boy who made it into South Africa's under-20 national team despite an HIV infection. Shooting had taken place in South Africa in summer 2009 – a moving experience that had taught me but one thing: I was never going to be an actor.

I was, though, determined to do my badges, even if the DFB had made the conditions extremely demanding for former professionals. I was sure that sooner or later, there would be another solution than this everlasting seminar with compulsory attendance in Cologne. At the time, rules dictated that you needed to acquire a basic licence before coaching a fourth-tier side for a year. If you managed to get your team promoted, your reward was not being allowed to continue coaching them until you had earned the corresponding badge. It was anything but logical. Next, you had to complete a second year-long internship before obtaining your manager's certificate across another eleven months' time. Based on this, I thought there should be individual solutions for some pros like Michael Ballack, Christoph Metzelder or myself, who had played a high international class. I wrote a letter to the DFB president with regards to this but did not receive a response.

For me, football was a good school for life; it teaches you how to deal with different characters. One needs a kick up the backside, another needs stroking. Without tolerance for your team-mates' approach to life, however, nothing will work, especially when it comes to players from other continents. All training and talent aside, a player's ability to work in a team still remains the most important prerequisite for success; without the often-invoked camaraderie, nothing will go to plan on the pitch. I was able to see myself leading the life of a manager; it would allow me to influence everything myself, at least until kick-off.

It is important to love your players and to try to make them better every day. Jürgen Klinsmann was derided for this attitude, but I too was convinced it could be achieved. Besides, I could imagine it to be a very fulfilling task. But all this was still up in the air; the great challenge now was going to be finding something I would enjoy just as much as playing football. First of all, I was going to pick up my education again, so that I could deepen the knowledge acquired during my studies of economic sciences. In fact, I had already commenced this shortly after my retirement, under the supervision of a professor. In order to manage a club, this might not be necessary, but it could not hurt, even if one day I decided to do something completely different.

At this point, I knew I was not going to miss one thing in particular: the training camps, the endless days in hotels before the games, and processing piles of man-high autograph cards in the space of a day for the club to sell. Drawing the line under my career, however, these things had represented a vanishingly small part of it all. Altogether, I was deeply grateful for everything I had been allowed to experience as a footballer. After all, the fact that I had been able to earn a living doing the thing I loved most was not to be taken for granted.

Besides, not only had I witnessed my sport's absolute athletic highlights but other things too of which I hoped to tell my grandkids one day. When Arsenal had won the league unbeaten, for instance, we had been given an audience with the Queen. Like schoolboys, excited and dressed up, we had stood in a row, along which she had strode as if she were taking a salute. Our captain had introduced each player to her with their names and nationalities. Before me in the row had stood three Brazilians. Upon hearing the country mentioned for the third time, the Queen had asked cautiously, 'Are there any English?' Then, it had been my turn. 'You are not from Brazil,' she had said. 'No, from Germany,' I had replied. The way in which she had said, 'Aaaah, Germany!' had seemed to envelop her entire memories of the Anglo–German relations of the past seventy years. When I finally shook her hand, I had been forced to think, awestruck, of the fact that I had been a touch away from Winston Churchill, Roosevelt, Kennedy, Nixon and Carter. It had been as if I had shaken hands with history incarnate.

A similar situation had occurred when I had met Helmut Kohl for the first time, albeit this had been a more informal setting. I had gone to France in 1998 as third keeper and had been the first at afternoon tea one day, when the Chancellor had entered the room. 'May I sit here?' he had asked in all modesty, leaving me flabbergasted. The Chancellor of the German reunification, the man who had been representative of the entire newly united country, had asked me a question. As if that were not enough, he had been quite in the know about me, even though being third keeper had meant my being the last number in the squad. 'Is the Milan transfer home and dry?' he had inquired, taking me in completely, regardless of whether or not an aide had been whispering the necessary details into his ear.

Moreover, the banquet held after the 2002 World Cup final had been attended by Chancellor Gerhard Schröder and his wife Doris. 'You have played a great World Cup and we at home have taken much joy in your performances,' he said in his address. 'We are also a little proud that you reached the final, even if it was not enough for a victory.' Following his speech, he had sat for quite a while at one table with the Bierhoffs and the Bodes, as well as my wife and me. Eventually, the mood had become so relaxed that Conny had suddenly said, 'My husband wants to be Chancellor one day too. How do you get to do that?' 'Well, first of all,' Schröder had replied, quick as a shot, 'you need to be good-looking. Then, you need to be in the right party, but that is easily done. Finally, you need to have a good, simple name. That is where you might struggle.' 'Yes, well, what about your name?' my wife had retorted, followed by a round of great laughter. After all, in what way was Lehmann more complicated than Schröder?

Angela Merkel, too, had always been very pleasant, human and sociable whenever I had met her in the setting of the 2006 World Cup. During the tournament, she had invited us quite privately to her office for potatoes and leberkäse. She herself had given us a tour of the house, showing us the flat in which her predecessor, Gerhard Schröder, had used to live: a terribly small place of perhaps fifty square feet, no larger than our massage chamber. Merkel had been utterly relaxed and very witty, a nonchalant woman with both feet on the ground. Somehow, I had expected it to be different standing next to the most powerful person in the country, but everything had been completely informal. During a subsequent event, after the premiere of Sönke Wortmann's World Cup documentary, she had even darted for the canapés in the same way as us, saying she had been glad to get something to eat; it had saved her from going home and having her husband make her some sandwiches. What a pleasant person this woman was.

All these anecdotes were only granted me because I had been throwing myself into my sport in such a way that allowed me to achieve something great. It had always given me special satisfaction to be able to share both the highlights and the nadirs with my team-mates. An individual athlete's fate certainly had to be more boring – with whom could he share what he had been through? It was much easier to process a depressing defeat with the help of ten others rather than walking around with it alone for days on end. This collectively experienced emotional roller coaster was certainly something I was going to miss in future.

I had not spent much thought on what people might say about me in ten years' time; I was not one for obituaries being given during one's life. I merely hoped that everyone with whom I had worked would be able to say I was a correct, reliable and above all honest person, who could nevertheless be headstrong. Furthermore, over the last twenty years, I had probably been one of the most entertaining players in Germany. My mistakes, antics, odd actions and my performances had given people lots of material for laughing, crying, happiness and anger. For that reason alone, I must have been worth my money.

Now, it was time for something new. I was looking forward to seeing what life might be like once I was no longer the footballer Jens Lehmann. I hoped, and at the same time was certain, I would not have to struggle with it. This was thanks to all the normal people around me and especially my wife, who even after big games and victories had always reminded me I still had to take out the bins and change my children's nappies.

# A Return
# To The Madness

IT IS STRANGE THAT MORE GOALKEEPERS HAVE NOT BECOME TOP class football managers. In theory, the goalkeeper should understand the game better than anyone else because they stand watching it more than any other player on the pitch. There can be games when a goalkeeper is waiting for 95 per-cent of the time for something to happen but the goalkeeper's concentration nevertheless needs to be even more intense than an outfield player because if he is not ready when the ball comes his way, he might make a mistake and he'll have to explain why a goal has been scored against him. It means goalkeepers are almost students of live football. Theoretically, we should be able to smell danger because the game unravels in front of us.

Additionally, goalkeepers are used to isolation – much like managers, I guess. We spend a lot of time training alone and managers are alone because no matter what advice they receive, the most important judgements are made by them, nobody else. You would think, then, a goalkeeper would suit being a manager. We are in high risk roles.

All goalkeepers are very different, of course. My biggest strength was organising the team from the back and interpreting what was happening in front of me.

I have thought a lot about this since retiring from football. As it happened, my final game was not in 2010 and rather in 2011. After leaving Stuttgart, there was one final game for Arsenal which came about because of a goalkeeping crisis. Three were injured and this left the club with one fit goalkeeper: Manuel Almunia. When Almunia injured himself during the warm-up in a game at Blackpool, I returned to the pitch once more. It was my 200th appearance for Arsenal and at 41 I became the oldest player in the club's history. The final score? Blackpool 1, Arsenal 3.

For several years after my second retirement at the end of the 2010/11 season, I worked in Germany as a match analyser – something I really enjoyed. I found that the most important thing to have in the media is not only an opinion but also an argument and reason – to try to explain the game from a professional's point of view rather than merely criticise like so many do. Otherwise, the public will see through the raw opinion very quickly and they will let you know about it. That is why Jürgen Klopp became very popular very quickly. In 2006 when the World Cup was being held in Germany, he was still a manager at Mainz. Viewers could see through his work as a pundit that Jürgen had a huge personality but also he thought deeply about the game and had different ideas about the way it should be played.

I can understand why more ex-players turn to media work and fewer ex-players are becoming football managers like they did in the past. Football at the highest end over the last twenty or thirty years has been lucrative financially. For many, there is no demand to work at all in many cases. I think many footballers see the hours coaches and managers have to put in and it frightens them.

If you have a great job in the media, why would you dare to coach every day instead? Media work means you can stay in one place and set down roots. Kids don't have to move schools. Coaching means travel and inconvenience. Particularly when you have earned enough money from the game – particularly when many players have travelled around countries between many clubs – they decide upon the more relaxing life. That is not to say media work is easy because there are excellent pundits, good pundits and bad pundits. It is an easier life rather than an easy life.

The pressure in management, of course, is now greater than it has ever been because of the money in the game, the new wealthy owners, a more aggressive traditional media and then social media. Did he have the chance to change anything? Maybe the people running Crystal Palace recognised a mistake in appointing him. It would only be fair if they admitted it. Outcomes like this can ruin reputations.

So, people ask me why coaching, why management – why now, especially at this time where so many get sacked so quickly? I have always liked challenges and pressure. You only get one life. My best moments so far have happened when I've been under pressure. I react well to pressure, being tested: trying to prove myself on the biggest stage – stretch my limits. I don't like to choose an easier life.

Three offers came for me to be a sporting director at clubs in Germany since retirement as a player. As supporters will know in England, the structure in Germany is slightly different. You have the coach who is responsible for choosing the team and taking the training. Then you have the Director of Football who hires and fires the coach and signs and sells the players. The Sporting Director supports the Director of Football. In England, clubs have chief executives and some sporting directors but many seem reluctant to announce a Director of Football. In England, the manager is king.

In the summer of 2017, I was very close to joining one of these Bundesliga clubs but I decided to withdraw because I think I can be a better trainer than a suit worker. You see so many examples of sporting directors who have not played football. It was my instinct that I would be better on the grass. Out of respect to those clubs – each of them in the Bundesliga – I'd rather not say who they are in print at this moment. The offers were very flattering.

My thoughts were on a return to Arsenal. I was always in touch with Arsenal, ever since I left the club for that second brief period as a player. I was invited over from Germany to play in staff games. It was a good way of keeping in touch with old friends. It made me realise how much I missed competition. I knew that the boss wanted to change something on his staff. So, I asked him to consider me. He called me back and said that he was interested. He gave me the opportunity to return. I'm really grateful for that opportunity. It is a role that allows me to study and contribute as much as I can without the focus being on me.

The expectation when you come to Arsenal is to always try and help the team to win games. I am still learning about the role but what I do know for certain is, coming back to Arsenal – a club I understand – has made my progression into being a coach a lot easier. Eventually, I will go my own way – wherever that will be, maybe back in Germany; maybe here in England.

I write this passage after being back at Arsenal for twelve weeks or so. Even in those twelve weeks, I have learnt a lot. I now have a completely different perception of the coach's and, indeed, the manager's responsibilities as well as the pressures they face. I think I was an easy player to manage because I liked to train. My career has taught me a lot of details about the game. I have seen a lot of things. I had played in three different countries for five different clubs, as well as the German national team in a couple of big tournaments. I have learnt a lot through those experiences. I recognise too how quickly football is changing, even since my own retirement as a player.

One thing that hasn't changed is the importance of recruitment, as well as media relationships. There are examples of coaches who are great with the media but have little else to offer in terms of man-management, tactical understanding and vision. These coaches do not last for long. The players won't believe you. Then, you are in trouble. You can be as great with the media as you want but sooner or later, the media, the fans and the club will find you out.

More and more managers and coaches have limited if no playing career to reflect on. That is a reality. It is not an absolute rule, of course, but I think it is better if a manager or a coach has experienced what the players are going through. It is a big advantage. This is the base I will start from. Another life begins.